The Green Cockade

The Irish in the French Revolution 1789-1815

By the same author

Soldiers, Scholars, Priests. Paris, 1985.
The Irish-French Connection 1578-1978 (Ed.). Paris, 1978.

The Green Cockade

The Irish in the French Revolution 1789–1815

LIAM SWORDS

GLENDALE

First published in Ireland by
GLENDALE
1, Summerhill Parade
Sandycove
Co. Dublin, Ireland

British Library Cataloguing in Publication Data
Swords, Liam
The green cockade : the Irish in the French revolution, 1789 – 1815.
1. Irish persons. Implications of French Revolution, 1789-1799
I. Title
944.04

ISBN 0-907606-69-5 pbk

Cover and line drawings by Rai Uhlemann
Typeset by Wendy A. Commins, The Curragh
Make-up by Paul Bray Studio
Printed by The Camelot Press plc, Southampton

To my father
who taught me my first lessons in history
and my mother
who loved us both

When every thing else is ready, let them send in a large quantity of wine and brandy, a fiddle and some French *filles*, and then when Pat's heart is a little soft with love and wine, send in two or three proper persons in regimentals and *green cockades* in their hats to speak to them of whom I will very gladly be one.

Wolfe Tone, *Diaries*, 1 p30.

Contents

Abbreviations

A.A.E.	Archives des Affaires Etrangères, Paris.
A.N.	Archives Nationales, Paris.
A.P.	Archives de la police judiciare.
Arch. Hib.	Archivium Hibernicum.
A.S.P.	Archives de la Seine, Paris.
B.H.V.P.	Bibliothèque Historique de la Ville de Paris.
B.N.	Bibliothèque Nationale, Paris.
B.L.	British Library, London.
Coll. Hib.	Collectanea Hibernica.
C.D.A.	Cashel Diocesan Archives.
D.D.A.	Dublin Diocesan Archives.
I.C.P.	Archives of the Irish College, Paris.
I.E.R.	Irish Ecclesiastical Record.
K.D.A.	Kerry Diocesan Archives.
N.L.	National Library, Dublin.
Prop. Fid.	Propaganda Fide Archives, Rome.
P.R.O. FO.	Public Record Office, Foreign Office, London.
R.I.A.	Royal Irish Academy, Dublin.
W.D.A.	Westminster Diocesan Archives.

Foreword

For the Irish community in Paris the French Revolution could scarcely have happened at a more ill-chosen moment. If many of them were aggrieved by its untimely arrival they could hardly be blamed: after almost two hundred years of precarious existence they had finally carved for themselves a modest niche in the French capital only to see their hard-won respectability swept away in the revolutionary upheaval. Refugees themselves from the kind of tyranny the Revolution aspired to eradicate, they expected, not unreasonably, that the French should make their omlette without breaking any Irish eggs. The revolutionaries, in the early years at least, were not insensitive to their special pleading when it was forcefully and repeatedly expressed: the Irish ecclesiastical institutions were accorded special status which was only rescinded with the advent of the Terror itself.

Although for the most part no more than reluctant and marginal participants in one of the great events of modern times their story is nonetheless worth recording. Their special status made of them unique witnesses, and *The Green Cockade* attempts to document their experiences, their small successes and their large tribulations. The salient events of the Revolution are chronicled only to the extent that they affected them and as they experienced them; and if too frequent use of their verbatim accounts renders the story at times indigestible I can only plead that the truth is traditionally reputed to be unpalatable. No one is obliged to write history but those who do are solemly obliged to tell the truth; and there is no surer way to achieve this than to let the witnesses speak for themselves. Hindsight is of no value to historians. After two hundred years the French Revolution continues to excite considerable passion among its proponents and antagonists and I have no desire to contribute my meagre offering to that particular debate.

That the core of this study is centred upon the vicissitudes of the two Irish colleges in Paris rather than the wider Irish community in the capital merits perhaps an explanation though certainly not an apology. Numerically they represented the largest concentration of Irish in the city and, more importantly, all the other Irish were in one way or another linked with them and regarded them as the focus of Irish society. Above all their fate could have entailed potentially catastrophic consequences for the Irish Church: all the other continental colleges together could not easily or adequately have compensated for the loss of Paris.

It is more difficult to explain why the French attached so much importance to the Irish colleges. Much bureaucratic ink was spilt over them, and relatively insignificant institutions are not normally accorded such inordinate attention. It was due, perhaps, in large part to the successful lobbying of the government by the Irish superiors and particularly by Dr Walsh, who argued convincingly that the Irish college was crucial in determining how Catholic Ireland would react to Revolutionary France, a reaction which might serve to widen its traditional breach with Protestant England. It was an argument which was later to make some impression on Napoleon.

As to the time-span of this book, there are reputable precedents for making bedfellows of the French Revolution and the Napoleonic era. Napoleon was created by the Revolution and continued to pay a certain lip service to the less radical aspects of its ideology; and Waterloo marks a definitive cut-off point in the history not only of the Irish College but in that of the wider Franco-Irish tradition.

The history of the Irish in Paris is a field well charted by some notable earlier explorers who provide a valuable guide to newcomers. The great pioneer was Patrick Boyle CM, rector of the Irish College at the turn of this century. His deceptively slight volume contains a mine of precise information; and during the course of the longest rectorship in the history of the institution he produced numerous articles, particularly on the revolutionary period. What Boyle did for the history of the Irish College Richard Hayes achieved for that of the wider Irish community in Paris. He had a keen eye for the colourful, well illustrated in his *Ireland and Irishmen in the French Revolution*, and his *Biographical Dictionary of Irishmen in France* is an essential *outil de travail* for anyone venturing into this field. While eminently readable his books are, however, very often poorly referenced, an omission which is more than adequately compensated for by Sister Mary O'Riordan in her unpublished thesis on the Irish colleges during the Revolution. Her comprehensive bibliography was an invaluable guide for me through the labyrinth of Parisian archives and contributed enormously to my meeting the bicentenary deadline imposed on this work. Other contributions, such as those of Mary Purcell and Marianne Elliot, are duly acknowledged in the appropriate sections.

Archivally the subject of this work suffers from almost an embarrassment of riches. The *Archives Nationales* contain an impressive amount of material dispersed over numerous areas, while both the *Archives des Affaires Etrangères* and the *Archives de la Seine* have considerable holdings. For the earlier chapters the *Archives de la Préfecture de Police* were particularly important. To the staff in all of them I acknowledge my indebtedness. They were invariably courteous and helpful, especially those in the police archives whose cheerfulness made my numerous visits there a pleasure. Dublin Diocesan Archives and Maynooth College Archives hold small but very important collections which in some instances filled large gaps in the story. To my knowledge much of this material has not been used before and I am grateful to the staff in both and especially to David Sheehy who kindly provided me with a detailed catalogue of the material in the Dublin archives. The Parker papers in the Benedictine Abbey of Douai, near Reading, proved very useful for the later chapters and I am deeply grateful to the Abbot and Dom Geoffrey Scott for their kindness and hospitality.

My gratitude is due also to Professor Louis Cullen who read the typescript and offered many useful suggestions with all the diffidence of an accomplished scholar. I thank too Bishop Joseph Duffy, Rev. Professor Brendan Devlin and Dr Frank O'Reilly who have been unfailingly supportive of my Irish College ventures. If this book contributes in any way to the prosperity of that institution I will be happy both for them and for myself. I wish also to thank Joseph Lynch and the Cultural Relations Committee of the Department of Foreign Affairs, Dublin, whose generous subvention made this publication possible, and Tom Turley and The Glendale Press for whom it constitutes a sizeable act of faith. I am grateful to Bernard Share for his long-standing friendship and skilful editing which removed so many of the lumps and bumps which peppered the original typescript and to Rai Uhlemann whose illustrations do so much to enhance the written word.

There are others who will be surprised to find their names acknowledged here—which only indicates their special relationship to the work. Bill Bolger always refused to allow me become discouraged and Sean O'Boyle, I am convinced, would never have allowed it remain unpublished. Declan Hurley, Mary Cheyrou-Lagreze and Sister Elizabeth Whyte helped to ensure that my chaplaincy service was maintained when I needed time to write. Martin Wickham found time to guide my first faltering steps in the world of cybernetics. Johnny Granville was generous as well as encouraging. Lastly, I thank my sisters, Terry, Olive and Brenda, whose hospitality have always been generously provided and often inadequately acknowledged.

1
Greening the Latin Quarter

I am told those of this house are at present called the Jesuits of the secular clergy

–Dr Patrick Joseph Plunkett, August 1775.

In the autumn of 1775 the Irish student community took up residency in their new college on the top of Mont Sainte-Geneviève in a street aptly named the 'street of the Green Horse'. For over a hundred years they had shared cramped quarters with the community of Irish priests in the medieval Collège des Lombards, halfway down the hill near the river. Founded originally by Italians, the Irish acquired it in the middle of the seventeenth century and had it restored but it never quite catered for the numbers or the temperaments of its residents. For most of its history it was friction-ridden. The community of priests and the community of students had little in common apart from their nationality. The practice of the Irish church during the seventeenth and eighteenth centuries was to ordain first and then send the clergy abroad for education, inspiring a French wit to describe them as 'the poor Irish who come to Paris to live on Masses and arguments.'[1] While the priest-students managed to eke out a modest existence with the help of their Mass-stipends, many of the younger students were reduced to living on their wits. One of their provisors or superiors, Dr Plunkett, observed that 'this very difference between those who are bred here and them is a cause of unaccountable animosity.'[2] Cohabitation only exacerbated the genuine or alleged grievances of each group. In any case, the sheer numbers in search of places made the acquisition of a new college imperative. The student community moved to the new Collège des Irlandais with its large courtyard and two wings, the work of the prestigious architect, François Joseph Bélanger. The priests continued to be housed in the mother-house, Collège des Lombards.

Correspondence during the decade leading up to the French revolution gives the impression of a rather donnish world deeply immersed in the academic disputes in the university of Paris and inordinately concerned about the number of prizes the Irish carried off each year. The latter was particularly important, because as Plunkett pointed out, a student 'will be received gratis as soon as he shall win a premium in the university. Should this happen the first year he will have nothing to pay during the course of his studies.'[3] The pressure on the students to gain results was enormous. Whatever harassment they were subjected to by their superiors was understandable. Irish catholics—or at least the strong farmers and well-off shopkeepers who insisted on sending their sons to Paris to be educated—were very loath to pay for them. Dr Charles Kearney, who became superior of Collège des Irlandais in 1782, complained that often they sent their sons of thirteen or fourteen years of age with only one half-term or quarter-term's fee and that nothing ever followed despite frequent solicitations. Kearney had not the heart to send these boys back to Ireland. The archbishop of Paris told him not to admit anyone 'but such as had bankers here to be responsible for their fees' which provoked Kearney's rueful comment: 'So little did they understand, so little do they still understand our countrymen.'[4] Even more embarrassing for Irish priests was the acceptance of such an Irish student by an English college abroad. The president of the Irish college in Douai wrote in 1781 to Dr Plunkett, now bishop of Meath, to request his influence on one of his flock 'to engage him to pay without any further procrastination' what he owed the English college for four years' bed and board for his son. 'The gentlemen superiors of that excellent and respectable establishment,' he added, 'have been very generous to this seminary and I can't help being concerned at the many losses they sustained from the Irish.'[5] In 1789, Abbé Edgeworth wrote to his friend bishop Moylan of Cork on behalf of one Fitzgerald, a medical student who was obliged to borrow five guineas, to persuade his father to send him money to pay his debts and return fare home.[6]

Despite their continuing financial problems, the Irish colleges had achieved a modest status in the French capital by the end of the eighteenth century, their members occupying chairs in the major colleges of the university. Plunkett himself had been royal professor of theology at Collège de Navarre before returning to Ireland as bishop of Meath and his theological expertise was frequently sought by the archbishop of Paris for his pastorals.

Peter Flood, later president of Maynooth, succeeded him in that post. Richard Ferris from Kerry became procurator of Collège de Montaigu and as such one of the key figures of that prestigious college: his career illustrates well what could be achieved by an Irish student of talent and ambition. His early academic success earned for him the post as master of the *cinquième* and soon after master of rhetoric. From here he progressed to procurator, the most lucrative and influential post in the college. Many of the best French families had their children educated in Collège de Montaigu and Ferris had himself appointed tutor to the son and heir of Prince de Craon.

Irishmen were particularly strong in the medical faculty, an invaluable asset in institutions where sickness took a constant toll. 'I consulted Dr MacMahon on Mr Fleming's disorder' the superior wrote in 1780. 'He tells me the remedy most universally approved of is an infusion of wild valerian root, which is well-known in Ireland ... Such is the opinion and firm persuasion of Mr. Bouvard, M. Belletête, M. Joachim and the whole of the faculty of Paris.'[7] Irish doctors also achieved prominence in court circles: John MacSheehy and John O'Reilly were both physicians to Louis XVI. As well as theology and law, medicine and surgery could be studied by burse-holders in the Irish college and Irish doctors had established a number of substantial foundations there expressly for these disciplines.

The other sizeable Irish community which sought the services of the Irish colleges was that of the officers serving in the Irish regiments in the French army. Many of the students who entered the Irish college at a tender age did not persevere to the priesthood and some opted for a military career. Then, as now, France was highly bureaucratic and all promotional heights were scaled over paper mountains. The requisite papers could not be acquired from official sources in Ireland for obvious reasons and the French authorities readily accepted the testimonials signed by the Irish superiors. General Count Daniel O'Connell and Charles Jennings, later General Kilmaine, were among the many officers for whom the Irish college issued certificates.[8]

One incident illustrates the efficacy of what might be termed the Irish 'mafia' in pre-revolutionary France. Patrick Joseph Plunkett was consecrated bishop of Meath on the last day of February 1779. On his way home to Ireland that summer his ship was commandeered by the famous American privateer, Paul Jones, then engaged in daring raids on English shipping. The bishop was despoiled of his goods, including an episcopal ring presented to him by Marie Antoinette. On reaching London, Plunkett dispatched a hurried message to the Irish college detailing his loss. Word was sent from there to the archbishop of Paris but more profitably to Dr Cahill, the superior, then taking the waters at Passy to alleviate his swollen glands. He immediately approached Dr Benjamin Franklin, the American envoy in France, who was also taking the waters at Passy. Franklin promised to raise the matter with the captain. Another message was dispatched to Mr Moylan, brother of the bishop of Kerry, who was commissioner of the marine for the Americans in the port of L'Orient, where Jones had towed his prize. The boat had been sunk in the harbour with most of its cargo still aboard. Undaunted, Moylan had the ship raised off the sea-bed, the bishop's five large, dripping trunks full of books and vestments dried out and dispatched to Mr Guernon in Bordeaux to be conveyed to Ireland with the apologies of the gallant captain. To raise an English ship hijacked by Americans off the sea-bed of a French port and return the cargo to Ireland and all in a matter of months required some armtwisting![9]

Whatever about their influence in France, the contribution of the Irish colleges in Paris to the Irish church was enormous. In all there were some 600 Irish students, secular and regular, studying for the priesthood in some thirty Irish colleges in Europe, stretching from Lisbon to Prague. Of these, France acounted for over a half and Paris one third. About 11,000 Irish students were educated in Paris in the seventeenth and eighteenth centuries, equalling the number of priests ordained in Maynooth during the two centuries of its existence to date.[10] Lecky said of them that they returned to Ireland 'with a real and varied knowledge of the world ... the manners and feelings of cultivated gentlemen and a high sense of clerical decorum.'[11]

On the eve of the revolution the Irish college in Paris had become a virtual nursery of the Irish episcopacy. In 1788 fifteen of the Irish bishops were Paris-trained, about half of them in Collège des Lombards and the other half in Collège des Irlandais.[12] When Dublin became vacant in 1786 both the university and the archbishop of Paris took a lively interest in the succession. The university postulated Rome in favour of their own man, Peter Flood. The archbishop of Paris divided his advocacy between Plunkett, bishop of Meath and the Abbé Edgeworth, son of a protestant minister from Co Longford who had converted to

Catholicism, left his ministry and taken his young family to Toulouse where he was educated. Edgeworth became a life-long friend of Moylan, the future bishop of Cork then a student at the Irish college in Toulouse, later moving to Paris to continue his theological studies at the Collège des Trente-Trois which was back-to-back with Collège des Lombards. After ordination he joined the Missions Etrangères society and ministered in Paris, taking a special interest in the poor and needy Irish in the city. The archbishop of Paris, having already postulated Rome in favour of Plunkett asked his vicar-general to write on behalf of Edgeworth, indicating his preference for the latter. 'One cannot speak too highly of this virtuous priest' the vicar-general wrote, 'who combines irreproachable morals with zeal and talent.' His only reservation was that Edgeworth was 'shy and excessively humble which might affect the strength of character necessary for the government of a church'. He pointed out that Edgeworth, not knowing Irish, would not be suitable for a diocese in rural Ireland 'where the use of this language is absolutely necesssary for a bishop to instruct his people' which was not true of Leinster or Ardagh 'where English was the dominant language.'[13] In the end Rome decided in favour of Thomas Troy, a Dominican who had been attached to San Clemente in Rome and the official agent of the Irish bishops there.

The Irish superiors provided an important service to the wider community of the Irish both at home and in Paris. They acted as the agents of the Irish bishops in France, handling their investments and rendering numerous little services designed to curry favour with their Lordships. 'A good and excellent gold repeating watch you will get for twenty-five louis,' Dr Kearney informed Dr Plunkett in 1788. 'Let me know your intention and I shall get you one from the first watchmaker in this city. Any other commission which you may have I beg you will employ me with.'[14] More importantly, they sought decisions from the theological faculty on questions which troubled Irish episcopal consciences, such as the morality of taking interest on money lent, then allowed by the government in Ireland. 'The opinion of the doctors seems to be unanimous in looking on the taking of that interest as lawful,' Kearney wrote to the archbishop of Cashel in 1785.[15] Their roles as financial advisors brought them into close association with the surprisingly numerous group of Irish bankers in Paris: it was, in fact, an Irish banker, John Waters, who actually acquired the present Irish college for Dr Kelly in 1769. So greatly did Waters admire the business acumen of Dr Kelly that he stipulated in his will that his executors should undertake no major financial venture without first consulting him.[16]

Two events took place in the summer of 1787 that can only be described as providential. The Book of Lecan, which had been housed for almost a century in the library of Collège des Lombards, was returned to the newly established Royal Irish Academy in Dublin.[17] A few years later, during the height of revolutionary turmoil, the library of Collège des Lombards disappeared without a trace.

Equally providential was a royal decree of that year ordering the suppression of the offices of the four provisors or superiors and their replacement by a single superior to govern the college: John Baptist Walsh, a priest of the diocese of Killaloe and superior of the Irish college in Nantes, being brought in to fill the post.[18] The decision was not popular with the Irish and gave rise to considerable bitterness. Six students signed a protest against the intrusion of Walsh,[19] four of them–MacMahon, O'Neill, Walsh and Delany–medical students. Together with Cruise and Ahern, they claimed that the four superiors had been expelled and a usurper put in their place. This accusation was to haunt Walsh for the rest of his long life. As little as a year later Walsh's appeal for funds for Collège des Lombards encountered a hostile reception in the diocese of Kildare and Leighlin, particularly from the former Lombardians. 'Dr Walsh's later contemporaries' Bishop Delany informed Archbishop Troy, 'are strangely and truly, I believe, filled with unconquerable prejudice against him and all his undertakings and which they never fail to reprobate with a very unbecoming degree of acrimony whenever I chance to mention them or hazard a word in their favour.'[20]

Much later, when Walsh's star was about to set, Comte Lally Tollendal harped on this theme in a confidential report to the minister of the interior. He was the grandson of Thomas Lally from Tullynadala, Co Galway who had left Ireland in 1691. A frequent visitor to Collège des Lombards himself, he followed the tradition of his father and grandfather who had always taken an active and benevolent interest in its affairs. He claimed that Walsh 'by underhand intrigues' had taken advantage of the 'too accommodating' archbishop of Paris, 'to supplant the former superiors grown grey in the exercise of their pious ministry.'[21] Be that as it may, it was unquestionably providential as Walsh was to play a lion's share in saving the Irish college during the French revolution.

An early challenge to his authority came from James Coigly, an Armagh priest who arrived in Paris in June 1785 and shortly afterwards found accommodation in Collège des Lombards. Later a burse became vacant which Coigly claimed. It had been established by Patrick Maginn, one of the founders of the college, to whom Coigly claimed relationship on his mother's side. He initiated a lawsuit against Walsh who had installed two priests, one from Dromore and the other from Down and Connor, in the vacant burse. 'John Baptist Walsh left no means untried to persecute me and ruin my character:' Coigly later declared, 'he even wrote to my bishop in Ireland, praying to have me removed to some other college; and this fact he denied upon oath, until I produced my bishop's letter against him.'[22] Walsh disclaimed all knowledge of such a letter. Having settled the matter of the burse to his satisfaction, Coigly then turned his attention to the regime of the college itself. His researches had brought to light the practice of the election of the superiors by the students every three years which had obtained up to the early decades of the eighteenth century. His struggle to politicise the students to reclaim their right was cut short by the revolution but he had stepped on a hornet's nest which was to threaten the survival of the college long after Coigly had left and found larger causes on which to expend his crusading energies.

Apart from a few straws in the wind, there is little awareness of an impending upheaval in the correspondence of the period. Mass-stipends became scarce and Flood wrote to Plunkett decrying 'the wretched and distressed situation of our poor Lombardians.' The annual income of the priest-students had fallen by one-third. 'The sensible decay of piety and religion in every order and description of the people,' he explained, 'render the calls to the altar less frequent and less beneficial.'[23] Kearney touched on another area of anxiety in 1788: 'every article of consumption is growing daily dearer.' Later, with the benefit of over a quarter of a century's hindsight, he explained the inflation with the observation: 'The grand agents of the revolution were preparing their batteries.'[24] But on this occasion he ended his letter to Plunkett on a more optimistic note: 'The States-General are soon to be assembled ... They will reform some abuses and put an end to the arbitrary disposal of the finances of the State ... and I am confident the funds will rise wonderfully immediately on the assembly of the states.'[25] He even suggested that Bishop Plunkett might consider buying some shares. Little did he suspect then that the States-General, elected between February and April

1789, would, on the initiative of the Third Estate, have constituted itself the National Assembly by the middle of June. The French revolution had begun.

NOTES

1. Qtd Boyle, *The Irish College in Paris 1578-1901*, p18n.
2. Cogan, *The Bishops of Meath*, 3 p6.
3. Ibid.
4. I.C.P. 3W 1. 5 Aug. 1807, qtd Boyle, I.E.R. May 1908 pp461-5.
5. Cogan, op. cit. 3 p67.
6. England, T.R. *Letters from Abbé Edgeworth*, p47.
7. Cogan, op. cit. 3 pp45-6.
8. Walsh, Micheline, 'Irish soldiers and the Irish college in Paris' in Swords, *The Irish-French Connection*, pp63-87.
9. Cogan, op. cit. 3 pp46, 48, 66.
10. Brockliss & Ferté, 'Irish clerics in France in the seventeenth and eighteenth centuries: a statistical survey.' Proc.R.I.A. pp536-7.
11. Lecky, *History of Ireland in the eighteenth century*, 3 pp354-5.
12. Prop. Fid. SC Irlanda 1788-1801, fos.85-6.
13. Prop. Fid. SC Irlanda, 16 fos.191-2 & 238. I am indebted to Fr Eoin Devaney for photocopies of the relevant folios.
14. Cogan, op. cit. 3 p127.
15. C.D.A. Papers of Butler 11, 9 Aug. 1785. I am indebted to Frs Mark Tierney OSB & Christopher Dwyer for photocopy.
16. A.S.P. DC6 252 f205.
17. The minutes of that body for 6 August 1787 'orders that Dr Ussher be desired to draw up a Latin letter of thanks to the Lombard's College.' I am indebted to Prof. Proinsias MacCana for this information.
18. A.N. F17 14764, cf F19 6237C & I.C.P. 3L 11 & 12.
19. A.N. F17 14760.
20. D.D.A. 4 Nov. 1788 Delany to Troy.
21. A.N. H3 2561A Lally Tollendal to Interior, Mar. 1811 pp1 & 2.
22. Coigly, *Life*, 1978, p12.
23. Cogan, op. cit. 3 pp88-9.
24. D.D.A. 121/9 29 Jan. 1816.
25. Cogan, op. cit. 3 p128. Kearney to Plunkett, July 1788.

2
A La Bastille!

The alarming ringing of the bells in the beginning of the disturbances made the very blood almost freeze in our veins with fear.

–Irish priest, Collège des Lombards, 13 September 1789.

Mob violence–that element which was to become synonymous with the revolution–soon made its appearance on the streets of Paris. The causes were manifold, not least of which being the sharply rising cost of living of which the Irish superiors were only too keenly aware. A serious economic crisis developed in 1788-89. Unemployment grew considerably and bad grain harvests aggravated matters. In July 1789 the price of bread in Paris reached record heights. The Irish students, however, were not yet feeling the pinch. 'Thank God we are not stinted yet' one of them wrote early that autumn: 'this scarcity in my opinion did not so much proceed from a want of corn as from a want of wind and water for the mills.'[1] Whatever caused the shortage, the lower classes in Paris were suffering real need.

On 23 June, after the Third Estate had proclaimed itself the National Assembly, the king ordered the troops to Paris. On the following day the French Guard refused to perform their duty and began fraternising with the crowd outside the Palais Royal, apparently won over by revolutionary propaganda. Two days later six regiments were ordered up to Versailles and on 1 July ten other regiments, mostly foreign, were called in from the provinces to throw a cordon round the capital. A newspaper report, naming the Irish together with the Swiss and the German regiments, did little for the peace of mind of the residents in the Irish colleges.[2]

> But of all things nothing alarmed us more than the expection of the Irish Brigades being ordered here to force the people to their duty and if they were, every Irishman in Paris would be infaillibly murdered. Our superiors were so convinced of this, that they desired us as soon

> as we heard the Brigades to be on their march for Paris, to quit immediately. The Brigades never march without three pieces of cannon at their front, so that if they came here they would strew the streets with dead bodies; however Providence has wisely ordered things otherwise.[3]

General Daniel O'Connell was commander of one of the German regiments and he is credited with advising in favour of the foreign regiments moving into the city to snuff out incipient revolutionary riots.[4]

When news reached Paris on 12 July of the king's dismissal of the popular finance minister, Necker, the populace took to the streets urged on by the gifted orator Camille Desmoulins. A large crowd which the guards failed to repel invaded the garden of the Tuileries. The army was no longer reliable. 'The French Guards, the Swiss Guards, the Hussars in short the entire Guards of the city either thro' fear, or not willing to spill the blood of their fellow subjects lay down their arms and left the city to the mercy of a mob ever capricious and ever guided by the violence of their passions.'[5] Some citizens armed themselves spontaneously and organised patrols to restore order and the electors of Paris considered giving them official status by creating a bourgeois militia. A priest from Collège des Lombards encountered them early on Monday 13 July on his way to the church of Saint Gervais:

> Next morning I went out half an hour after five to say Mass and was astonished I did not meet the guards in the streets as usual. Not thinking it prudent to enquire the reason I went forward till I came to Place la Grève (the place of execution opposite the Town House) thro' which I was to pass in order to go to the Church. To my great wonder I saw there thousands of people armed with pikes, poles, spits, sticks, swords, guns etc. They immediately cried out: 'Voilà un pretre: arretez lui!' Upon hearing these words I believed my end was at hand, as they detested the sight of a priest; however when I told them I was an Englishman (sic) and a real lover of liberty they let me pass but God knows, what a slender thread supported my existence that moment; others attempted to go out that morning, but were obliged to make off with their lives, and until they saw me were convinced I was killed. We remained afterwards within our walls for a few days, every moment in expection (sic) of the College being set on fire, or that the King would burn or starve the city if they continued to disobey him.[6]

That day the crowd at Palais Royal sent a deputation of six citizens to the Hôtel de Ville to impress on them the necessity of creating a bourgeois militia. One of the six was Joseph Kavanagh, a bootmaker from Lille. He played an active role in the events leading up to the taking of the Bastille, earning himself a pamphlet with the title: *Exploits glorieux du célèbre Cavanagh. Cause première de la liberté française.*[7] There was an acute shortage of arms for the new militia and Kavanagh was very active in seeking out guns and ammunition. He was among the huge crowd who went on the morning of 14 July to the Invalides, forced their way in and seized 40,000 muskets that were stored there, along with twelve cannons. At some point he commandeered a carriage and drove through the streets of Paris with two others, shouting 'A la Bastille! Let us take the Bastille!'

The Bastille, a state prison, contained a sizeable quantity of ammunition, including 250 barrels of powder. In the popular mind it was a symbol of royal despotism, as illustrated by the Irish student's comment: 'Whatever the designs of the founders the use of it is in the end a disgrace to any nation.'[8] At the time there were, however, only seven inmates, though the staff were quite numerous. In addition to the garrison of 30 Swiss soldiers and 80 veterans they included a doctor, a surgeon and even a midwife, though all prisoners were male. There was also an architect, two archivists and an *entrepreneur des bâtiments*. The spiritual welfare of the prisoners was even better assured than their physical needs–by no less than four ecclesiastics, a chaplain, a confessor, and two titular chaplains. One of the latter was a Clonfert priest, Thomas MacMahon from Eyrecourt, Co Galway. The 70-year old MacMahon, who had taken his doctorate in the Sorbonne and now resided in the nearby rue St Antoine, was paid 40 *livres* a month plus a *livre* for Masses. His salary for June, the last month for which such records were kept, indicates that he said one of the last Masses, if not the last, there.[9]

On that occasion his congregation of eight consisted of two madmen, two *débauchées* and four swindlers. The Bastille's most notable prisoner, the Marquis de Sade, was transferred to an asylum in Charenton just two weeks before 14 July, thus narrowly missing one of history's most momentous occasions. During his five years detention at the Bastille de Sade had been singularly well-treated, receiving frequent visits from his wife. This did not, however, prevent him howling from his sixth-floor window that the prisoners were all being strangled and urging passers-by to come and rescue them. De Sade's detention career is closely linked in the records to that of another prisoner, listed as Comte Whyte de Malleville. Whyte, a 60-year old Dubliner, and former officer in an Irish regiment, had originally been committed to Vincennes by his family after they had him declared insane. When Vincennes was closed in 1784 he was transferred with de Sade to the Bastille. His name was destined to follow de Sade's once more in the register of Charenton.[10] Of the other prisoners Claude Tavernier had been committed for an assassination attempt on the king and Comte de Solange committed by his father for dissipation.

When the attackers reached the Bastille that morning they were confronted by a formidable fortress. With its 30 metre high walls, its turrets and its mounted cannon, it was not going to be easily taken. 'I was in some of the appartments' the Irish student wrote, 'but not in the dungeons, it was a square building and on two sides eight towers, it was like a solid rock, I am certain the strongest building in the world.'[11] The governor was requested to hand over his powder and withdraw from the towers the cannons trained on Paris. While negotiations were going on shots were exchanged between the garrison and the besiegers. The latter believing they were betrayed, attacked the fortress, 'determined to take it or lose their lives.'

> Notwithstanding the continual fire from the garrison they got in as far as the third Court, which is next the Fosse; to cross the Fosse to the Bastile they did not know how, as there is only one passage and that is the great Gate of the Bastile, which let down, forms a bridge across the Fosse. One experienced man among them seeing the gate was held up by a large chain ordered the cannons to be brought up and levelled at it. They were accordingly kept playing at the chain until they broke it, and immediately the gate fell down and formed a passage for them into the Bastile ... Hardin who first mounted the Bastile is ennobled by the nation, he ascended with two hangers, 4 pistols slung to his side, one in each hand and one in his mouth. He would have been swept away and most of those who were ascending with him had it not been for a boy of about 14 years, who fortunately found a gun on the top of the Bastile, fired it off, killed two soldiers and the engineer who was at that moment putting the match to the cannon levelled at them as they mounted.[12]

In the excitement, the attackers almost forgot to free the prisoners. When they did the four petty swindlers, with the ease of professionals, melted into the crowd and disappeared from history, arguably the earliest beneficiaries of revolutionary *liberté*. Whyte, a fragile little figure with a beard almost a yard long and what one eye-witness described as 'the smile of an idiot'[13] was borne in triumph through the streets of Paris, blissfully unaware of his role in one of the revolution's most momentous occasions. Some kind soul lodged him for the night and had him committed next day to the asylum at Charenton which his family had initially tried to avoid because of the harshness of its régime.[14]

The taking of the Bastille constituted the first great *journée* of the French revolution, marking the collapse of absolute monarchy. It resulted in 98 killed, including the governor, 73 wounded, seven freed and several unemployed. To the latter the government was surprisingly generous. Abbé MacMahon was accorded a pension of 500 *livres* which was slightly more than his salary.[15] He lived another five years, died intestate, and his estate devolved upon the government.[16] The fall of the Bastille also produced an official list of heroes, *les vainqueurs de la Bastille*, 863 in all.[17]

The king was forced to return to Paris where he accepted the tricolour cockade, symbol of the revolution: blue and red for the city of Paris and white for the Bourbons.

> The King came here the 24th of July guarded by two hundred thousand bourgeois under arms. I did not see him for I was afraid to go out that day; it was said he signed four propositions; viz. permitting the Bourgeois or Commons to guard the city of Paris, sending away his troops from the environs of Paris and Versailles, consenting to the erasing of the Bastile, and to the beheading of his representatives here. The city is now guarded by the bourgeois and all things seem to go on very well. They make the patrol every day and night regularly; they are getting a blue uniform faced with red and white, gold epaulets and white small cloths.
>
> It was reported here that tythes were abolished, a number of benefices retrenched. Convents and some Colleges to be suppressed etc; however we have every reason to hope we will not share in this general wreck as we are not supported by national or royal munificence and as we are of local utility as being all priests.

The Irish priest penned his letter on 13 September 1789, taking care to leave it unsigned for 'political reasons'. It had all been very exciting and very frightening. 'You see what dangers we have escaped and what we have to fear.' Dr Walsh had read a letter to them from the archbishop of Cashel who had heard that the Collège des Irlandais had been suppressed. 'If I live to go to Ireland' he concluded, 'you shall see me an honest but not a great man. I see now the shallowness of my understanding, the great depths of learning and how difficult to be acquired, how easily forgot.'

Whatever the taking of the Bastille may have contributed to the national morale, it contributed nothing towards solving the great problem confronting the National Assembly, the enormous national debt. In 1789 it stood at five billion, double the amount of money in circulation. Necker, now restored to his functions, proposed that citizens of means should contribute one-fourth of their income to relieve the exchequer. It proved ineffectual. Early in August, the church agreed to the suppression of ecclesiastical titles and a decree was passed on 29 September asking it to send in its silver ornaments to the national mint. The Irish colleges apparently anticipated the decree, handing theirs in to the Paris mint on 24 and 28 September. A week later the offering of Collège des Irlandais was recorded in the parliamentary archives.[18] The presentation was made by Comte Lally Tollendal, one of the notable orators in the Estates-General and the National Assembly in the early years of the revolution. His oratorical flair is amply illustrated in his presentation of the receipts of the Irish silver to the assembly.

> The students and clerics of the Irish college established in Paris, rue du Cheval Vert, charge me to lay at the feet of the King and the National Assembly the product of all their plate and of all the silver vessels of their church. They point out to me that their offering seems to them too small to warrant them to address it directly to you, President. It is in truth the widow's mite; but they give much for they give all they possess. Moreover, they point out to me that, in their poverty, they feel too happy to offer to France this small tribute of their gratitude for her benefits. I am bound to them by ties of a common origin, conducted hither all of us a century ago, by our fidelity to the worship of our fathers and the line of our kings, we have sworn the same sentiments to our new fatherland and to the prince who adopted us. Never, gentlemen, has any of us proved false to these sentiments and we never will.[19]

It was indeed the widow's mite, worth less than 300 *livres* but, surprisingly, almost double that of Collège des Lombards, the mother-house. But the National Assembly was not going to be fobbed off by such paltry offerings from the clergy. It decreed that all ecclesiastical establishments should make a detailed declaration of their property and followed that on 2 November with a decree nationalising all ecclesiastical property. John Baptist Walsh submitted the declaration of the properties and revenues of Collège des Lombards early in 1790.[20] Two other colleges had their declarations signed by Irish priests, Collège de Navarre by

Dr Peter Flood and Collège de Montaigu by Abbé Richard Ferris. Walsh's five-page declaration hardly bears close scrutiny. It was obviously in his interest to play down the Irish assets, though parts of his statement can be confirmed from independent sources, e.g., that the library comprised only about a thousand volumes donated by various individuals and that both staff and students provided their own furniture and books. He emphasised that the college subsisted on external help only, all derived from outside France. But Walsh was worried, advising Bishop Plunkett: 'If the prelates of Ireland could influence government to demand a translation of the national funds, they would act very properly in my opinion.' He added, rather pessimistically: 'Human means afford no solid hopes and we look to God alone for happier times.'[21] But characteristically, Walsh was prepared to lend God a hand, and in the early months of 1790 he addressed a *mémoire* to the ecclesiastical committee of the National Assembly, the first of a flood with which he was to bombard the various French governments in defence of the Irish properties. In it he leans heavily on anti-English sentiments in France. 'The English government' he declared, 'detests the revolution which has regenerated France. It will do everything in its power to prevent Irish students acquiring those principles which sooner or later will germinate the seed of liberty.'[22] A second *mémoire* underlined the financial benefit to France of preserving the Irish colleges. They were no charge on the state. The superior acted as general agent for Irish catholics who invest their funds in France in addition to the considerable sums remitted annually 'for the support of a thousand students.' In the circumstances, a little exaggeration was forgivable! He added: 'Irish priests do not require the intervention of the British ambassador.'[23] When it came to nationality, Walsh made most of whatever cards were trumps.

His persistence was rewarded. On 14 September the ecclesiastical committee of the National Assembly handed down a decision stating that Collège des Lombards, being a house of education of young Irish ecclesiastics, should retain the management and administration of its properties.[24] Not satisfied, Walsh rushed off another *mémoire* requesting that the decision be confirmed by a decree of the National Assembly. The matter was urgent as the English government was about to introduce a bill providing education for catholics in Ireland with the object of inducing them to renounce their French establishments. 'But the Irish *timentes Danaos et dona ferentes* will reject this insidious offer if the assembly decrees the retention of their establishments.'[25] The ploy worked. Chasset, who had been asked to submit a report on the matter, mounted the tribune of the National Assembly and delivered an oration in favour of the Irish petition, heavily laced with phrases borrowed from Walsh's *mémoires*. 'Rivals of the Athenians in science, arts and good taste' he declared, 'the French will always glory in having foreigners come to them for education.'[26] The Assembly decreed that 'houses of study, of education or simply religious, established in France by foreigners or by themselves, shall continue to exist as in the past.'[27] Walsh had won an exemption not only for the two Irish colleges in Paris but also for the five others at Toulouse, Bordeaux, Nantes, Douai and Lille and for the three religious houses at Wassy, Boulay and Bar-sur-Aube. Not only that, but also for 17 British colleges, religious houses and convents, which they duly acknowledged. It was confirmed by a royal decree, the first of some thirty issued between 1789 and 1815 regarding the government of the Irish college in Paris.

NOTES

1. This letter is among the family papers of Col. Eoghan O Néill to whom I am deeply indebted. For full text see O Néill, *Gleann an Óir*, pp94-7.
2. *Moniteur*, 4 July 1789.
3. As 1.
4. Hayes, *Ireland and Irishmen in the French Revolution*, p23n.
5. O Néill, op. cit. p95.
6. Ibid.
7. B.N. 395. The pamphlet by P. Cressonier is subtitled: 'Pour faire connaître comment le sieur Cavanagh a influé puissement sur l'immortelle journée du 14, et l'importance du service rendu par lui à la Nation ...' Cf Hayes, op. cit. pp23-8. Kavanagh's name is not listed among the official list of the Vainqueurs de la Bastille, which surprised the archivist of the revolution, M. Tourneux.
8. O Néill, op. cit. p96.
9. Bournon, F. *La Bastille*, pp68-9, 203, 296. A.S.P. DQ 10 791 & 1312, 603 doss.751.
10. A.N. C. 134 doss 5, Tuetey, A., *L'Assistance publique à Paris pendant la révolution*, pp453, 458, 492. *Moniteur* 1 p195, 24 July 1789. Bournon, op. cit. pp103, 196-7.
11. O Néill, op. cit. p96.
12. Ibid.
13. Hayes, op. cit. pp42-3.
14. A.N. C.134 doss.3; cf. Tuetey 1 p30 & Bournon, op. cit. pp196-7.
15. Bournon, op. cit. p203.

16. A.S.P. DQ 10 603 doss. 751.
17. James Bartholomew Blackwell from Ennis a medical student of the Irish college is credited with playing an active role in the taking of the Bastille. His name is not on the official list. Cf. Nolan, Pierce L. *Dublin Review* 1890 & Hayes, op. cit. pp28-9.
18. Archives parlementaires, procès-verbal de l'Assemblée Nationale, V, n95, p8? 8 Oct. 1789.
19. For full text see I.E.R. (Jan-June) 1904, pp49-50.
20. A.N. T.1636. 20 Feb. 1790.
21. Cogan, op. cit. 3 p147, Walsh to Plunkett, 2 June 1790.
22. A.N. DXIX. 30 doss.472 nd. qtd Daumet, op. cit. pp201-203.
23. A.N. DXIX. 30 doss.472.
24. A.N. DXIX. 44 no.702.
25. A.N. DXIX. 30 doss.472.
26. *Moniteur*, p1250-1, 29 Oct. 1790.
27. A.N. F 19 6237A. 7 Nov. 1790.

3
Incident on Champ de Mars

By night it was being said that sacrilegious priests with swords ensconced in their walking-sticks, mutilated the national monument, tore down the trophies and murdered the sentries.

–*La Feuille du Jour*, 8 Dec. 1790.

The Irish college had to face another enemy, this time within its own walls. On 8 December 1790 some 30 pamphlets were cried up through the streets of Paris on foot of an incident involving Irish students on the Champ de Mars.[1] This was, and still is, the military parade ground, stretching from the front of the École Militaire to the river Seine opposite the Palais de Chaillot. It was the site chosen for *la fête de la Fédération* on 14 July 1790 to commemorate the first anniversary of the taking of the Bastille. It was near the city and capable of accommodating 300,000 spectators. Architects transformed the space into a vast amphitheatre. A bridge of boats was constructed across the river, leading to an *arc de triomphe*. At the opposite end, near the École Militaire, a vast covered gallery was erected with a throne for the king and a seat for the president of the Assembly, on the same level side by side, flanked on either side by places for the deputies of the National Assembly and the municipal officials of Paris. At the very centre of the amphitheatre a civic altar, *autel de la Patrie*, was erected with a statue of liberty on the northern end and another representing the genius of the constitution on the other. The words of the oath of federation were inscribed on its base.

All classes participated in the construction of the amphitheatre, the work becoming a communal festival in itself. Whatever their motives were, families and groups marched out to work at Champ de Mars to the accompaniment of fifes, drums and flags: even General Lafayette put in a few hours there. Contemporary engravings show all classes, aristocratic women working side by side with the common folk. The Irish students also made their civil contribution.

> Abbé Kearney, assisted by ladies of his acquaintance, performed this task and thereby obtained for them in the evening a civic card signed by one of the representatives of the people, which at that critical period was one of the causes of saving them from persecution. By showing this card to patrols and frequent domicile inspectors, they escaped being arrested as suspected persons.[2]

It rained on the day of the festival. Nevertheless, the long cortège of National Guards from all over France, units of the regular army, municipal officials and members of the National Assembly marched through Paris, across the pontoon bridge under the triumphal arch into the Champ de Mars, where some 350,000 people had congregated. The banners of each contingent were blessed in turn. Talleyrand, leader of the new constitutional church, celebrated Mass. Then, dramatically, the Marquis de Lafayette drew his sword and swore the oath 'to be faithful forever to the nation, the law and the king.' And then the king, Louis XVI himself, took the oath. Champ de Mars became consecrated ground for the partisans of the revolution.

It was here, less than six months later, that a group of Irish students provoked an incident. Of the 30 pamphlets published as a result, seven still exist as well as two newspaper accounts.[3] For the most part, they are highly propagandist in tone, giving disappointingly few details. Some are violently anti-Irish; others try courageously to exonerate them. One is a poem of truly epic proportions.[4] 'The whole world knows' the poet wrote in his preface, 'about the horrible attack made on the altar of the fatherland and the superhuman courage of the troops who defended it; these unprecedented deeds deserve to be transmitted to posterity by way of our poem, whose glory, by identifying with theirs, will no less endure.'

Some factual details can be gleaned from the pro-Irish pamphlets, possibly because the anonymous authors consulted the college, and it is not beyond the realms of possibility that one of them may have been written by Kearney or Walsh or at least at their request. The incident took place on Monday 6 December, the feast of St Nicholas, traditionally a school holiday. Thirty or forty Irish students were present on the Champ de Mars, and in the course of a game—football is suggested—damage was done to the altar of the fatherland, which varied in the accounts from the overthrow of the statue of liberty to knocking off a piece of wood supporting a corner vase. An angry exchange followed between the sentry and a student, exacerbated by a language problem. Other students and guards became involved in the argument, attracting a large number of very partisan spectators. Fearing the worst, the Irish students took to their heels and fled. Six of them were cornered and conducted to the nearest police station where they were interrogated. Later they were escorted by a detachment of the National Guard to the Hôtel de Ville where they were again interrogated. That evening they were detained at the De La Force prison. One pamphlet mentioned that the Irish students wore black and had their hair closely-cropped in traditional Irish clerical fashion.

Their defence lawyer, M. Buirette-Verrières, was a member of the Cordeliers Club and was in fact author of one of the pamphlets in favour of the students.[5] Verrières claimed in his address to the court that in undertaking the defence of the Irish students he ran the risk of sharing their fate should the verdict go against them.[6]

The six in question were Thomas MacKenna, Jeremy Delany, Peter Ingolsby, William Costello, John Hickey and Francis O'Beirne. Three other participants were named in the course of the interrogation: Hurley, Maginn and Aurelly (sic). The latter was possibly Charles O'Reilly from Co. Louth, featured in a later published account of the incident as the main culprit.[7] They ranged in age from Ingolsby who was twenty-three to Maginn who was fifteen or sixteen.[8] The date of their arrival in France varied from two weeks previously in the case of Hurley to five years in the case of Thomas MacKenna, who acted as spokesman for the group. Three of them, MacKenna, Delany and Costello, gave their evidence in French, two others through interpreters, MacKenna acting for Ingolsby and Costello for O'Beirne. Hicky, only two months in France, was not called upon to give evidence. There was only one ecclesiastic in the group: MacKenna, who was a tonsured cleric.

From the statements made, both at Gros-Caillou police station and at the Hôtel de Ville, it emerged that between 30 and 40 Irish students left the Irish college at 2pm and made their way to the Champ de Mars–as they did frequently on free days–led by a senior theologian. When they arrived about 3pm the Champ de Mars was thronged with tourists, strollers and about a thousand workers. The incident occurred at about 3.30. About 15 Irish students approached the altar of the fatherland in the centre of the ampitheatre. Something was knocked down and a row developed with the sentry. MacKenna claimed in his statement that 23-year-old Ingolsby had climbed the steps of the altar and that the sentry brusquely ordered him down. Ingolsby remonstrated with the sentry. Realising that Ingolsby did not understand French, MacKenna rushed over to explain matters. The sentry refused to listen, pushed MacKenna back violently and struck him with the flat of his sword. MacKenna could not remember whether the sword was sheathed or unsheathed. 18-year-old Jeremy Delany stated that he approached the altar of the fatherland with about 15 students, among whom were Hurley, O'Reilly, O'Beirne, Hicky and Ingolsby. He admitted seeing Hurley picking up a support for the incense vase but had not seen it being knocked down. Delany was himself knocked down by the sentry and sustained an injury to his nose. He admitted picking up a stone to defend himself.

In their defence the Irish students claimed they were the victims of brutality on the part of the sentries. MacKenna was struck several times with the flat of a sword; Ingolsby on the bottom with a musket butt; Delany twice knocked down and struck with a gun butt. Hicky was also knocked down and struck with a shoulder-belt. O'Beirne tried to ward off blows from a sword with his walking-stick and the sentry struck him with his fist on the right side of the head. Both Delany and Ingolsby admitted picking up stones but claimed it was in self-defence. At this point, the incident was attracting a large and nasty crowd and the Irish took to their heels. A running battle developed with a large number of workers joining in the chase. Six of the Irish were cornered just at the exit of the Champ de Mars.

They were taken first to the guard house and then to the police station at Gros Caillou in the Invalides section. A large crowd followed. Apart from the Irish students, statements were taken from seven others, including a barge-man, a shop foreman, a journeyman and some soldiers. Their accounts of the event differed substantially from that given by the Irish. From these statements, an indictment was drawn up charging the Irish with tearing down the inscriptions surrounding the altar, throwing down a wreath, seeking to rip out the planks, maltreating and disarming the sentry and throwing stones at the National Guard. As a result it was decided to commit them to De La Force prison.

Outside the police station the crowd was growing and turning extremely ugly. They were trying to force the door, calling out for the prisoners to be handed over to them to be hung from lamp-posts. Already a dozen of them had forced their way into the courtyard. The commandant of the 9th battalion offered to convey the prisoners to the Abbaye prison. He went out and exhorted the mob to respect the law but to no avail. Reinforcements were sent for. A troop of cavalry arrived and were ordered to draw up in battle formation. Twice they charged to clear a passage so that the Irish could be taken out. Some of the riders were unhorsed and injured. Finally, the authorities were forced to concede that the ringleaders of the mob be allowed to escort the prisoners to the Hôtel de Ville with the mounted National Guard.

At the Palais Bourbon they were joined by General Lafayette, who headed the cortège. The march lasted about an hour, each Irish student held tightly by his French captor like a bounty-hunter. All Paris was thus alerted to the 'Irish plot'. As one newspaper reporter commented: 'in the interval between the departure from the Champ de Mars and the arrival at the Hôtel de Ville the incident had been falsified beyond recognition.' He noted pointedly that 'one witness repeated from memory a fairly long dialogue between the seminarist and the sentry–and this in spite of the fact that ... this cleric neither spoke nor understood French.'[9] When they arrived at Hôtel de Ville MacKenna was knocked down, beaten and almost hanged, which prompted the defence lawyer to remark later: 'So much for confidence in General Lafayette!' Statements were again taken at Hôtel de Ville and eventually the students were committed to De La Force prison.

That evening, the reporter for *La Feuille du Jour* entered a well-known café where a very excited crowd were heatedly discussing the incident. People were shouting 'The rope! The gibbet! Public apology!' He left this 'den of furies' and wrote in his report that 'by night it was being said that sacrilegious priests with swords ensconced in their walking-sticks mutilated the national monument, tore down the trophies, and murdered the sentries.'[10] Collège des Irlandais became the immediate target for their anger, a mob riot taking place outside in which Kearney nearly lost his life. He was held responsible for the rash behaviour of his students and later claimed that he owed his life 'to the generous efforts of the National Guard.'[11]

Well aware of the volatility of the Parisian populace Walsh

immediately sent an urgent message to the municipal authorities requesting police protection for the colleges. On the following day, M. Bailly, the mayor of Paris, instructed Lafayette 'to take efficacious measures to insure that their houses and persons will be respected.' The mayor included the Scots and English establishments, which he said, 'the people are accustomed to regard as identical.' As to the incident itself, he informed Lafayette that, after hearing all the witnesses, it was concluded that 'the Irish ... were guilty only of a slight act of rashness, for which they were at present atoning.'[12] They were left in prison for two weeks to cool their heels. Ingolsby, whose behaviour was, to say the least, provocative, was probably rusticated by the superior as his name disappears from the college records. All were fortunate to escape so lightly. The battalion commandant involved felt obliged to enter into his statement that 'they owe their lives to the prudence and firmness of the National Guard, who behaved with all the wisdom and zeal possible.' A little over six months later the same National Guard put down a protest in the Champ de Mars which resulted in a large-scale massacre.

The Irish colleges were beginning to acquire a notoriety among Parisians that was distinctly unhealthy. The adoption of the Civil Constitution of the Clergy by the National Assembly in the summer of 1790 and the subsequent imposition of an oath to support it split the French church. The following spring, when Pius VI finally condemned it and threatened the French clergy who took the oath with excommunication, the two Irish chapels in the capital became unique. Not included in the terms of the Constitution, the priests there could continue to perform their functions and attracted a number of the French faithful to their services. Irish priests working in French institutions were proffered the oath. Abbé Richard Ferris in Collège de Montaigu refused it and lost his considerable financial emoluments, which included those of the vicar-general of Amiens. Dr Peter Flood of Collège de Navarre also refused but remained on the staff of the Irish college. The Civil Constitution, however, struck a mortal blow at the financial underpinning of Collège des Lombards. There, the priest-students supported themselves on their Mass-stipends, which mostly entailed saying public Masses in the Parisian churches. Walsh informed Bishop Plunkett 'of the local events which put the students of this house under the cruel necessity of finishing their education in a more Catholic country.' A number of Meath students penned a postscript to the same letter, hoping 'your Lordship will be sufficiently sensible of our distressed situation when informed that the municipal officers have debarred us from celebrating in any church or private chapel without a special licence from our intruded and anti-canonical prelate, whose jurisdiction we must disavow.' They concluded the letter by informing their bishop: 'The greater part of our subjects have disposed of their little effects and are resolved to set out immediately.'[13] The final retreat from Collège des Lombards was already under way. Early in May, Archbishop Troy wrote to Archbishop Butler: 'The situation in France is becoming alarming and the sixth year students at the Lombard College ought to be called home.'[14]

Walsh, never the most popular of clerics, was worried 'at a report which was industriously propagated in Ireland—that of my deviating from canonical authority and swallowing the constitutional pill.' His appointment to Collège des Lombards was neither forgotten nor forgiven. 'Thank God' he told Plunkett, 'I am innocent of this foul imputation and I trust that the prelates on whom the vile calumniator dared to impose will bring him to condign punishment.'[15]

Walsh had to solve a more pressing legal problem to keep his house functioning. Under the old régime, all financial transactions of the college were countersigned by the abbots of Ste Geneviève and St Victor. These gentlemen were no longer legally recognised in France. But rents had to be collected, debts paid and bursaries administered. Walsh petitioned in turn the Paris Directory and the financial committee of the National Assembly for permission to administer his properties under his own signature. The National Assembly issued a decree granting him sole administratorship, on condition that the original deeds be placed in the Paris departmental archives.[16]

By now the police were taking a sinister interest in the foreign colleges. A police commissioner made a tour of inspection of the English college, just a hundred yards around the corner from Collège des Irlandais. Just before he had completed his inspection in the company of the superior he noticed a door which had not been opened. Inside, he found an ordination service in progress, involving a large group of French clergy, all of whose names were taken, including that of the bishop[17] The Irish colleges could justifiably be suspected of housing similar activities, as future events would show.

Some confusion reigned in police circles regarding the areas of application of the law. A printed list of churches and chapels belonging to the nation, to be closed by the decree of the Paris Directory, mentioned Collège des Lombards but not Collège des Irlandais.[18] On 15 April the police visited Collège des Irlandais and placed seals on the chapel.[19] The following day, it was the turn of Collège des Lombards where the police found 62 occupants including Walsh who declared his intention of making representations to the Department. The matter appears to have been rapidly cleared up, as the seals were lifted the next day, Sunday, at 7am, in time for the usual Masses.

A week later Troy proposed to Butler that the name of Abbé Edgeworth be inserted in all the official documents of the Irish college,[20] presumably because of his influence in court circles as confessor of Madame Elisabeth, the king's sister. Fortunately for the future of the Irish colleges this proposal was never implemented. The fortunes of the royal family took a decidedly downward turn a month later, when they were apprehended on their flight to Varennes and brought back in disgrace to Paris.

On Bastille Day 1791, Kearney painted a gloomy picture of events in a letter to Plunkett:

> Nothing has remained free from the evil influence of our famous revolution ... religion lost–impiety trumphing–the Sees occupied by schismatic, immoral, irregularly consecrated bishops–the true ones dispersed, persecuted, outlawed–parishes abandoned to the wolves–the true pastors obliged to hide themselves–the churches deserted–everything, in a word, that hell can invent, put into execution to discourage the faithful and absolutely overturn religion.

And after all that he added: 'Our house is quiet.'[21] It was the proverbial calm before the storm.

NOTES

1. Tuetey, A. *Répertoire général des sources manuscrites de l'histoire de Paris pendant la révolution*, 2 p423. Tuetey lists this as one of the ten major incidents of 1790.
2. Byrne, *Memoirs*, 3 p200.
3. B.H.V.P. 12272. *Grand Tumult arrivé hier au soir à l'occasion d'une insulte faite à l'Autel de la Patrie, au champ de la Fédération, et Beau Trait du général La Fayette qui s'empare des coupables et les conduit lui-même à l'Hôtel de Ville.*

   B.N. Lb39 9585. *Détail de l'horrible assassinat commis hier au soir au*

Champ de la Fédération, sur la personne d'une sentinelle et Insulte faite à l'Autel de la Patrie par une troupe d'aristocrates et d'abbés.

B.N. Lc2 2453. *Fureur du Père Duchesne contre les soixante calotins qui ont saccagé et profané l'Autel de la Patrie, assassiné la sentinelle du Champ de Mars et désarmé le corps de garde.*

B.N. Lb39 9586. *Récit véritable de ce qui s'est passé au Champ de Mars.*

B.N. Lb39 4407. B.H.V.P. 953548. *Adresse au peuple de la capitale sur l'événement du Champ de Mars, le 6 décembre 1790.*

B.N. Lb39 4408. B.H.V.P. 959779. *Justification des écoliers irlandais, sur l'événement qui s'est passé au Champs de Mars, le lundi 6 du mois. La Feuille du Jour*, 8 Dec. 1790; *Mercure de France*, 18 Dec. 1790.

4. B.H.V.P. 959784. *Grand poème epi-civique où l'on célébre la grande victoire des citoyens soldats et des soldats citoyens sur les abbés aristocrates qui voulaient pulveriser l'Autel de la Patrie.*
5. This club, named after the Franciscan monastery where it had been founded the previous April, was more formally the Society of the Rights of Man and the Citizen. Its most prestigious members were Danton, Marat and Camille Desmoulins, and amongst a preponderance of lawyers and journalists was James Ruttledge, a prolific pamphleteer of Irish extraction. B.H.V.P. 953548.
6. A.N. F7 4624.
7. O'Reilly, *The Irish Abroad and at Home*, pp215-6.
8. In this tiny sample, the age of entry into Collège des Irlandais varied between 13 and 21.
9. *La Feuille du Jour*, 8 Dec. 1790.
10. *La Feuille du Jour*, 8 Dec. 1790.
11. D.D.A. 121/128, 18 Nov. 1801.
12. B.N.P. *Fonds Français* 11697 fos.109v & 110r. 7 Dec. 1790.
13. Cogan, op. cit. p190-1, Walsh to Plunkett, 18 April 1791.
14. C.D.A. Troy to Butler, 5 May 1791. cf Coll. Hib. 20 pp102-3.
15. Cogan, op. cit. p194, Walsh to Plunkett, 14 July 1791.
16. A.N. C58 no. 590, 31 Mar. 1791.
17. A.P. A A/198 *Observatoire*, 19 Mar. 1791.
18. Ibid. 11 April 1791.
19. Ibid. 15 April 1791.
20. C.D.A. Troy to Butler, 25 April 1791.
21. Cogan, op. cit. pp194-5, Kearney to Plunkett, 14 July 1791.

4
'Our House is Quiet'

I ask you, gentlemen, to take prompt, certain and efficacious measures to protect us henceforth from insult and outrage, or else pronounce our expulsion from France. We shall leave it without a blush.

–Walsh, *Mercure de France*, 15 Oct. 1791.

Early in the autumn of 1791 Abbé Edgeworth wrote to Bishop Moylan of Cork:

> All our churches shut up; a considerable number of our late labourers obliged to flee; those who remain, compelled by necessity to exercise their functions in private rooms, and to go about from house to house ... Both civil and religious matters go every day worse and worse in this unfortunate country ... God alone can know what our doom may be ... We have therefore, according to me, a more cruel winter to pass than any of those we have yet seen; and during that space of time, how many assaults will be given to the feeble remains of Christianity in this unfortunate kingdom![1]

The next assaults were destined for the Irish colleges, for whom the winter was to prove very cruel indeed.

Sunday 25 September marked their re-opening after the summer holidays. As the faithful were emerging from Sunday Mass in Collège des Lombards, they were attacked by a large crowd which had gathered outside. The Irish chapels had now become targets for extreme revolutionaries. The police report states that there was a 'considerable gathering' of men and women in rue des Carmes.[2] When the police detachment arrived they were informed that a number of women were seen entering the chapel. It was now midday and Mass was finished. The police commissioner informed Walsh that the law required that the outside door be kept shut during religious services, which were authorised for the Irish occupants and not for outsiders. Walsh invoked certain treaties to which the commissioner replied that they did not authorise him to allow certain women into his chapel. Walsh said they entered without his knowledge and that his house deserved special indulgence as there were in Paris a large number of Irish people who did not understand French and could only communicate with their own priests. That, the commissioner replied, was a matter for the Directory to decide. In the meantime, the law was to be scrupulously observed. The police now turned their attention to 'managing' the crowd, whom they feared would only turn ugly if force were used to disperse it. Walsh was asked to withdraw the women as the commissioner did not wish to enter the chapel out of respect for the exposed Blessed Sacrament. If they persisted, an 'irruption' on the part of the crowd was to be feared. The women were duly escorted to the street. Later that day other women presented themselves for Vespers but Walsh kept the door shut.

Walsh at once demanded a transcript of the police report which was not forthcoming and which he claimed was not drawn up until three days later. When he did get it he immediately contested its version of the event. In a two-columned printed reply, which Walsh addressed to the Directory, the police and the *procureur-syndic*, he pointed out factual errors and alleged the police 'treated the disturbers gently while denying justice to the persecuted'.[3] This also formed part of an *exposé*, which he addressed to Madame.[4] He gives his own account of the event in a long letter to the newspaper, *Mercure de France*:

> ... several of them [Irish] accompanied perhaps by some French friends or servants assisted at our Mass and on leaving were pursued, hooted and maltreated by individuals who emerged from a neighbouring wine-shop, and as if insults and threats were not enough, they laid hold on a respectable woman (she is said to have been pregnant) and whipped her cruelly; This scandalous scene was applauded.[5]

When the police commissioner arrived on the scene with a detachment of the National Guard he immediately promised the mob satisfaction and reprimanded Walsh in the presence of four of the ringleaders. The commander of the National Guard was equally partisan. 'In the name of the law, I order you to follow me to the church of Saint Etienne or I will abandon you to the people'. Walsh ended his letter on a high note: 'I ask you then, gentlemen, to take prompt, certain and efficacious measures to protect us henceforth from insult and outrage, or else pronounce our expulsion from France. We shall leave it without a blush ...'

By this time the violence had spread to rue du Cheval Vert where Collège des Irlandais became the new target. Here, Walsh's allegation of the partisan behaviour of the National Guard is explicitly mentioned in the report of police commissioner Simon, of the Observatory Section. While commending the battalion sergeant of the regular army stationed at Val-de-Grace for his zeal and intelligence and for his firm, moderate and prudent action, he added pointedly, 'feebly supported' by the National Guard. He went on to state: 'We would have liked that the zeal of those who were there to assist him was equally impartial and moderate but we were informed that several of the National Guard illegally entered the Irish seminary ... and forced those they found there to leave without escorting them, thus exposing them to the fury of the crowd.'[6]

The incident took place on Sunday 9 October. The police were astonished by the enormous crowd gathered in Place de l'Estrapade. They were informed that the cause of the disturbance was the anger felt by the populace about the Mass in the Irish seminary, attended by a considerable number of outsiders, particularly women. Both entries into rue du Cheval Vert were thronged, while soldiers and National Guard occupied the street itself and the entrance to the seminary. The police called on the people to disperse but were largely ignored. Some individuals were inciting the crowd, depicting the conduct of the Irish seminary as a rebellion and declaring that if the magistrates would not enforce the law the people would. Meanwhile, from inside the Irish college, the students were provoking the crowd with threatening and insulting gestures. One of them tried to detach a slate to throw at the crowd, but was prevented by a companion. The crowd claimed an earthenware vessel had already been thrown but the police failed to find any fragments on the street. The crowd eventually began to disperse from rue du Cheval Vert but still thronged the adjacent streets. No sooner had the military chiefs decided to raise the guard and retire than they had to be called out again. It was between 7.30 and 8pm before the streets were cleared.

Further details can be gleaned from the statements taken by the police from the battalion sergeant and five witnesses on Sunday evening. These included two second-hand dealers, a bookbinder (all three, interestingly, from rue des Carmes, near Collège des Lombards), a shoemaker and a former cavalry officer. The latter had been dismissed for refusal to take the oath and arrived at the Irish college armed with a rosary-beads, loudly declaring to all and sundry that he was a 'Catholic, holy, Roman and apostolic.' The police arrested him for his own safety and later released him, declaring 'that his mind had become deranged by fanaticism'. According to the second-hand dealers, the cavalry officer had been present a fortnight earlier at the disturbances outside Collège des Lombards, making signs of the cross and offering to conduct the women to safety. He behaved similarly outside Collège des Irlandais. When interrogated the 40-year-old former captain, a native of Languedoc, declared that he used these occasions to exercise his religion and to prevent the women being whipped by the crowd. He was accompanied by the shoemaker, Claude Michel, whom he considered to be a pious catholic.

The battalion sergeant alleged that Michel Renaud, one of the second-hand dealers, had hooted and obstructed him. The police, not considering him one of the ringleaders, dismissed him with a warning that if he were caught again in similar circumstances he would be charged with disturbing the peace. The police commissioner described the event as one 'of such great importance' and concluded his report by warning the police department to 'take all the precautions necessary to prevent the dangerous consequences of disorder by a headstrong people'.

The importance of the incident in the popular mind is borne out by the title of a pamphlet about it: *Exact account of the great revolution which took place at the Irish seminary, rue du Cheval Vert, at Estrapade, faubourg St Marceau, where 27 bigoted counter-revolutionaries were whipped by the holy anger of the people, as well as the superior of the seminary with the list of names and status of all the arses whipped.*[7] In fact, only 12 names are given, the others being almost all housekeepers of refractory parish priests, one of whom collapsed three times 'when she saw they were about to whip the superior of the seminary.' The pamphlet claimed that the Irish seminary had become a refuge for the refractory priests of Paris. 9 October was the feast of St Denis, patron saint of the clergy and all the non-juring clergy of Paris and its environs came to celebrate it at the Irish college. For the occasion the Irish provided a moving statue in the form of a large crucifix whose head could make the yes and no signs. The author explained that it was all very cleverly contrived with wire and springs. All this proved too much for 'the decent patriotic ladies of faubourg Saint-Marcel'. They apprehended the women leaving Mass, 'whipped their bare bottoms publicly in the middle of rue du Cheval Vert,' after forcing them to apologise loudly and clearly. The action began at 2pm and continued until after 6pm. The guard were forced to remain very late, because, after they had completed this correction, the people wanted to enter the college 'to destroy this den of superstition'.

The police report does not record the whippings but a newspaper report does mention that 'a woman was snatched from a confessional'.[8] In a further statement on the following day the battalion sergeant, Jean-Louis Duschaisne, declared that he was called out at 3.30 by the porter of the Irish college and remained on duty there until 8pm. He mentions the porter of the house opposite the Irish college among the main culprits and, particularly, his wife 'who displayed the greatest fieriness, declaring that they should whip all the women found in the college'. The guards themselves were treated 'as vermin and crooks'. A young woman with five or six others said they should force their way into the college, whip the women there and chase them out. With reinforcements from rue Mouffetard, he cleared the entrance to the college, but the young woman forced him and his 'feeble detachment' to give way. Further reinforcements were summoned from faubourg St Jacques and Val-de-Grace and the crowd were dispersed. With the street evacuated, the people in the chapel were brought out. He formed a passage-way through the crowd, still filling the corner, to escort the women to safety. Nevertheless a woman was knocked down by a young man of about 18, dressed in green. He arrested the young man and handed him over to a guard, who later, inexplicably, released him. A woman from Mouffetard kept shouting: 'Whip them!', but he did not succeed in arresting her. The sergeant added that there was no provocation by the people inside the college, although stones were fired at the students' windows to provoke them.

Passions were inflamed. The slightest incident could re-ignite the fuse. On Monday afternoon a drunkard from rue des Carmes banged loudly on the Irish college door, claiming he saw two women go in. When his condition was realised, he was hustled out, 'receiving or giving himself a blow on the head'. The door was locked with the drunkard's hat inside. He started to shout and in no time a huge crowd had gathered. Taking no chances this time, the police called in reinforcements, including a detachment of cavalry. The crowd were promptly dispersed. Having retrieved his hat, the drunkard was led away in the direction away from the crowd. A foreigner, a knight of the order of St Louis, continued to incite the crowd. Charles Kearney, the superior, emerged and began to remonstrate with them, insisting forcefully in the name of the law, on the right to liberty and security of persons. He soon became involved in an argument with one of the National Guard[9] and the police persuaded him to retire.

The police, with an official, M. Joly, entered the Irish college, where they discovered nothing to justify the riotous behaviour of the crowd. A domestic servant, Marie Cirret, was taken to the police station and charged with inciting the people. She had resisted arrest, striking the battalion sergeant in the stomach with her fist. She had been one of the principle trouble-makers on the previous day. The maid denied everything and her employer, an assistant police chief of the section, gave her a character reference, stating that she was 'good-hearted but pigheaded'. She was released on his assurance that she would be made available to the police on request. She was however denounced to the police department.[10]

Marie Magdeleine Lamotte rose at dawn on Tuesday 11 October and performed her morning ablutions in her apartment, 14 rue Bordet. She was 52, a spinster, a teacher and devout, with a definite penchant for martyrdom. A formidable combination in any age. At 8am she set out jauntily to attend Mass, as was her wont, at the Irish college. Swinging round the corner from Place de l'Estrapade, her flat heels beat out a military tattoo on the cobblestones of the battle-scarred rue du Cheval Vert and alerted the neighbourhood of her arrival. She knocked loudly on the great door of Collège des Irlandais. From inside, the plaintive voice of the concierge pleaded with her to go away or 'she would have us all murdered in our beds'.[11] Disappointed that the Irish had no longer the stomach for war, she decided to carry the battle across the road to the chapel of the Eudists, about a hundred yards away. On the way she stopped to gossip with Marie Magdeleine Robinaut, the maid of M. de la Noue, a deputy of the National Assembly who had come down to collect the milk. They both hailed from the same part of the country.[12]

Catherine Gerome, a turner's wife from rue des Ciseaux, heard about the woman who went every day to Mass at the Irish college, and decided it was time to put a stop to it. Spotting the two women chatting, she launched her attack. 'Here are two more bigots to be whipped!' She claimed she was goaded into it by the National Guard saying that she hadn't the courage to whip them. The maid went to the police station at 5 rue des Postes. The policeman's wife and the local town-crier, who was visiting, came to arrest Gerome. In the ensuing scuffle, Gerome lost her bonnet, but was finally dragged to the commissariat. From there she was conveyed to De La Force prison. Rioting continued outside the Irish college and later a hawker from rue des Carmes was taken in for questioning. He was selling broadsheets, including, presumably *The Great Revolution*, on Sunday's riot, and became obstreperous when the police requested him to retire. At the station he apologised and pleaded for leniency, claiming he was his family's only support. He was released with a caution.[13]

Had these incidents taken place outside a French religious house it is highly improbable that the municipal authorities would have bothered to intervene. But the Irish colleges gave them an international dimension. The Directory of the Department issued a decree on Wednesday 12 October strongly condemning the outrages 'which violated at the same time natural justice, civil liberty, treaty obligations and the law of hospitality'. It ordered that the municipality should see to it that there would be no further violations of religious liberty and 'charged especially the procurator of the commune to denounce and pursue all civil and military officials who refused or neglected to guarantee full religious liberty with all the means provided by the law and to pursue also all persons who by act, insult, threat or provocation, attempted to violate it.'[14] This decree was printed and posted throughout the Department. On Saturday, notifications of the decree were sent to the Observatory and Panthéon sections, where the two Irish colleges were situated, by Desmousseaux, procurator of the commune. In his accompanying letter he said that 'fanaticism and intolerance appear to agitate the people' and he urged the sectional administrators to use all the means at their disposal to preserve public order, concluding: 'I rely entirely on your zeal, firmness and prudence'.[15]

All three were put to the test on the following day. The crowd gathered again to harass the people attending Mass at the Irish college and bouts of fisticuffs took place between women, an elderly lady being seized and violently shaken. A nun was also struck. Jeanne Michelle Pothain, a lacemaker, accompanied by her friend, Antoinette Augustine Soullignan, the daughter of a timber wholesaler, was heading hurriedly into rue du Cheval Vert when she was seized by the arm. She was grossly insulted in the foulest of language, called a 'whipped arse', and accused of going to the Irish college 'to see her pimps'. Held by her scarf, she was struck so violently in the back that she could not breathe. Finally, in an effort to escape she hit her attacker as hard as she could on the left jaw. A Justice of the Peace, M. Bosguillon, who was standing guard outside the college door, saw what had happened and came and arrested the assailant. She was a cotton-spinner, called Jeanne Paret, a widow who lived in rue Mouffetard. At the commissariat she declared loudly that 'nobody should be let into that house' and that 'she wasn't going to prison for some whipped-arses.' But to prison she went, at first to the Concièrgerie to await her trial at which she was given three months hard labour.[16]

On 6 October the catholics of Paris had sent an address to the king through the Internuncio in which they specifically referred to the outrages committed outside the Irish chapels. But on this occasion, the police had acted firmly and promptly and on the following day Kearney and Walsh wrote to the Department expressing their appreciation. They gratefully acknowledged the decree issued on 12 October and its firm and impartial execution the day before. They even paid a special tribute to the National Guard.[17] Two days later, the Directory of Paris wrote to M. de Lessart, Minister of the Interior, in reply to the latter's enquiry about the measures taken to prevent outbreaks at the Irish chapels. The minister was informed about the decree of 12 October and that it was proposed to confer with the Mayor, the municipal officials, the police department and the officer commanding the army regarding further measures. The Irish superiors themselves were invited to the Department on the following Friday where 'it intends to take in their presence ... the necessary measures to provide them with all the rights the law guarantees dwellers in France.'[18]

The decree of 12 October had authorised the opening of some chapels under the supervision of the local parish priest who had accepted the Civil Constitution. The Internuncio informed the Holy See that Walsh 'loudly protested against the clause and threatened the intervention of the British Ambassador. As a result of this threat, Montmorin took fright at the thought of English cannon and the clause was speedily removed for everybody'.[19] Blondel, the secretary of the Department wrote a letter to *Le Moniteur Universel* requesting them to publicise the new decree and in it he acknowledged the part played by the Irish incidents in obtaining this decree.[20] A new decree was issued on 19 October stating that 'all secular and religious could open their churches ... without submitting to any other surveillance than that of the police'.[21] A letter was addressed to Walsh on 23 October by several Irish and French citizens congratulating him on his courage and tenacity, in obtaining this decree. In thanksgiving he had Masses offered for the prosperity of France.[22]

The diocese of Kerry was at this time vacant and among the names proposed to fill it was that of Charles Kearney. Surprisingly, in view of all he had been through, Kearney wrote to Rome on 25 October: 'With all power of mind and sincerity ... I ask that [I] be not named'.[23] Little did he suspect then that whatever horrors the unruly canons of Kerry at their worst might provide they would be nothing compared to those in store for him from the growing reign of terror in Paris. Kearney and Walsh proposed to the Internuncio the name of a former student of the Collège des Lombards, the Abbé Cook, then living in some style in Paris, judging by the inventory of his silverware in his residence in the fashionable rue du fabourg St Honoré. An anonymous correspondent in Collège des Lombards advised him in verse to be wary of his sharp wit and his sharper quill, concluding:

> Whilst most that are or would be great
> Must dread your pen, your person hate;
> And you on Draper's-hill must lie,
> And there without a mitre die.[24]

Walsh went on to press Rome for a fairer share of episcopal honours for the alumni of Collège des Lombards. He pointed out that the last seven appointments were all former students of Collège des Irlandais while the great majority of priests for the Irish mission came from his college. 'They form, with their confrères in Nantes, two-thirds of the secular clergy of Ireland', he stated. He emphasised the importance of the Irish language, 'the strongest barrier against heresy'. His students, arriving in Paris as mature adults, retained their fluency in Irish, while the younger students of Collège des Irlandais soon forgot whatever Irish they had.[25]

Meanwhile, in Paris, the Irish colleges were enjoying a temporary respite from riots. Parisian suspicions that they were providing refuge for refractory priests were indeed justifiable: Walsh organised retreats for them in Collège des Lombards in November and December. This was a daring undertaking and one not supported by all the Irish priests. Abbé O'Brien, chaplain to Monsieur 'protested vehemently against it and Walsh denounced him to the Internucio, Abbé de Salamon. 'Under the influence of fear and panic himself, he sought to inspire the students with his own alarms, saying that they would get themselves massacred if the retreat took place ... he burst out publicly, and threatened to denounce to the new magistrates my unpatriotic conduct, in authorising meetings which compromised the existence of the house.'[26]

But O'Brien's fears were justified. Trouble flared up again on 8 December, outside Collège des Lombards, while one of these retreats was in progress. The crowd coming from Mass were attacked and insulted; an old man was knocked down and a woman was thrown in the gutter. Two individuals were denounced to the police by Walsh for inciting the riot and two French priests, Abbé Lodier and Abbé Dutouche, made corroboratory statements. Walsh insisted on the right to freedom of worship accorded him by the decree of 12 October. Two young men were taken in for questioning. Both of them, François Pierrot, an apprentice tailor, and Jean Baptiste Catois, a journeyman binder, were near neighbours of the college in rue des Carmes. They pleaded innocent and were released with a warning 'to be more circumspect in future in their language and never to be found again in a crowd outside Collège des Lombards, with intent to disrupt religious services'.[27]

The retreats however, continued: six in all between the end of 1791 and the early months of 1792. Abbé de Floirac, vicar-general of Paris, attended. The Internuncio wrote to Cardinal Zelada in Rome: 'I was truly edified by their fervour. I can assure your Eminence, that they renewed in a special way their oaths of loyalty and obedience to the Holy See'. He added that at the December retreat they decided 'to unite themselves more closely to the Sacred Heart of Jesus' indicating the presence of Père de Clorivière, founder of the Society of the Heart of Jesus and Daughters of the Heart of Mary.[28] Abbé O'Brien must have decided to move out as in January 1792, the mayor and officials of St Denis issued him a certificate stating that he was resident in the cloister of St Paul, where he was a canon.[29]

The police reported trouble again on 2 February when women were insulted going into Mass. The crowd were informed in the presence of Walsh that the religious services were within the law and they issued orders to the barracks at Place Maubert, to mount frequent patrols in rue des Carmes.[30] On 22 February the Internuncio wrote again to the cardinal, enclosing a letter from the retreatants for the Pope. 'Clergy of the second order' he wrote, 'are behaving in a truly heroic manner in the midst of all the dangers that surround us'. He added: 'Abbé Walsh is the soul of these good works'. Cardinal Zelada replied: 'Say to Abbé Walsh how much his zeal and edifying piety are appreciated'. On 4 March, probably after the fourth retreat, Mgr de Bonald, bishop of Clermont, ordained several young Frenchmen in secrecy in the library of Collège des Irlandais. One of them was Pierre de Coudrin, the future founder of the Order of the Sacred Heart, which was to give to the world the leper priest, Damian of Molokai.[31]

As the political climate worsened, such ceremonies were bound to compromise the Irish colleges. Aware of the approaching doomsday, Charles Kearney wrote to Bishop Teahan of Kerry. The latter relayed the message to Moylan of Cork: 'By a letter I had last post from Dr Kearney he wishes most earnestly that we should endeavour to establish seminaries in this kingdom which might be supported, he says, by yearly remittances from our colleges abroad. That by this means those funds, the income of which would be forthcoming, tho' the principal cannot be got out of France, might become of real use to our Mission. This business he earnestly recommends for the Bishops to revolve in their minds. And it may now be more necessary to take up, if on account of the Emperor's death, the project of the Counter-revolution drops.'[32] The emperor's death worried also Abbé Edgeworth as he conveyed to Bishop Moylan: 'This delusive hope, kept up from week to week by foreign letters, has supported our spirits, under the rod of iron that sways at present.' However, he expected the new emperor to act decisively and he was correct. Francis II was young, impetuous and had a taste for military adventure. 'I think him bound in honour to make good all the promises of his father', Edgeworth remarked, adding: 'it is evidently in his interest; ... he cannot expect to enjoy peace in his own dominions, if the spirit of insubordination that now prevails in France is not effectually repressed.'[33]

A month later France declared war on Austria. Prussia joined Austria and the war of the First Coalition began. Abbé Richard Ferris from Kerry had exchanged his cassock for a military uniform. He rejoined Berwick's Regiment where he had been a cadet 20 years earlier and was quickly promoted to captain and aide-de-camp to the Duc de Fitzjames.[34] When war broke out in April 1792, he was stationed at Bingen on the Rhine. Count Bartholomew O'Mahony was the brigadier-general of the regiment, which was assigned as bodyguard to the Bourbon Princes, including Monsieur, brother of the king and future Louis XVIII.

While many of the Irish officers joined the Army of the Princes across the Rhine, others like the two Dillons, Arthur and Theobald, Oliver Harty and the future General Kilmaine opted to serve revolutionary France which was totally unprepared for active military operations and with its officer ranks considerably depleted by emigration. Dumouriez established three armies, under Custine, Lafayette and Rochambeau. An army corps of the latter, under Theobald Dillon at Lille was directed to attack Tournai, but no sooner had Dillon's troops advanced beyond the border than they were surprised by Austrian detachments. A partial withdrawal ended in confusion and the French retreated into Lille, where the cry of 'treason' was raised and Dillon was massacred by his own troops.[35]

These disasters reacted immediately on the political situation in France. Counter-revolution was in the air. The deteriorating international situation was bound to change what was hitherto a privileged position for the Irish colleges into an acute embarrassment. Xenophobia was beginning to spread in Paris. On 21 May a certain M. Minot made a complaint to the Mayor of Paris that 'a large number of false devotees of both sexes assiduously frequented the services celebrated by the Irish priests, rue du Cheval Vert, to the great indignation of the whole neighbourhood against those hypocrites of whom society should be purged'.[36] Such statements were beginning to be taken seriously in high places. M. Pétion, Mayor of Paris, instructed the police to have the English seminary, just round the corner from the Irish college, placed under surveillance, as rumour had it 'refractory priests were engaging in military exercises there'.[37] The Departmental authorities were empowered to deport refractory priests who were denounced by 20 'active' citizens.

On 13 June Louis imposed his veto on the decree against refractory priests and dismissed his Girondin ministers. The Girondins retaliated by supporting a popular demonstration to celebrate the anniversary of the Tennis Court Oath on 20 June. About 8,000 people, many of them women and all carrying pikes, invaded the Tuileries Palace and held Louis captive for several hours. Many of them had come from the radical faubourgs of St Antoine, St Marceau and the Observatory, where the Irish college was situated. Public opinion outside France was aghast at the treatment of the king. Writing from Tipperary to Abbé Cook, Fr Carroll alludes to Cook's 'minute and circumstantial detail of the tumultuous proceedings of the Parisian rabble on the 20th of last month: our publick prints here were sufficiently replete with all their diabolical manoeuvres'. Carroll added optimistically: 'We have very strong hopes that the approach of the foreign troops to the frontiers will bring about some happy change.'[38]

On 28 July news of Brunswick's Manifesto reached Paris. The Duke of Brunswick was the commander of the Prussian and Austrian forces then preparing to invade France, and his manifesto proclaimed that the allies were invading to suppress anarchy and restore the king's authority. Any National Guards who offered resistance would be shot and their homes demolished. It also declared that, if the Tuileries were invaded again or the slightest violence offered to the royal family, the city of Paris would be held specifically responsible, on pain of 'military punishment and total destruction.' Two days later the *fédérés* arrived from Marseilles, and Paris heard for the first time the stirring music of Rouget de Lisle's marching song, known to history as the 'Marseillaise'. A popular insurrection was now in the making. The Irish in Paris, in common with all foreigners, had further reason for disquiet. 'It is to be feared that they will be revenged on such as they think anyways attached to former principles,' Kearney informed Plunkett. 'In a word', he continued, 'the situation we are in is desperate beyond expression.'[39]

NOTES

1. England, op. cit. pp67-9, Edgeworth to Moylan, 20 Sept. 1791.
2. A.P. A A/200 *Panthéon,* 25 Sept. 1791.
3. D.D.A. 121/8, 25 Sept. 1791.
4. Possibly Marie Antoinette or Madame Elisabeth, the king's sister.
5. *Mercure de France*, 15 Oct. 1791. cf I.E.R. 1904, pp58-60.
6. A.P. A A/198 *Observatoire*, 9 Oct. 1791.
7. B.H.V.P. 7502. Qtd Boyle, I.E.R. (Jan-June) 1904, pp60-1.
8. *Mercure de France*, 15 Oct. 1791.
9. A militia force whose functions were limited to maintaining order locally. Established in July of 1789 and recruited locally, they were noticeably partisan, tending often to favour, as in this instance, the rioters at the expense of their victims.
10. A.P. A A/198 *Observatoire*, 88-9, 10 Oct. 1791.
11. 'que le peuple faisait de mauvais partis à tous ceux qui venaient entendre la messe aux Irlandais.'
12. A.N. Z3 84.
13. A.P. A A/198 *Observatoire*, 11 Oct. 1791.

14. A.N. F19471, 12 Oct. 1791. D.D.A. 121/8. A.N. F17 1162.
15. A.P. *Butte-des-Moulins*, 15 Oct. 1791. Qtd Amadou, op. cit. p50.
16. A.P. A A/198 *Observatoire*, 93-4, 16 Oct. 1791. A.N. Z3 81.
17. A.N. F17 1162, 17 Oct. 1791. D.D.A. 121/8.
18. A.N. F19 470 f209r.
19. *Correspondance secrète de l'Abbé Salamon*, 1 p119.
20. *Moniteur* 23 Oct. 1791.
21. *Moniteur* X p126. Cf Amadou, op. cit. pp49-50.
22. D.D.A. 121/8, 23 Oct. 1791.
23. Arch.Hib. VII pp11-13.
24. A.N. T452. nd.
25. Arch.Hib. VII pp4-5, 8-9.
26. Arch.Hib. VII pp13-14.
27. A.P. A A/200 *Panthéon*, 201, 8 Dec. 1791.
28. Ledré, Ch. *L'Abbé de Salamon*, p157.
29. A.N. F7 4474 59, doss.1. Jan. 1792.
30. A.P. A A/200 *Panthéon*, 2 Feb. 1792.
31. Commemorative plaque.
32. Teahan to Moylan, 20 Mar. 1792. cf. Coll.Hib. XIV pp110-111.
33. Edgeworth to Moylan, 21 Mar. 1792. England, op. cit. p72.
34. P.R.O. London, FO.27,43. Cf Purcell, op. cit. p34.
35. Hayes, *Irish swordsmen in France*, pp22-38.
36. Qtd I.E.R. 1904, p63.
37. A.N. DXL 3 no 60. Cf Tuetey, op. cit. 4 p90.
38. A.N. T452. Carroll to Cooke, 10 July 1792.
39. Cogan, op. cit. 3 p196. Kearney to Plunkett, 2 Sept. 1792.

5
Kerry Coup d'Etat

Know, Citizens, that this college was founded to educate the sons of victims of despotism and tyranny; they suffered martyrdom for the sake of equality and the rights of man.

–Thomas MacKenna, August 1792.

Rumours were rife in Paris about the impending escape of the king. Lafayette and others had made preparations for his flight to Rouen or Compiègne. Lally Tollendal claimed that Charles Kearney together with a few others including Abbé Edgeworth and the queen's principal page, Swinburne, planned the king's escape. A boat was bought and was lying off Le Havre. The boat waited a long time 'on the tragic indecision and the more tragic refusal of this unfortunate Prince: they would or could only take the King and he would not leave without the Queen.'[1] Later Kearney was to admit 'From the beginning of the Revolution I was pointed out as a man devoted to the cause of the Bourbons.'[2]

Popular fears and suspicions of counter-revolution galvanised the *sans-culottes* into action. On the night of 9 August delegates from the Parisian sections displaced the legal municipal authority at the Hôtel de Ville and formed an insurrectional Commune, ordering the sections and the *fédérés* to march on the royal palace the following day. When the armed mob tried to enter the palace, the Swiss Guards fired on them. The palace was set on fire and 600 of the Swiss Guards massacred. Kearney described 'the second revolution ... by far a more bloody one than that of '89.' Louis and his family had taken refuge at the National Assembly, where he was suspended from his royal functions. The royal family were later imprisoned in the Temple.

Kearney kept Plunkett up to date with the events:

The new constitution was ... quite overturned. The kingdom is now divided into three parties–those who call for the return of the old

> monarchy, all abuses corrected, those who would wish to adopt the constitution as formed by the first assembly, and those who are determined to dethrone the king. This last is actually the reigning party; no man dares to say a word against them. The strictest inquisition is made use of to find such as may be opposite to their system. Such as are suspected are cast into prison ... [3]

The Irish college must have been high on that list. On that very same day, Friday 10 August, it was invaded at 11am by 'a troop of disreputable people, armed with guns, swords, sabres and batons, who forced the entrance door and heavily infiltrated the interior. They roughed-up several of the students while others escaped over the walls into the neighbouring gardens and houses.'[4] Under pretext of searching for arms they broke into several apartments. The arrival of police commissioner Simon and the National Guard put an end to the pillage.

It was probably at this period that Thomas MacKenna, of Champ de Mars fame, armed with two pistols, primed and loaded, held the invading mob at bay, threatening to shoot the first one who dared to cross the threshold. Stopping them in their tracks, he addressed them:

> Know citizens, that this college was founded to educate the sons of the victims of despotism and tyranny; they suffered martyrdom for the sake of equality and the rights of man, and many of those who studied here are now in the French ranks of the army fighting on the frontiers against the European tyrants, to prevent them profaning the sacred land of liberty in France. As for me, I am going to embark on board a French warship where I expect to have an occasion to fight our worst enemies the English. [5]

The mob were appeased and melted away, exclaiming that he was a '*brave bon diable*.' MacKenna was then the second senior student in the college, having spent seven years there. Miles Byrne met him at Boulogne-sur-Mer in 1807, when the Irish Legion was stationed there. MacKenna was then a wealthy merchant, married to a widow and living in some style, and enjoyed entertaining the Irish officers. The story has some of the exaggerated flavour of an officer's mess. MacKenna was to spend more time than he then realised in Collège des Irlandais.

Worse was to follow. On Sunday 12 August at 5pm another crowd, larger this time, stormed the college to the cries of 'liberty and equality'. They began by pillaging the cellar and consuming the wine. Intoxicated, they broke into and looted Kearney's apartment, 'led by unknown individuals, who seemed to be perfectly informed on the lay-out of the house.'[6] They removed all Kearney's papers and registers. The students were forced to flee again, pursued by the mob screaming: 'Take Kearney dead or alive!' According to Lally Tollendal, the leader was a certain Truchon, nicknamed Longbeard.[7] He was, in fact, a member of the Paris Commune. There were 23 students in the college at the time, the older ones in their early twenties.

At this time, too, Abbé Edgeworth's house in rue du Bac was broken into at midnight by about 40 or 50 men, their leader demanding to see his papers. Edgeworth was terrified as he had 'papers of some importance; and many of them, if too nicely viewed, might have brought me to the block:' He managed to produce some of the less significant ones and they turned their attention to another occupant of the house on whom they discovered a letter recently arrived from Germany. He was taken away and executed a few days later. Severely shaken, Edgeworth spent the next two days destroying all his papers. Shortly afterwards, his house was broken into again by over a hundred men and this time thoroughly searched. Nothing was found and Edgeworth was left at liberty. One letter, from an agent of Monsieur, which had escaped the notice of both Edgeworth and his inquisitors 'betrayed in very clear terms all my connections with the court.'[8]

One of the results of the revolution of 10 August was that the Department of Paris was completely overshadowed by the Commune, whose members belonged, for the most part, to the lower middle class of small shopkeepers and artisans. They controlled the police and the National Guard, now under the command of the brewer, Santerre. The prosecution of political crimes was transferred from the courts to the local administrative authorities, thus making the Commune in Paris the final authority for all matters of internal security. They delegated their responsibility to the sections, who set up vigilance committees to carry out house-to-house searches and interrogate and arrest suspects. Between 10 August and the end of the month about 520 persons were arrested in Paris, of whom a half were refractory priests. Kearney informed Plunkett that 'all priests that have not taken the oath were taken, locked up in different monasteries and are to be gradually transported. Their fate is truly deplorable.'[9]

To prevent the escape of suspects the Commune suspended internal passports. To travel within the country it was necessary to have an identity card or *certificat de civisme*, granted only by the vigilance committees. Abbé Cook, still nursing hopes of getting Cashel, obtained his certificate in July. He was probably the last Irish priest to leave Paris as his Tipperary correspondent, Fr Carroll wrote: 'you give me the greatest of pleasure by the hint you have given in your letter of your determination to leave Paris by the beginning of August ...'[10] Dr Bray in fact was elected Archbishop of Cashel, although Cook tied with him in the voting.

By now most of the priest-students of Collège des Lombards had left, many of them more than twelve months previously. One of the first to leave was James Coigly. 'Having run many great risques and narrowly avoided being lanternized in the commencement of the Revolution, I, with great difficulty made my escape from Paris on the 12th of October 1789, and came as far as Dieppe unmolested; but the morning after my arrival there I was arrested and with great difficulty obtained permission to embark in the Brighton packet-boat.'[10a] At that time one of them, Charles MacCarthy, wrote to the Fr Leahy in Louvain:

> As we have lost every prospect of future existence in this unhallowed city and our house being now on the very brink of utter ruin, our society begins to disperse. Some are already gone to Antwerp, others are going to Louvain, and those who are in any measure advanced in their studies, are determined for Ireland.[11]

Only six, Robert Meagher and William O'Donnell of Cashel, Edmond O'Leary and O'Shaughnessy of Killaloe, Edmond Murphy of Kildare and Monk of Ardagh attended the final retreat at the end of April.[12] Walsh gave what he could to some 60 students to pay their return fare to Ireland. Later, he claimed he could not take signed receipts from them as they could be used as proof of contributions to the *émigrés* which would have meant certain death for Walsh.[13] Some of them had very narrow escapes. Fr Kearns, later executed as a Wexford insurgent, was caught by the mob and hoisted on to a lamp-post. A powerfully built man, the weight of his body broke the rope. When the crowd had departed, an Irish doctor, lurking in the shadows, succeeded in reviving him.[14] Fr Stephen Tobin of Roscarbery, managed to obtain a passport from the authorities by posing as a carpenter. His father had been a wheelwright.[15]

As Collège des Lombards was easily the most important seminary on the continent supplying priests for the Irish mission its closure would in a short time have catastrophic consequences for the Irish church. Kearney thus suggested to Plunkett that 'two or three houses might be established in Ireland for such as are intended for the church. Funds could be sent over yearly from France, whither it will be for many years improper to send persons for ecclesiastical education.' With regard to Collège des Irlandais, of which he himself was superior, he thought 'a few boys of talent may be sent over for classical education, and the study of languages, then sent home to pursue the study of theology.'[16] Bishop Bellew of Killala proposed establishing a seminary in Connacht. Wolfe Tone thought it would be advisable to educate all the Catholic clergy at home and that with the breaking up of the seminaries in France the bishops would be forced to adopt this line, adding 'that in that light, as in ten thousand others, the Revolution was of infinite service to Ireland.'[17]

With the abolition of the monarchy and the arrest of the king, those with the slightest royalist sympathies had reason to fear for their safety. Lafayette had defected on 19 August. Lally Tollendal had been arrested as a royalist shortly after. He was released the day before the massacres and made good his escape to England. The following day, Kearney wrote: 'it is said that this day all the prisoners have been murdered.' He was, in fact, writing when the September Massacres had already begun. On 1 September news arrived in Paris of the imminent fall of Verdun to the invading armies. The following morning the Commune called on the citizens to arm themselves, closed the barriers and ordered the volunteers to assemble in the Champ de Mars. 'Men, women and children are under pain of death,' Kearney wrote, 'to march out to meet the enemy, and to act according to their respective abilities–the men of any strength to fight; the weak and women, to dig up entrenchments. No besieged town was ever under such real apprehensions.'[18]

It was a fine Sunday. The crowds were out of doors and at 2pm the alarm cannon was fired and the tocsin sounded by the church bells. One of the municipality, on horseback, proclaimed in different parts of the city that the enemy was at the gates, that Verdun was besieged and could only hold out a few days. At 4pm the massacres began. George Munro, an English agent in Paris gave a graphic account of the 'scenes of horror' to Lord Grenville:

> A party, at the instigation of someone or other, declared they would not quit Paris as long as the prisons were filled with traitors ... A large body of *sans-culottes*, attended by a number of Marseillais proceeded to the Church des Carmes, rue Vaugirard, where amidst the acclama-

tions of a savage mob they massacred a number of refractory priests ... exceeding in all 160.[19]

Abbé Edgeworth, hearing the fire-bells, sent a servant-boy to see what was going on. He came back 'half dead with fright', told the Abbé about the massacres at the church des Carmes of several of the Abbé's most intimate friends, and that their house in rue du Bac was the next target. Disguising himself, the Abbé made his way to his mother's lodgings where he remained in hiding for several weeks.[20]

The Commune dispatched commissioners in an effort to save those imprisoned for civil offences and thus limit the ferocity and extent of the massacres. Notwithstanding, the murders resumed that evening at the Abbaye prison. Munro went to see for himself what was happening. He arrived there at 7am:

> ... a single file of men armed with swords or piques, formed a lane of some length, commencing from the prison door ... Two of the municipality were there in the prison with some of the mob distributing their justice. Those they found guilty were seemingly released but only to be precipitated at the door on a number of piques and among the savage cries of 'Vive la nation!' to be hacked to pieces by those who had swords and were ready to receive them. After this their dead bodies were dragged by the arms or legs to the abbaye which is distinct from the prison. Here they were laid up in heaps til carts could carry them away. The channel was swimming with blood and a bloody track was traced from the prison to the abbey down which they had dragged these misfortunate people.

Munro ends his gruesome account by apologising to Lord Grenville for detailing 'such an uncommon barbarity which I am sure, must be as disaggreeable for your Grace to read as it is for me to commit such acts to paper, but they ought to be particularised to the external disgrace of the people who pretend to be the most liberated among the nations of Europe.'[21]

In Dublin, Wolfe Tone thought differently. Writing in his diary a fortnight later, he commented:

> The devil to pay in Paris. The mob have broken open the prisons and massacred all the prisoners with circumstances of great barbarity, but robbed no one ... Strange mixture of cruelty and sentiment! An Irish mob would have plundered but shed no blood. A Parisian mob murders but respects property; which is best? I lean to the Frenchman; more manly. Our mob, very shabby fellows.[22]

Even while Tone was writing, revulsion had already set in among the revolutionaries in France, each group trying to saddle their political opponents with responsibility. Abroad, the impression created by the massacres which continued from 2-6 September, robbed the revolutionaries of their early friends and sympathisers. Peter Flood had a remarkably narrow escape. He was rescued 'from the sword of the armed mob' by M. Guiraut, one of the commissioners of the Commune and presented the following day at the bar of the National Assembly as proof to the English people 'of fraternity and generosity'. A request to the Assembly to furnish him with the means of returning to his native land was greeted with applause. It decreed that Flood be placed under the protection of the French nation and that Guiraut's name be entered in the minutes for saving a man's life.[23]

On 20 September the French army under Dumouriez won a decisive victory over the Prussians at Valmy. On the same day, the National Convention met for the first time in the palace of the Tuileries and its first act was to abolish the monarchy. The students who had fled the Irish college on 12 August did not return. They found furnished lodgings in the neighbourhood. Kearney, fearing for his life, went into hiding though some students later asserted that he had already fled before the invasion of the college. The Commune assigned the supervision of the building to Citizen O'Donnell, prefect of studies for the previous few years. He decided, however, to quit the post and try to return to Ireland.

Before leaving he gave a dinner in the college to a number of his compatriots in Paris[24] and a small group of the more politically-conscious students, hearing of this, decided to lodge a complaint with the Commune, thus hoping to get control of the college and its revenues. Most of them were from Kerry and were led by William Duckett from Killarney, who had completed his studies and left the college in July 1789. Of the four involved Bartholomew Murry alone was the holder of a bursary, while Edward Ferris, Jeremy Curtayne and Bernard MacSheehy were fee-paying students. All of them attended the meetings of the Society of the Friends of the Rights of Man held on Thursdays and Sundays at White's Hotel, 7 Passage des Petits Pères. The Society was composed of Irish and English residents of Paris who supported the revolution.[25]

In their complaint to the three commissioners of the Commune who visited the college the students stated that Kearney had squandered the revenues to the tune of 50,000 *livres*; that he had offered money to those willing to return to Ireland but nothing to those who refused his 'perfidious' offer; that he entertained daily refractory priests and put the chapel at the disposal of non-conforming bishops for their ordinations, thus 'exposing the students to the fury of a people justifiably angered'. Furthermore, he had, in violation of the rules, recently obtained an enormous loan. This probably refers to the loan made in July by Abbé MacDermott of Nancy, then in Paris, of 50,000-60,000 *livres*. Kearney, hard-pressed at the time by creditors and suppliers and by students demanding their return fare to Ireland, was at a loss as to how 'to shut so many mouths'. He later declared that 'his students and himself owe their lives to the timely help provided by MacDermott.'

But the chief complaint of the students was directed at Walsh. They maintained that in 1786 the rules of the college were 'grossly violated' when Comte Walsh de Serrant, intriguing at Court, had the four *proviseurs* removed and replaced by his 'creature' whom they stated was his cousin. Comte Walsh de Serrant, an ardent royalist, was then serving with the army of the Princes. The students pointed out to the Commune that a decree of 1728 accorded them the right to elect their superiors and that this decree had been violated by Walsh's appointment.[26] Fr James Coigly had resurrected this old decree and tried to rouse the students to re-activate it before he left Collège des Lombards in October 1789. He claimed that he would have succeeded 'had not the revolution in France put a period to our efforts.'[27] But the decree and its import was still obviously on the minds of the students who thought the moment opportune to promote it. Kearney's absence gave them their chance.

Fortunately for Kearney the students were not aware of the real reason for his absence. He had gone to London, ostensibly on college business, but the real purpose of his journey was kept a closely guarded secret. It took almost another quarter of a century before Kearney himself felt safe enough to commit it to paper. In 1816, after the restoration, he wrote that he had been 'sent by the Court here to England. It was the Abbé Edgeworth who had me named to go as an interpreter to a French nobleman'.[28] He spent three weeks in London but when exactly is not clear. Assuming that the students were correct when they stated that he was absent when the college was invaded on 10 August and as the royal family were detained in the Temple from that day, it is likely that Kearney left for London about the end of the first week in August. He was back in Paris, though not in the Irish college, at the start of the September Massacres as his letter to Plunkett is dated 2 September. It is possible that the nobleman in question was M. de Sainte Croix, one of Louis' ministers who escaped after 10 August. Lord Grenville, the British Foreign Secretary, requested the king to grant him an audience early in October.[29]

Kearney remained in hiding until the end of September when he was arrested and brought before the Tribunal of 17 August, established on that date to try political suspects, particularly those associated with the fallen monarchy. He wrote that 'he was singled out for victimisation by the famous Fouquier-Tinville but fortunately the tribunal was suppressed by the Committee of Public Safety'.[30] Walsh too went into hiding that autumn, finding a refuge in the house of Montesquiou-Fésenzac. While there, his health broke and he later claimed that he owed his life to the care he received there.[31] In his absence, he placed Patrick Murphy of Dublin in charge of Collège des Lombards. The sudden disappearance of the bursar and the students caused alarm among the college suppliers. Murphy warned Walsh that there was a 'public outcry'. Walsh wrote to the president of the section requesting him to assemble the suppliers on a fixed day when he would return to settle their accounts if given a safe conduct. This he did on 1 October,[32] remaining to turn his attention to quelling the student rebellion in Collège des Irlandais.

Both sides in that dispute now had recourse to Lebrun, who had been named Minister of Foreign Affairs on 10 August. James Maher, who had taken over as prefect in Kearney's absence wrote first, complaining that the commissioners of the Commune who had visited the college to hear the complaints of the students had acted illegally by placing seals on Kearney's registers and demanding the accounts.[33] This letter was followed two days later by a *mémoire* from Walsh and a letter from the students, with the heading: 'Read, Citizen, you have been deceived'. They claimed that the founders of the college had established it as 'a little republic', giving the students the right to elect their superiors. The superior was obliged to reside in the college under pain of deprivation. In 1789 the students numbered 70, a total now reduced to between 20 and 25. Yet the debt had risen to over 54,000 pounds, evidence of 'palpable theft'.[34]

On 13 October Maher declared that Kearney would make a complete statement of accounts if his safety were guaranteed. Maher himself had been suspended from his functions by the Commune, who appointed O'Donnell to supervise the college.[35] Seals had been placed on 12 August and remained until 1 October, during which time Maher had been relieved of his responsibility.[36] The commissioners made their report and the municipality decided to dismiss Kearney, authorising two of their deputies to supervise the election of a new administrator by the students.

At 8am on 29 October the two deputies arrived at Collège des Irlandais and called upon Truchon, substitute procurator of the Commune, to join them.

> We assembled all the young Irish bursary-holders of the said establishment in the chapel, we read to them there out loud article 8 of the rules of the establishment and in pursuance of the said article obtained from them the prescribed oath, by which they swore to elect, according to their conscience, the most suitable persons, swayed neither by personal interest nor solicitation and we then proceeded to the nomination of a Provisor-Superior, by means of a ballot. There were nine voters present: Murray, Duckett, Mac Sheehi senior, Mac Sheehi junior, Curtayne, B. Blackwell, J Oneill, Ferris, MacMahon; and on counting the ballot, MacMahon received four votes, and citizen Duckett five votes, and considering that citizen Duckett had five votes which are the majority of nine, the number of voters, he was nominated and elected Provisor.
>
> The voters then proceeded to a second ballot, to choose an administrator of the temporalities of the said establishment. This second ballot completed, the count revealed the name of citizen Nicholas Madgett, an Irish priest, former Curé and Prefect of Studies, in one of the Irish houses situated in the provinces.[37]

Nicholas Madgett was a strange choice, to say the least, as his subsequent career as an English agent and bitter opponent of the revolution was to demonstrate. Nephew of the former bishop of Kerry of the same name, he was educated in Paris at the Collège de Ste Barbe where his uncle had been president. He was acting as curé of Blaignon near Bordeaux when the Civil Constitution of the clergy was introduced. He refused the oath and made his way to Paris. His role in this affair seems completely inconsistent with the rest of his life.

On 3 November the committee of the Observatory section ordered Ducros, porter at the Irish college to hand over the keys to Duckett.[38] Two days later, two of the students, Edward Ferris and Jeremy Curtayne, invited Jean Baptiste Lafitte, justice of the peace, to the college, to place seals on Kearney's effects to prevent their being removed. They opened a door on to a passage where they were shown a straw-covered basket containing 24 bottles of a yellowish liquid. They decided to taste it and concluded 'it resembled whiskey of a considerable age and very high quality'. Afterwards they visited the cellar where they found several empty wine barrels and two half hogsheads almost full. There was a small cellar at the end locked and Kearney had the keys. When the seals were placed, Ferris, Curtayne, MacSheehy and Duckett signed the official document. Fr Maher signed after writing: 'I protest against this imposition of seals.' The Kerry coup-d'état was complete.

At this point Citizen MacKenna presented himself and with characteristic independence insisted on signing in protest 'against all that had taken place at the request of the above citizens' whom he declared were not bursary-holders as they claimed to be. He was backed up by Citizen Murphy, who declared that the four in question held their bursaries from Collège des Lombards and not from Collège des Irlandais, and supported by Citizen Moriarty. Citizen Cruise, who had been in charge of the cellar for six years, declared that it was a lie to assert that the superior had no more right than the students to drink the special wine, because it was in fact specially intended for him. A veritable war of signed declarations ensued. The gang of four drew their quills once more, declaring that Collège des Lombards and Collège des Irlandais formed one and the same establishment. Furthermore, Citizen Cruise had forfeited all right to protest, as he had received Orders 'from the hands of a refractory bishop.'[39]

Kearney immediately wrote to Lebrun, Minister of Foreign Affairs, protesting against the action of the Commune and begging him to intervene with the Minister of the Interior. 'If I have not presented myself at the college' he explained, 'for the two months since my return from London where I spent three weeks on seminary affairs, it was because I was informed that my life was in danger'.[40] He was prepared to return as soon as the law would guarantee his safety. Lebrun, himself a former priest, of obscure origins, proved more than sympathetic. The same day he wrote a strongly worded letter to the Minister of the Interior protesting against the illegal actions of the municipality. The Irish colleges, he declared, were under the direct administration of the archbishops and bishops of Ireland, 'a friendly country'.

He pointed out that 'elections, whether internal by the students, or external by whatever political group, were expressly forbidden'. Referring to 'the special affection we have for the Irish nation', he requested his colleague to intervene promptly and secure Kearney's restoration.[41] Roland, the minister, replied that he had ordered the implementation of the Departmental decrees of 27 October and 3 November. The former stated that the Irish colleges 'will continue to be provisionally administered in conformity with the laws of 7 November 1790 and 6 April 1791.'[42]

Citizen Cournand of the Department had been commissioned to make a report on the dispute and this was sent on 3 November to the municipality of Paris. As a result they withdrew their protection from the newly elected and Charles Kearney and James Maher were restored as superior and procurator respectively and the seals lifted.[43] This was carried out by the same justice of the peace, Jean Baptiste Lafitte, who was 'astounded to find only twenty-one bottles of whiskey instead of the original twenty-four, which we could not account for as we had checked the seals before raising them and they were unbroken. So this swindling must have been achieved by sleight of hand ... before we imposed the seals'. The finger points to Jeremy Curtayne and Edward Ferris, probably during the tasting operation.

Meanwhile, the young rebels were fast maturing politically and in the best of company. They attended the banquet given by the English-speaking residents of Paris in White's hotel on 18 November. Here they mixed with the emerging Irish patriots, Lord Edward FitzGerald and the Sheares brothers, John and Henry and pro-revolution Irish officers, like Colonel Arthur Dillon, fresh from his triumphs on the eastern frontier. The French had won a decisive victory over the Austrians at Jemappes[44] on 6 November, which placed the country at their mercy and made clear their intentions of carrying their revolution abroad. These were heady times, especially for Irish college students just cutting their first political teeth. At the banquet toasts were drunk to the young new republic and its victorious armies. Military bands played the *Ça Ira* and the Marseillaise. Lord Edward Fitzgerald proposed 'the abolition of hereditary titles' and publicly renounced his own, adopting instead 'Citoyen'. Dillon proposed the toast to 'the people of Ireland', offering to place his own sword at their service. It was decided to draw up an address and present it to the National Convention, congratulating the French nation on its victories over the enemies of liberty.

On the following day, the Convention issued its first propaganda decree offering fraternal aid to subject peoples. Irish patriots in Paris were caught up in a tide of euphoria. On Wednesday 28 November a large deputation arrived at the bar of the Convention and were greeted with prolonged applause.

> You have taken up arms for the triumph of liberty and reason. We hope that the armies of liberty will not lay down their arms until tyrants and slaves are no more. Soon, there will only remain a shameful memory of all those would-be governments, fraudulent creations of priests and tyrants combined.[45]

Following the signature of Lord Edward FitzGerald came those of William Duckett, J. O'Neill, Edward Ferris and B. Murry and a little further on those of Bernard MacSheehy and Jeremy Curtayne. It was also signed by Nicholas Madgett, a cousin of the usurping priest of the same name,[46] who was one of the students' chief mentors in their dispute with the college administration. He was a man of considerable influence in Irish-French affairs, holding the position of head of translation in the Department of Foreign Affairs.

It was probably Madgett who advised the rebels to appeal the decision to restore Kearney to the National Convention. In this they were supported by two deputies, Santhonax and Léonard-Bourdon.[47] The latter had been a teacher in Paris before the revolution and had subsequently become commissioner of the Paris Commune in Orléans. Now back in Paris as a deputy at the National Convention where he always voted for extreme measures, he took a special interest in the Irish colleges on which he seemed particularly well-informed. Later, William Duckett acted as his secretary in Hamburg. The students personally presented their case at the sitting of the Convention on 2 December. Their petition was sent back to the Committees of Education, Alienation and Domains.

Kearney and Maher wasted no time either in making their case to the Convention. They sent in a printed statement claiming that the illegal act of the Commune permitting the election 'sent a ripple of alarm through all the foreign establishments.' They exposed 'the partiality and indecency of a secret meeting at which the so-called electors and elected belonging for the most part only to a small canton claimed the property of a whole kingdom'. The commissioners of the Commune had read the text of the 1728 decree on which the rebels based their election, with 'inconceivable carelessness' as article 17 states clearly that the prefect of the community is nominated by the archbishop of Paris. Finally, they asserted that the denunciation made against them to the criminal tribunal was 'belated and after the event' and was inspired by the desire for vengeance on the part of advisors who had led the students astray.

Five or six Irish students had denounced Kearney to the Committee of Public Safety, accusing him of encouraging the students to join the army of the Princes and of giving them money and letters of recommendation for that purpose; of receiving refractory priests, giving them food and lodgings, allowing them to preach against the constitution and 'poison the minds of the students with aristocratic maxims' and permitting ordinations by refractory bishops; of misappropriating and squandering college revenues, running the college into debt, reducing the bursary-holders to destitution and failing to present accounts; and finally of receiving and harbouring the property of *émigrés.*[48] It was an impressive list of charges, any one of which could cost Kearney his life. However, the most serious of all, his recent royal mission to London, had escaped the students' vigilance.

On 6 December the Committee of Public Safety commissioned Citizen Rovère to compile a report for the National Convention on 'the superiors of Collège des Irlandais, suspected of secret machinations for a counter-revolution'.[49] Kearney addressed his defence in a printed pamphlet on 20 December, claiming that the recently overturned student election occasioned his denunciation and then proceeded to answer his denouncers charge by charge. He was not aware of any student who had defected to the princes. If his accusers were so aware they should have alerted the authorities then. The only money he gave to students was their return fare as well as a letter of recommendation on the completion of their studies. He could not be held responsible for the use they might make of these. Regarding refractory priests, he did not deny the charge, stating simply, 'our house was always open'. Religious services took place openly, with the approval of the Department, under the supervision of the municipality and local police who 'heard and saw everything'. 'Is it possible that in such circumstances one would risk speaking against the government?' he asked. If such had happened, why had his accusers waited so long to exercise their patriotism, as outsiders had been coming to the Irish chapel for the past fifteen months? If refractory priests occasionally dined in the college, Kearney also received constitutional clergy there. The only ordinations held in the college were Irish. No law prevented the French making use of these occasions.

Tackling the charge of financial mismanagement and malfaisance, Kearney stated that since he took over in 1783 over 50,000 *livres* was due in unpaid student fees–a very modest 100 *écus* per annum. 'In no Paris seminary are they better-off than in ours', he declared. He admitted receiving the property of de Juigné, the former archbishop in March 1792, who was not then an *émigré.*[50] It was left in the most 'frequented' place in the house. De Juigné chose the Irish college 'as one supposed a foreign house would attract less notice'. When the law required it Kearney declared its presence and it was taken away by the municipality. 'I have no doubt', Kearney concluded his defence to the National Convention, 'that you will guarantee me the peace and security, which every citizen, French or foreign, has the right to expect from you.'[51] But the National Convention had a far more important trial on their hands: that of the king, Louis XVI.

NOTES

1. A.N. H3 2561A, Mar. 1811 p28.
2. D.D.A. 121/9, 29 Jan. 1816.
3. Cogan, op. cit. 3 p196.
4. D.D.A. 121/9.
5. Byrne, op. cit. 3 pp158-9.
6. D.D.A. 121/9.
7. A.N. H3 2561A, Mar. 1811, pp31-2.
8. England, op. cit. pp83-6. Edgeworth to Usher Edgeworth, 1 Sept. 1796.
9. Cogan, op. cit. 3 p196, 2 Sept. 1792.
10. A.N. T 452, 5 July 1792.

10a. Coigly, *Life*.

11. Jennings, B. *Louvain Papers 1606-1827*, art. 696 p492.
12. Prop.Fid. SC Irlanda, 1788-1801.
13. A.N. F19 6237A, p35, 8, 10 Feb. 1812.
14. Hayes, op. cit. p198.
15. Ibid.
16. Cogan, op. cit 3 p196, 2 Sept. 1792.
17. Tone, *Memoirs*, 2 (appendix) p415, 16 Oct. 1792.
18. Cogan, op. cit. 3 p196.
19. P.R.O. London FO. 27, 40. Munro to Grenville, 4 Sept. 1792.
20. England, op. cit. pp87-8.
21. P.R.O. London FO. 27, 40. Munro to Grenville, 4 Sept. 1792.
22. Tone, *Memoirs*, 2 (Appendix) p405, 17 Sept. 1792.
23. A.N. C 163 f 6624 v; Tuetey, op. cit. 5 p30.

24. A.A.E. Corr.Pol.Angl. 582 fos.359-60, 13 Oct. 1792.
25. *Moniteur* XV, p58.
26. A.A.E. Corr.Pol.Angl. 582 fos.341-2, 12 Oct. 1792.
27. Coigly, *Life*, p12.
28. D.D.A. 121/9, 29 Jan. 1816.
29. Brit.Lib. Dropmore Papers, 58857. King to Grenville, 5 Oct. 1792.
30. Maynooth, Papers of I.C.P. Ms.60, 18 Nov. 1801.
31. A.N. F19 6237A. p15.
32. Ibid. He payed a total of 10,403 pounds, 18 shillings.
33. A.A.E. Corr.Pol.Angl. 582 fos.330-1. 10 Oct. 1792.
34. Ibid. fos.341-2. 12 Oct. 1792.
35. It was used as a depot for papers seized from the English college and the Eudist house which might explain the presence there of the belongings of Monsignor de Juigné, former archbishop of Paris.
36. D.D.A. 121/8. 1792.
37. I.C.P. 14 A. Mémoire pour Walsh, pp27-8.
38. D.D.A. 121/8, 3 Nov. 1792.
39. A.S.P. D.13..U 1. 5 Nov. 1792.
40. A.A.E. Corr.Pol.Angl. 583 fos.106-7, 27 Oct. 1792.
41. A.A.E. Corr.Pol.Angl. 583 fos.110-111.
42. Ibid.
43. *Patriote Français*, 21 Nov. 1792.
44. Capt. Blackwell had as his lieutenant the famous Murat, later king of Naples. cf. Hayes, op. cit. p29.
45. *Moniteur* XIV pp592-3, 29 Nov. 1792.
46. A.N. C 241, 28 Nov. 1792.
47. Maynooth, Papers of I.C.P. *Mémoire à consulter* p9.
48. D.D.A. 121/8, 21 Nov. 1792.
49. A.N. AF 11. 288; Tuetey, op. cit. 8 p64.
50. De Juigné resided at 9 rue des Postes, now the property of Collège des Irlandais.
51. D.D.A. 121/8. Kearney to Convention, 20 Dec. 1792.

6
The Altar and the Throne

The few honest people who continue faithful to their God and king keep silence and weep daily over the ruins of the altar and the throne, without the least hope of seeing the re-establishment of things.

–Abbé Edgeworth, 2 November 1792.

'I am almost the only man I know of', Abbé Edgeworth wrote to Moylan, 'who dare raise up his head and hope for happier times.'[1] He was then in hiding at Choisy, nine miles outside Paris, posing as an Englishman 'of small fortune and quiet disposition.' The exiled archbishop of Paris had entrusted Edgeworth with the care of the diocese but he had hesitated over accepting this enormous responsibility. His decision was overtaken by events.

The National Convention decided to begin the trial of Louis XVI on the day after Christmas. Saint-Just proposed to the Convention that Louis be tried for being a king, which to Saint-Just was the worst crime of all. Robespierre claimed that Louis' conspiracy to use armed force against the nation was sufficient to execute him without a trial. In the event, the discovery in the Tuileries of an iron chest containing incriminating documents detailing Louis' intrigues with foreign powers sealed his fate. The trial proper ended on 7 January. Beginning on 15 January three questions were put to a roll call of the Convention. The first was: Is Louis guilty of conspiracy against the nation? Of 745 members, 671 voted guilty. On the question of submitting the judgement to the people, the vote was 424 against, 283 in favour. On 17 January, the third question, that of the penalty, was put to the Convention. The straight death penalty received only 361 votes against the combination of reprieve and negative votes totalling 360, too close to be politically safe. It was decided to take another vote on the question of the reprieve. On 20 January the reprieve was rejected and the execution set for the following day.

Louis addressed a letter to the Convention, asking for a delay of three days to enable him to prepare himself 'to appear in the presence of God'.[2] He asked for a priest whom the Convention would undertake to protect, 'free from every fear and anxiety resulting from this charitable act'. He handed a note to one of the commissioners of the Commune, with a name and address written on it: *M. Edgeworth or Fermon N° 483 rue du Bac.* It was not in the king's handwriting but, most probably, that of Madame Elizabeth, his sister. Edgeworth had become her confessor a few years previously and visited the palace once or twice a week. He had spent a good part of the morning of 9 August with her, the day before the royal family had been arrested. He was not known personally to the king or queen, though he later observed: 'They were indeed no strangers to my name; and in those latter times, had often expressed their astonishment, on hearing how freely I resorted to the palace, whilst round about, all was terror and woe.'[3]

Weeks before the final summons Edgeworth had already been approached on behalf of the king. Louis had asked M. de Malesherbes, who helped him prepare his defence, to go and see the man who had been recommended by his sister, adding: 'It's a strange assignment for a philosopher ... but I assure you, my friend, the consolations of religion are very different from those of philosophy.'[4] Malesherbes arranged a meeting with Edgeworth in the house of Madame de Senosan, where he handed him a letter from the king. In it Louis asked Edgeworth 'as a last pledge of my affection for him, as a favour which he hoped I would not refuse' to attend him in his last moments. He added: 'as the service was likely to be attended with some danger for me, he dared not insist, and only prayed (in case I deemed the danger to be too great) to point out to him a clergyman worthy of his confidence.'[5] Edgeworth accepted without hesitation. 'A king even in chains had a right to command', he later wrote.[6]

Edgeworth returned from Choisy to Paris and rue du Bac to await the summons. At 4pm on 20 January a messenger arrived with a note: 'The Executive Council, on a matter of the greatest importance, requests the immediate presence of Citizen Edgeworth de Firmont at its chambers.' A carriage was waiting in the street. When he arrived at the Tuileries all the ministers were assembled. Garat, Minister of Justice, informed him that Louis Capet had requested his presence for his last moments and asked Edgeworth whether he consented. Edgeworth replied that since the king had expressed this wish and designated him by name his consent was a duty.

The minister and Edgeworth left the Tuileries together and went, under mounted escort, to the Temple. Edgeworth was in lay dress, which was then obligatory for the clergy. Considering that 'for the first time, religion itself was receiving a sort of tribute from the government', Edgeworth asked the minister for permission to wear clerical dress, which was unequivocally refused. In the carriage, the minister felt extremely uncomfortable. 'My God!' he exclaimed, 'What a frightful mission I have been assigned!' At the Temple, both Edgeworth and the minister were searched by the guards. Even the Abbé's snuffbox was opened and the snuff meticulously sifted.

First the Minister of Justice, accompanied by several members of the Commune, entered the king's apartment and read to him the decree of the Convention, fixing irrevocably his execution for 10am the following day.[7] When Edgeworth was brought in the king made a sign requesting the others to leave. The Abbé broke down in tears 'at the sight of this prince, once so great and now so unhappy', causing Louis to weep also. 'Forgive me' he said, 'forgive this moment of weakness ... I have lived so long in the midst of my enemies ... that the sight of a loyal subject moves me deeply.' The king then drew his will from his pocket and read it twice to the Abbé. He had drawn it up on Christmas Day, the day before his trial began. While waiting for the royal family to join him he asked the Abbé for news of the clergy and the church in France. He knew that great numbers of them had fled to England and were well received there. He enquired in particular for the bishop of Clermont, who had attended the retreats and performed the ordinations at the Irish college. He also spoke of Mgr de Juigné, archbishop of Paris. 'Tell him' he said, 'that I die in his communion and that I have never recognised any other pastor except him. Alas! I'm afraid he will be a little annoyed that I did not reply to his last letter.' Their conversation was interrupted by the arrival of the royal family. Leaving Edgeworth alone, he met them in a little outer room. For almost a quarter of an hour the Abbé heard nothing but 'piercing cries'. The meeting with his family lasted an hour. When he returned to Edgeworth the king collapsed in a chair, shattered. His valet, Cléry, proposed that he should eat something and he agreed.

Abbé Edgeworth was anxious as to how he might bring the king holy communion and decided that the only possibility was to say Mass in the king's chamber. This required official authorisation and the king was not optimistic. 'They will never give what they can refuse,' he said. Edgeworth put his request to the commissioners, disconcerting them somewhat. One of them suggested that Edgeworth was planning to poison the king under the guise of giving him communion, adding that 'history provides enough examples to require them to be circumspect.' The Abbé pointed out that what he required to say Mass would have to be brought in by them. He had been searched so rigorously coming in that if he was found in possession of poison tomorrow, then it could only have been delivered by them. The Minister of Religion had to be consulted and permission was granted on two conditions, firstly that the Abbé sign an official request and secondly, that Mass would have to be finished by the latest, at 7am because Louis had to leave at 8am for the place of execution. Edgeworth drew up his list of requirements, which was sent to the Constitutional curé of the parish of St Francis of Assisi.[8]

It was now after 10pm and seeing that the king was tired the Abbé suggested that he should get some sleep. He agreed. The Abbé spent the night in Cléry's little room which was only separated from the king's room by a partition. The king rose at 5am and sent immediately for Edgeworth and they remained in conversation for an hour. The altar had been set up in the king's chamber. The king heard Mass on his knees and received communion. Afterwards, the Abbé left him alone to finish his prayers.

Day was breaking and drums could be heard beating all over Paris. 'Probably the National Guard who are starting to assemble' remarked the king. A little later detachments of cavalry entered the Temple courtyard and they could hear perfectly the voices of the soldiers and the hoofbeats of the horses. 'It seems that they're here,' Louis said. Between seven and eight several people came and knocked at their door with various enquiries. Louis said to the Abbé with a smile: 'These people see daggers and poison everywhere. They are afraid I am going to kill myself. How little they know me! To take my own life would be a weakness. Since I must, I will know how to die.' Finally, there was one last knock on the door. It was Santerre, the brewer from faubourg Saint Antoine, who had recently been appointed chief of the National Guard. He asked the king to follow him. 'I'm busy' replied the king, 'wait another few moments and I will be yours.' He shut the door and threw himself at the Abbé's knees. 'It's all over,' he said. 'Give me your last blessing and ask

God to support me to the end'. He stood up and approached the guards. When he saw that they were all wearing hats, he asked his valet, Cléry, to bring him his too. Tears streaming down his face, Cléry ran to find his hat. He asked them to give Cléry his watch and all his belongings both in the Temple and those deposited with the Commune. The king and Edgeworth entered the carriage between two gendarmes, the Abbé still hoping that a last minute attempt would be made to rescue the king. He gave him his breviary and indicating the psalms 'best suited to his situation', they recited alternate passages.

The journey lasted almost two hours. All the streets were lined with citizens armed with pikes and guns. The carriage stopped in place Louis XV in a large empty space surrounding the scaffold. It was lined with cannon and as far as the eye could see there was a huge armed crowd. As soon as the king realised that the carriage had stopped, he turned to Edgeworth and said: 'Here we are, unless I'm mistaken.' One of the executioners opened the door and the gendarmes made to get out but Louis stopped them. 'Sirs' he said, putting his hand on the Abbé's knee, 'I recommend this man to you. See that after my death, no harm comes to him.' There was no reply and the king insisted a second time. One of them cut him short, saying: 'Yes, yes! We'll look after him. Leave it to us.' At this remark Edgeworth froze.

When the king had got out three executioners attempted to undress him but Louis pushed them back and undressed himself. According to Charles Kearney, Samson, the executioner, then approached him with a large pair of scissors to cut his hair. 'He had a large head of hair confined by a ribbon according to the fashion of the day.' Then they tried to tie his hands but Louis would not have it. The executioners insisted. 'This was' as Edgeworth wrote later, 'the most horrible moment of this devastating morning'. Louis turned towards the Abbé as if looking for advice. 'Sire' the Abbé told him in tears, 'I see in this latest outrage another resemblance between you and the God who will be your reward.' Louis no longer resisted. 'Do what you will,' he told them, 'I will drink this chalice to the dregs.' His hair was cut off and thrown to the ground. The steps leading to the scaffold were extremely steep and Louis lent on the Abbé's arm as he climbed them. He crossed the scaffold confidently and silenced the drums with a mere look. In a loud voice he declared: 'I am innocent of all the crimes of which I am accused. I forgive those responsible for my death and I beg God that the blood you are about to spill will leave no stain on France.'

He would have continued, but Santerre drew his sword and ordered the drums to roll. The king's head was placed on the block and in an instant he was guillotined. The youngest of the executioners, no more than 18 years old, grabbed the head and displayed it to the people, to be greeted with cries of: 'Long live the Republic!' Edgeworth was sprinkled with the blood. He turned around, only to face twenty or thirty thousand armed men. Trusting to Providence, he approached the first line which to his surprise opened up before him, as did the second and third. By the time he got to the fifth line he 'was absolutely lost in the crowd, and no more noticed than if he had been a simple spectator of a scene which forever will dishonour France.'

There was another Irish priest present at the execution, in this case as a 'simple spectator'. Charles Kearney of the Irish college 'arrived in the Place de la Révolution' as he later recounted, 'before the king and managed to reach the scaffold just as the carriage in which he sat with the Abbé Edgeworth and the two gendarmes approached from the rue Royale.' He mentioned that the guillotine was so placed that the last gaze of the king was fixed on a statue of Liberty erected there and beyond that the palace of the Tuileries. Kearney mentioned that he made it back safely to the Irish college but that Abbé Edgeworth had to take refuge in a little milliner's shop in rue du Bac and later escaped through the back door.[9]

Edgeworth went immediately to Malesherbes, who advised him:

> Fly, my dear Sir, from this land of horror, and from the tigers that are now let loose in it: they will never pardon the attachment you have professed for the most unfortunate of kings; and what you have done this morning is a crime, which sooner or later they will resent.

Three considerations made Edgeworth hesitate. One was his commitment to the diocese of Paris; the second his duty towards Madame Elizabeth, and lastly, the commissions the king had entrusted to him. He hid out for three months in the home of a friend. A newspaper carried a story that he had crossed over to England and was conferring with Pitt himself. He wrote a letter to the archbishop, seeking advice but the letter was intercepted and fell into the hands of the Committee of Public Safety. His friend's house was raided but Edgeworth had already destroyed the letters written to him by Madame Elizabeth from the Temple. Having said goodbye to his mother, whom he was never to see again, and provided for the diocese as best he could, he made his way to Bayeux in Normandy, from which he could cross easily to England. Nothing held him now but Madame Elizabeth. She was guillotined on 10 May 1794. No sooner did he hear of her death than he took boat for England.

With the death of the king, the Irish colleges entered a crucial stage of their existence. From the autumn of 1792 they found themselves in an acute financial situation, exacerbated by the rapid depreciation of the French paper currency and sharply rising prices. The Irish budget depended almost totally upon investments and on the regular payment of dividends. Walsh had exhausted his liquid funds by his huge settlement of accounts with the college suppliers on 1 October: for current expenses he required the dividends now due. The Treasury withheld these claiming that the Irish colleges had been included in the law of 18 August 1792 suppressing secular religious houses and colleges and ordering the sale of their properties. This was followed by a decree sequestering the properties and ordering their rents to be withheld.

Walsh had the difficult task of convincing the government that the Irish and British establishments were excepted from this new law as they had been by that of 7 November 1790. In a *mémoire* to Lebrun, Minister of Foreign Affairs, he argued that a later law did not cancel an anterior one unless it was clearly so stated in one of its articles. He asked Lebrun to seek clarification from the National Convention so that their dividends could be released, pointing out that in his capacity as agent of the Catholics of Ireland he had invested in the previous June no less than 6,544 *livres* in France. This *mémoire* was jointly signed by William Hurst for the English college, Alexander Innis for the Scots college and R.A. Kellet for the English Benedictines.[10]

In a further *mémoire* bearing the same signatures as well as that of Charles Kearney, Walsh played the political card:

> The British government would like to educate its Catholic youth at home. Parliament is meeting soon and it will be a decisive time for our bishops. We love France and it is our most fervent wish to continue our institutions here.

Using his previously successful ultimatum, he concluded:

> Or else, if the legislators are not favourable, we expect with your typical candour, that you will notify us in time, so that our bishops may accept with good grace, the offers the British government is disposed to make them.[11]

The *mémoire* was sent both to Lebrun at Foreign Affairs and the National Convention. After receiving reports from the Committees of Education and Finance, the Convention decreed 'that the administrators of these establishments shall receive, until their fate is decided, the usual revenues for the first six months of 1793'.[12] A further decree of 8 March, relative to the sale of properties forming the endowments of colleges, expressly excepted the Irish and British colleges in article 6 and four days later in an addition to this article stated that 'the administrators are authorised to receive the arrears accruing up to now from all investments owed them by the Republic, as in the past.'[13]

One other problem was also resolved by the Convention at this time. A few of the Irish bursaries were administered by the suppressed colleges and were now threatened with extinction. Francis O'Beirne and O'Carroll held the Morveinagh and O'Carroll bursaries which were administered by the grandmaster of Collège de Navarre and they petitioned the Convention to have them transferred to the Irish college.[14] Terence O'Shaughnessy, James O'Moloney and MacMahon had O'Moloney bursaries tenable in Collège Louis-le-Grand and they made a similar request.[15] The Convention appointed Walsh administrator of these.[16] In the case of the O'Moloney foundation, Walsh had a special claim to the post as his mother was Joan O'Moloney.

The two laws of February and March were important additions to the earlier legislation of 7 November 1790 and 6 April 1791, providing protection for the Irish colleges from the revolutionary government. Unfortunately political events had already overtaken these legal guarantees. With the declaration of war by France on England on 1 February the position of the Irish colleges changed dramatically. The war was now going against the French. By March, the Austrians had taken Liège and crossed the Meuse. La Vendée revolted against the levy of 300,000 men and between 10 and 15 March the peasants of the west, who had been alienated by the rigorous measures taken against the refractory priests, rose en masse. The purchasing power of the *assignats* had dropped to 50 per cent of their nominal value and there was an acute shortage of coffee and sugar and, shortly afterwards, the familiar signs of bread scarcity in Paris.

All of this contributed to a series of insurrectionary *journées* in the capital organised by extremists known as *enragées*, forerunners of an institution later identified with the Terror. The Revolutionary Tribunal was set up on 10 March for the summary trial of those accused of crimes against the state. It was to have jurisdiction over

> all counter-revolutionary activities, all attacks on liberty, equality, unity, the indivisibility of the Republic, the internal and external security of the state, and all plots tending to re-establish the monarchy or any other authority hostile to liberty, equality, and the sovereignty of the people.

The tribunal was composed of five judges, a 12-man jury, and a public prosecutor with two assistants. One of the latter and the most famous was Fouquier-Tinville, before whom Kearney had appeared the previous September. The court was permitted to arrest all those denounced to it by public officials and private citizens. A further repressive measure was introduced which provided for the election in each section of a revolutionary committee of 12 members consisting of *sans-culottes* who were entrusted with the duty of rounding up foreigners and political suspects without passports.

The Irish superiors had as much to fear from their own compatriots as they had from the French. Nicholas Madgett of Foreign Affairs wrote to his minister warning him to keep a sharp lookout for British spies and pointed out that 'within four days the English minister had received an exact copy of the address presented to the National Convention by British citizens, with a list of all the signatories.'[17] He followed this with a *mémoire* naming Walsh, Kearney and Maher as spies. 'The denunciations made against them' he pointed out, 'to the general council of the Commune, to the Provisional Criminal Tribunal, to the Committee of General Security and elsewhere, show clearly that their houses have provided meeting-places for refractory priests, since the beginning of the revolution.' More seriously, he accused them of sending the revenues of the house to the army at Coblentz. Among the documents produced against them at the Criminal Tribunal was a letter from one of the *émigrés* thanking the superiors for the money they had sent.[18] According to Lally Tollendal the individual in question was the Duc de Fitzjames. Madgett was still seething over the fact that Kearney had managed through the intervention of his own minister to overturn the takeover of the college by a few of his protegés.

Earlier in the month, Madgett had formed a few of the Irish students into a mission designed to disseminate propaganda about the French revolution in Ireland. William Duckett was their leader. Now, three weeks later, Madgett had no word from them. 'One can hardly doubt' he wrote to the minister about the Irish superiors, 'that it was they who wrote to England and Ireland denouncing them as French spies.' He even suggested that they sent an emissary ahead of them to make sure they were caught. They were, in fact, arrested in London as Madgett suspected, betrayed by a former Irish priest, Charles Somers, who was a paid English spy in Paris. On 4 March he had written to Bland Burges informing him about 'a parcel of young fellows just escaped from an Irish seminary here.'[19] Detained for a while in London, they were eventually released, possibly because as Somers had observed 'they were not at all qualified for such a mission' and represented no threat to British security. They represented a first fumbling attempt at secret service by revolutionary France. Edward Ferris seems to have made it back to his Kerry home where he remained active in republican circles. His name disappears from the Irish college annals at this time as does also that of his fellow rebel, Jeremy Curtayne. The other two, Bernard MacSheehy and Bartholomew Murry remained. Duckett became one of France's most reliable and dedicated agents.

Following these denunciations Walsh was detained at the Mairie during March and April.[20] Before or after his release he produced another *mémoire* emphasising the difference between England and Ireland. Referring to England joining the coalition against France, he declared: 'It would be unjust to impute this coalition to Irish catholics as they have no part in the government and no voice in parliament.' Arrested himself on false information, he had been restored to liberty 'as a good citizen whose patriotism had been recognised'. He contributed to the national collection and to that for La Vendée. His house had been searched and nothing suspect had been found there. He fed and lodged the Evrard family whose two sons were serving under the French flag and the halls and refectory of Collège des Lombards were occupied by carpenters working for the army.[21]

Notwithstanding his protestation of civic-mindedness the Committee of General Safety of the Convention issued an order for the arrest of himself and Kearney on 8 May.[22] The commissioners were ordered to seize their papers and bring in any which appeared suspect. A similar order was issued for the arrest of Maher whose address was given as place Saint Michel, with the rider that the commissioners were empowered to commandeer whatever armed force might be necessary to execute the order.[23] Walsh and his papers were taken into custody on 12 May.[24] Kearney was arrested on 17 May on the instructions of Marat.[25] Lally Tollendal claimed that when Walsh was asked during the interrogation why he allowed fanatics to attend Mass in Collège des Lombards, he replied that it was not there but in Kearney's house that such Masses took place.[26] Kearney was kept in detention for a week on charges which he later described 'as vicious as they were abominable'.

NOTES

1. England, op. cit. pp76-7. Edgeworth to Moylan, 21 Nov. 1792.
2. *Moniteur* XV p256, 24 Jan. 1793.
3. England, op. cit. p81. Edgeworth to U. Edgeworth, 1 Sept. 1796.
4. Delarc, Abbé. *L'Eglise de Paris*, p360n.
5. Ibid & England, op. cit. p90.
6. Ibid. Edgeworth to U. Edgeworth, 1 Sept. 1796.
7. Edgeworth's account as qtd in Delarc, op. cit. pp360-77. Taken from *Relation des derniers moments de Louis XVI écrite par M. L'Abbé Edgeworth*, (Paris 1817) pp49-94.
8. It comprised a missal, a chalice, a corporal, a pall, a paten, an altar stone, a purificator, an amice, an alb, a cincture, a maniple, a stole, a chasuble, two altar cloths and large and small host.
9. O'Reilly, *The Irish Abroad and at Home*, pp223-5.
10. A.A.E. Corr.Pol.Angl. 583 f131, 30 Oct. 1792.
11. Ibid f266-7, 20 Nov. 1792.
12. A.N. F 17 2500, 14 Feb. 1793.
13. A.N. F 19 6237A, 8 & 12 Mar. 1793.
14. A.N. F 17 2500, 6 Feb. 1793.
15. Ibid.
16. Ibid. 14 Feb. 1793.
17. A.A.E. Corr.Pol.Angl. 587 f20, 13 Mar. 1793.
18. A.A.E. Corr.Pol.Angl. 587 f45, 22 Mar. 1793.
19. P.R.O. London FO 27, 42, 4 Mar. 1793.
20. A.N. F 19 6237A, *Administration*, pp13-14.
21. A.P. A A/200 *Panthéon*, 28 Mar. 1793.
22. A.N. F 7 4753 doss.1, 9 May 1793.
23. A.N. F 7 4774 39 doss.3, 10 May 1793.
24. A.N. F 7 4753 doss.1, 74, 12 May 1793.
25. Maynooth, Papers of I.C.P., ms.60.
26. A.N. H3 2561A, Mar. 1811.

7
Prison des Irlandais

Is there any Frenchman who does not easily understand what it must have cost certain persons at that time to keep clear of the road that led to the scaffold, to escape being cast into a dungeon, to mitigate the horrors of it when one was cast therein, to prepare the way to secure an escape from it.

–Charles Kearney, 5 August 1807.

Other Irish were being rounded up at this time. A Citizen O'Sullivan was arrested on 23 May and later released with a caution.[1] Three days later, an Irish Capuchin, 41-year-old Clement Murray, was interrogated.[2] In June, another Irish Capuchin, Peter MacDermott, petitioned the National Convention for his release. He had formerly been chaplain to the French embassy in London, and the Convention passed his case over to the Minister of the Interior to decide.[3] Another Irishman, G. O'Connell from rue Saint André des Arts, was detained from April to July. Christopher White, the owner of White's Hotel, was arrested in July with all his family.[4] In August another Irish Capuchin was arrested and lodged in Bicetre prison. He was 49-year-old John Joseph O'Guinnivan, former guardian of the Irish monastery at Bar-sur-Aube and now attached to the parish of Saint Roch. He was found in possession of English books and letters which was not surprising as he kept himself alive by teaching English.[5] Even Irish officers who had distinguished themselves fighting for revolutionary France were not immune from arrest, particularly when the French suffered any reverses in the war. Such was the case of Thomas Keating from Limerick who was promoted to the rank of General of Brigade for distinguished service at the battle of Neerwinden in March. Despite Robespierre's intervention on his behalf with the Minister of War, he was imprisoned at the Abbaye.[6]

Following the reverses suffered by the army of the princes Richard Ferris decided to abandon his captaincy in Berwick's regiment and try his luck once more in France, this time posing as an ardent republican. He went into hiding in Triel, a little town about 20 miles west of Paris, close to the home of one of his married sisters, and from there in July he sent a *mémoire* to Lebrun on Ireland and the prospects of a French invasion. Lebrun had been a student of his in Collège de Montaigu. Ferris was particularly disdainful of the Irish student mission in March. 'Is it with such feeble means' he asked, 'that the French ministry believes that entire nations are to be conquered?'[7]

Unfortunately for Ferris, Lebrun had been dismissed and placed under house arrest. Ferris's *mémoire* was lost in the office files. He wrote again to Foreign Affairs seeking an exemption from the decree against foreigners then being prepared by the National Convention,[8] and again six days later asking for a passport to come to Paris to explain himself.[9] On 12 August a decree was issued ordering the arrest of all suspected persons and the police in Triel began to take an unhealthy interest in Ferris. On that same day, Foreign Affairs eventually replied that they had no record of his correspondence with Lebrun and invited him to furnish them with proof.[10]

Finally, the persistence of Ferris paid off. Foreign Affairs wrote to the Committee of Public Safety on 26 August asking them to extricate him as quickly as possible from the dangerous situation he was in. They pointed out that he had submitted an interesting *mémoire* on the present situation in Ireland and that 'he had given several other proofs of his ardent zeal for liberty and his attachment to the French Republic.'[11] The Committee appointed Citizen Barère as *rapporteur* in the affair and Ferris continued to solicit him for another three weeks. He also wrote to another member, Herault de Sechelles, to whom he was known: one word from him would terminate the matter.[12] Finally, on 2 August, it was decided to send Ferris on a secret mission to England, 'a mission that required a certain latitude if it was to produce results.' For this purpose he was given 900 *louis d'or* and 1,200 *livres*,[13] and left Paris for London, with money, passport and secret code, just as most of his compatriots in Paris—and many of them with much better republican credentials than his—were about to begin their prison sentences.

On 5 September Terror became officially the order of the day. On Friday 6, Léonard Bourdon took the floor at the National Convention and launched into a tirade against Kearney:

> Citizens, there is in Paris an establishment known as the Irish seminary. The director of this seminary has given constant proof of his lack of patriotism and in spite of all his efforts he has failed to corrupt the young people placed in his care. Those patriots, indignant and weary of the aristocratic views of this man, revived an old rule which allowed them to elect their own superior. The Committee of General Safety concluded that this superior was justifiably suspect and as a result had him arrested. The Committee proposes that you confirm the nomination made by the students of this seminary.[14]

The proposition was adopted by the Convention which ordered the Committee of Alienation to present, within three days, a report on the establishments set up in France by foreign powers. The Convention then went on to decree that 'foreigners, born in the territories of powers with whom the Republic is at war will be placed under arrest in *maisons de sureté* until the National Assembly orders otherwise.' The decree contained in all 16 articles. Article 5 stated:

> Every citizen will have the right to attest against others any information they might possess which casts suspicion on the purity of their principles.'

More ominously, article 9 stated:

> Those who are convicted of spying or in communication with foreign powers or *émigrés* or any other enemy of France will be put to death and their properties declared forfeit to the Republic.[15]

Kearney was arrested almost immediately and at first detained at the Irish college guarded by 'two good citizens at his own expense'. A week earlier he had been named as the executor of the will of a friend named Commines involving the sum of 108,000 *livres*. The money was seized and put in the national treasury.[16] Kearney himself remained in jail for two years, moving to the Scots College and then to the Luxembourg. Among the documents produced against him were two letters, one from an English colonel describing the part he played in the plan for the king's escape to England and the other from the Duc de Fitzjames in thanks for the help he had given to many of his compatriots to save them from death and return them home. At one point he was confined for 36 days in a dungeon from which, he was informed, his only release would be the scaffold.[17]

Kearney was saved by the intervention of Camille Desmoulins whom the Irish priest had helped when he was a student at Collège Louis-le-Grand. To save his own life and the lives of others he had been obliged to disburse considerable sums. 'He could not' Lally Tollendal observed, 'see anyone suffering without opening his purse for him and when that was empty, that of the college.'[18] Describing his years in prison he himself later wrote:

> Is there any Frenchman who does not easily understand what it must have cost certain persons at that time to keep clear of the road that led to the scaffold, to escape being cast into a dungeon, to mitigate the horrors of it when one was cast therein, to prepare the way to secure an escape from it. Lavishing right and left all the money I could get my hands on to secure my own release and the release of others, I thought I was fulfilling a sacred duty.[19]

With Kearney arrested, the students of Collège des Irlandais were left to fend for themselves. The decree against foreigners expressly stated that 'the children of foreigners who have been sent to France for their education are free to remain there, provided that the persons in whose homes they live answer for their civic zeal.' Even had Kearney still been at liberty his word would scarcely have been acceptable. Obviously anticipating this problem the students themselves presented a petition to the National Convention expressing their 'deep anxiety' at the decree just issued against British subjects. The Irish colleges, they said, were founded over 200 years ago as a result of 'the most barbarous persecution' by the English. This persecution should entitle the Irish to the special favour already accorded to the Dutch. If Ireland had not openly pronounced itself in favour of the French revolution it was because 'it is occupied by a superior force' but there were happenings there every day which showed how eager they were to follow the French example. The earlier rebellion seemed to have divided the student body and those who remained aloof on that occasion must have believed themselves targeted in the subsequent denunciations:

> We have learned with deep sadness that certain malignant individuals of our own country have tried to cast suspicion on our sentiments towards the Republic. We protest solemnly against these infamous calumnies and we declare before this august assembly that we yield to no citizen whatever in our republican sentiments.[20]

They concluded that 'they could only see their studies interrupted with great regret' and hoped that the Convention would insure that they continued. The petition was signed by 13 students 'for all the Irish.' Among the signatories were Thomas MacKenna and

Francis O'Beirne, who had figured in the Champ de Mars incident three years earlier; but surprisingly, only six were listed among the 23 composing the student-roll in August 1792. It appears that at least seven new boys had entered the college since that date. Before his arrest, Kearney had placed some of the younger boys in a French boarding school run by François Cardinal in 7 rue Tracy where they spent six or seven months.[21]

Notably absent from the signatories were Bernard MacSheehy and Bartholomew Murry, who were admitted three weeks later to the bar of the Convention to present their own petition. They asked to be granted French citizenship and the enjoyment of the foundation money left by their uncles for the duration of the war until their studies were completed.[22] Both had contributed to the denunciation of the Irish superiors discussed at the meeting of the Committee of Public Safety on the previous day when the Committee had decreed that the denunciation by the students of their superiors as 'suspects and counter-revolutionaries be sent to the Committee of General Safety as serious'.[23]

The students' denunciation ran to three tightly-written pages and was signed by Bernard MacSheehy. The superiors, Kearney, Walsh and Maher were accused of opening their colleges 'to all the aristocrats and counter-revolutionaries of Paris.' Here, refractory bishops and priests, 'followed by a huge crowd of fanatics, celebrated baptisms, confirmations, secret marriages, and ordinations and 'launched tirades against the principles of the revolution.' This led to the invasion of the college on 10 August 'because public indignation had exposed them to the vengeance of the people.' They fled but returned a few days later and with the help of Truchon, then *procureur syndic*, they re-established the college which 'had been abandoned by the superiors.' With the help of Manuel, Pétion, Lebrun and Rolland, 'all-powerful at that time ... but whose lack of civism is today well known,' the superiors were restored. Cournand had the seals broken on the documents which contained 'information on fanaticism and counter-revolution.' Before Cournand's arrival there had been 30,000 *livres*' worth of property belonging to the former archbishop of Paris there. Truchon had already deposited at the Commune a large quantity of little emblems designed to be worn by the counter-revolutionaries. 'It appears the college was the principal depot for them or even the factory.'[24]

The procurator of the Commune had Kearney brought before the Criminal Tribunal of 17 August where he was charged with the foregoing as well as with encouraging several of the students to join the *émigrés* and giving them money to support the counter-revolutionary movement. Fouquier-Tinville would have had him condemned if Rolland had not had the Tribunal suppressed by a decree of the Convention. The students were obliged 'to abandon a refuge where they had become masters'. They had scarcely left Paris when the superiors circulated a rumour that they left as 'Jacobin emissaries to preach insurrection in Ireland.' The rumour preceded them to England where they were arrested and imprisoned. The denunciation also mentioned a letter from Edgeworth, 'confessor of the tyrant', and enclosed a copy of another letter to Kearney from La Villeurnay. The denunciation stated that Kearney and Maher had already been arrested. Maher had been arrested at Abbeville where he had gone to gather information on the army of the north which he planned to transmit to the Duke of York. Walsh was still at liberty.

On 7 September the *procureur général syndic* of the Department had issued stirring orders to the heads of the sections to seal the houses of foreigners. 'On this measure' he urged them, 'the safety of the fatherland depends and the slightest delay could entail enormous consequences.'[25] At six o'clock on the morning of 8 September commissioners of the Panthéon section arrived at Collège des Lombards to place their seals. Walsh was absent. The concièrge, Evrard, pointed out to them the door of Walsh's apartment and they placed their seal on it. Walsh returned at four o'clock in the afternoon and sent for the commissioners. They placed all his papers in a wardrobe and sealed the door. Walsh then requested them to witness his declaration, in which he stated that the previous May he had the sum of 20,000 *livres* in *assignats* which represented dividends he had received as administrator of the Irish foundations and representative of Irish catholics. The list of bursary-holders and investors was placed under seals. He stated that a watch and silver belonged to the estate of an Irishman, Christopher Hartford, rue des Sept Voyes, who had died on 26 March.[26] For some reason Walsh was not arrested on this occasion.

On that same morning the commissioners raided a house in rue d'Enfer. In a bedroom on the third floor they found an Irishman called MacSheehy, a 47-year-old Kerryman who had lived in Paris for 29 years. Seals were placed on his papers.[27] On the denunciation signed by Bernard MacSheehy three names and addresses were given: Kearney's, Walsh's and MacSheehy, rue d'Enfer. His age matches that of John MacSheehy, Bernard's uncle, who had been physician to Louis XVI.

Walsh was still at liberty at the end of September and seems to have taken refuge in the district of St Germain-en-Laye. He signed a certificate there for John Leyne, a Kerry priest who had entered the Collège des Lombards in 1769 at the age of 28 and had lived in France since.[28] To reach St Germain-en-Laye Walsh would have required a certificate of civism, provided by the municipal or sectional authorities as article 7 of the decree stated that a foreigner 'cannot leave or go anywhere without having the certificate, which will be required by the competent authorities. Those who violate this article will be arrested as suspects.' In his denunciation Bernard MacSheehy had singled out Walsh as a 'dangerous man', going on to describe him as 'more given to intrigue, more political and more counter-revolutionary than the other two ...a cousin of comte Seran Walsh, *émigré* or at least claims to be.' He claimed that Walsh 'was in the pay of the cabinet of St James' and pointed out to the intelligence committee of the Department that Walsh was still at large, whereupon they sent a copy of the denunciation to the Committee of General Security of the Convention on 2 October requesting them to treat the matter as serious.

The position of British subjects in France gave rise to a lively debate in the National Convention on 10 October, Robespierre pointing out that the past proved that delay in executing security measures had always disastrous consequences for the fatherland. 'I demand,' he said, 'that you order the arrest of all the English and the provisional seizure of their property.' His voice proved decisive and a decree which sealed the fate of the Irish colleges was adopted. Article 1 stated:

> All English, Scottish, Irish and Hanoverians of both sexes and in general all the subjects of the king of Great Britain who are at present on the territory of the republic will be, on reception of the present decree, placed under arrest in houses of security and seals placed on their papers. Their properties and those even of absent subjects will be seized and confiscated to the profit of the republic.[29]

Walsh had now no alternative but to give himself up or expose those who were sheltering him to severe penalties, the decree having specifically stated that whoever sheltered such people had to declare so within 24 hours under penalty of ten years in irons.

He was arrested on 15 October, 'stripped of his clothes and linen', and imprisoned in St Germain chateau,[30] which, ironically, Louis XIV had provided for James II when he fled to France after the battle of the Boyne and became the headquarters of the Irish Jacobites. In compliance with the same law Walsh made a declaration of all the properties in his possession, though nothing could shake his determination 'to run all risks to save the properties and press for the removal of their sequestration at the opportune moment'. He managed to persuade the governor of the prison ('the representative of the people') to change his confinement from inside the chateau to the outside area. He was obliged each day to report to the municipality and was even allowed to leave that district escorted by a gendarme.[31] Even during his imprisonment he continued to administer the college finances.

The law made no distinctions: neither age, sex nor politics offered immunity. A foreign name alone sufficed for condemnation and for the O's and the Macs their was no escape. On 23 September a petition was addressed to the National Convention in the name of all the English, Irish and Scottish residents of Paris and its environs.

> In the face of the misfortunes of which we are going to be the innocent victims we confidently claim your protection, the rights of justice and hospitality ... The unfortunate and persecuted came to France seeking a refuge: the friends of universal liberty came here by choice. We represent both.[32]

Their plea fell on deaf ears.

After having successfully defended Dunkirk, besieged by the Duke of York, General O'Meara, commander of the garrison, was deprived of his post and ordered to withdraw 20 leagues from the frontier.[33] General Thomas Ward, a former student of the Irish college, was arrested as a foreigner and imprisoned at the Carmes on 10 October. He had fought with distinction in the army of the north. His Irish valet, 25-year-old John Mallone from Limerick, suffered the same fate; both were later tried by the revolutionary tribunal, condemned and guillotined.[34] General James O'Moran from Roscommon was also relieved of his command and taken into custody, even though Carnot refused to sign the warrant for his arrest. From prison on the eve of his trial, he declared: 'Forty-one years of irreproachable service, marked by severe battle wounds, should establish my character.' He was brought before the revolutionary tribunal, charged with carrying out manoeuvres tending to favour the enemy, condemned and executed.[35]

The first Irishman to be brought before the tribunal in January 1794 and prosecuted by the dreaded Fouquier-Tinville was Dr Edmond Saint Leger. He was 41 and a former student of the Irish college who had been appointed commissioner of St Domingo with extensive powers in 1791, returning a year later to Paris to present his report. He was one of the very few to be acquitted.[36] Colonel Thomas MacDermot, also from Roscommon, who had signed the congratulatory address to the National Assembly from White's Hotel in 1792 was also arrested in spite of his declared republican sentiments.[37] James Bernard O'Dunne was 82 and had spent 73 years in France. He sent a petition to his local revolutionary committee, pleading that the law should not be applied to him. For 30 years he had served France as ambassador in several countries including Portugal and was in receipt of a small pension. He suffered from a painful and incurable disease which required daily treatment by a surgeon. He was imprisoned in his own house, under the supervision of two guards to whom he had to pay 10 *livres* a day plus their food. When he complained that he could not support them on his pension, the authorities withdrew one.[38]

Thomesson O'Ryan was a 62-year-old nun from Kilkenny who had been living in France for 42 years. She had been completely deaf for six years and, not surprisingly, 'had no pronounced opinions.' She was kept in custody in her convent room.[39] Another Irish nun, 28-year-old Anne Lonergan, was arrested as a foreigner and imprisoned in English convents, first at Charenton and later in rue fosses St Victor not far from the Irish college.[40] This was the prison chosen for Marie Louise O'Murphy, the former mistress of Louis XV, immortalised in the paintings of François Boucher, who was then 57, a widow and the mother of Général de Beaufranchet, a natural son of Louis XV. From the prison records it appears that she reverted to her Irish name (Lenormand was her married name) deeming perhaps her Irish connections less dangerous than her royalist past.[41]

A number of Irish medical students were also imprisoned, such as 19-year-old Thomas Barclay from Limerick and 25-year-old William Walsh.[42] Another escaped arrest by surreptitiously joining a group of volunteers heading for the frontier: he was Patrick MacMahon and had taken part in the attempted takeover of the Irish college in 1792.[43]

The growing number of arrests swelled the prison population, the laws against foreigners of September and October 1793 causing a dramatic increase. On 13 September, it was reported that there were 1,877 detained in the *maisons d'arrêts* in Paris; by 17 April 1794 that figure had reached 7,541. To accommodate these the revolutionary authorities commandeered a number of religious houses and convents, one of which was Collège des Irlandais.[44] The Irish students were detained, though probably not as prisoners, the law of 6 September excepting the 'children sent to France for their education' and that of 10 October excluding 'the children, born on the territory of the king of Great Britain, over 12 years of age and placed in French schools'. (Presumably the latter meant schools in France.) Now that their superiors were arrested some provision had to be made for their welfare and that responsibility fell to the local sectional authorities. The matter came up for discussion at the general assembly of the Observatory section on 15 December, where it was decided 'that provisionally ... the expenses of the seminary in rue du Cheval Vert will be paid by the more wealthy of the prisoners, in view of the fact that there are some who have no resources, and that the food will be the same for all.'[45]

On 25 October the first batch of prisoners arrived at the Irish college,[46] having been transferred from the Luxembourg palace which was already overcrowded. They were all English, Irish or Scots and in general of very modest means. Four of them, Charles Clutterbuck, Thomas Williams, James Lepinet, and Dominick Fitzsimons were English language teachers; the others included mechanics, servants, a groomsman and an earthenware dealer. Four were listed as Irish: Francis Woulfe, Edward Hunt, William Robert Lyster and Dominick Fitzsimons. Fitzsimons had been guardian of the Irish Capuchin monastery at Bar-sur-Aube. Woulfe was a servant in the house of La Tour du Pin.

Wealthier prisoners, mostly French, were interned in the Irish college between January and May 1794. Only one of these had Irish connections: John Baptist Lynch, a former president of the *parlement* of Bordeaux and a grandson of Colonel James Lynch, from Rahoon near Galway, who had followed James II to France. He later was to become Mayor of Bordeaux and a count of the empire. Lynch was arrested with the 84-year-old André Leberton, president of the *parlement* of Bordeaux. He requested that they be imprisoned together and designated the Irish college on account of the advanced age of his colleague, suggesting that conditions there were not as harsh as elsewhere.[47]

The French were nearly all former nobles such as Comte Jean Joussineaux la Tourdonnet and Comtesses Larbouste and de Laval. Others were royalist soldiers such as lieutenant general Paul François Gauthey and captain Louis Charles Chalendar. There were two refractory priests, Thomas Albin Joseph Audibert and Guillaume Auguste de Lort, former vicar general of the diocese of Valence. Nicolas Legaré Roland who was imprisoned with his wife, was described as a writer. Jean Charles Nazon was a planter from St Domingo and listed as an 'enemy of the people'. Three of them were subsequently condemned to death and guillotined, being moved from the Irish college on 17 May to the Luxembourg palace and later to the Conciègerie. One of them, Charles Vanhoff, was a 19-year-old Dutch clockmaker who had crossed the border from Holland in violation of the decree of 6 September 1793. Another, 40-year-old Antoine Tournon was a journalist and editor of the *Mercure Universel*. He was charged with taking part in a prison conspiracy. The third was Comte Jean Joussineau La Tourdonnet, former colonel of the carabineers.

On 13 November 1793 the Committee of General Safety of the National Convention issued a decree ordering that those under arrest in their own houses were to be detained in another *maison d'arrêt* in Paris. As a result Charles Kearney was transferred to the Luxembourg palace.[48] The police register listed the charge against him as conspiracy, a capital offence. It was probably here that he spent 36 days in a *cachot* or dungeon. Another Irishman was incarcerated there on the same day, also charged with conspiracy. Arthur Dillon had been colonel-proprietor of Dillon's regiment under the *ancien régime* and fought in the Americas. He became governor of the island of St Eustache and returned to France at the outbreak of the revolution as deputy for Martinique at the National Assembly, later returning to the army to fight for the republic and distinguishing himself at the battle of Valmy. Like other Irish soldiers he fell victim to the general xenophobia. During the trial of Danton and Desmoulins a rumour was circulated about a huge conspiracy in the prisons to surround the tribunal, murder the judges and free the Dantonists. Spies planted in the Luxembourg named Dillon as the ringleader and claimed that his room was the rendezvous for the conspirators. Brought before the revolutionary tribunal, he admitted organising the able-bodied prisoners to defend themselves in the event of another September Massacre, and to trying to communicate with Lucille Desmoulins. He followed Danton and Desmoulins to the guillotine on 13 April 1794.[49]

Apart from the long shadow of the guillotine prison life was not particularly harsh, especially for those with money or access to friends outside. Within they could move about freely, visiting each other in their rooms. Drinking parties were not unusual. Dillon at his trial stated that the spy who visited him in his room brought lemons to make punch and was already intoxicated. Charles Jennings, better known as General Kilmaine, was deprived of his command because he was Irish and as a report on him to the Committee of Public Safety stated, 'republicanism does not easily penetrate into Irish heads.'[50] He was imprisoned in the Luxembourg from where he wrote to his wife:

> Darling, Today I received the linen you sent and a bottle of rum and a bottle of champagne. I drank all that with a compatriot and to your health. Don't worry on my account but take care of yourself. Goodbye. I love you with all my heart.[51]

Fortunately for Kearney, who always seemed to keep one step ahead of the guillotine, he had been transferred to the Scots college before the prison conspiracy. He was certainly there by 2 February 1794 when commissioners arrived at the Irish college to seize his papers.[52] On the previous day the Convention had decreed that 'property belonging to foreign communities, will be ... sold like the rest of the national domain.' A commissioner of the Department of Paris assisted by two active citizens was 'charged with the removal of all titles and papers in the Irish, English and Scots houses whose properties had been confiscated to the profit of the French republic.' Starting at 9am they adjourned at 6pm, 'considering the needs of a house which served as a prison.'[53] They continued on 3 and 4 February, loading papers into boxes, having pruned away those which they considered of no importance. In all, they took away one large wicker-basket, seven large cartons, 18 small cartons, three boxes and eight registers which they put in a waggon and delivered to Citizen Duchatel, director of the office of liquidation of *émigrés*' property.

Two weeks later, the same citizens arrived at Collège des Lombards to remove the archives.[54] From here they took away one large wooden casket, six cartons, seven registers and one small bag, and delivered them to the same office. Between 15 February and 22 March an inventory was made of all these papers. Those found in Walsh's lodgings comprised 34 sets, totalling 757 documents, those in the lodgings of Murphy who was prefect were divided into 12 sets, totalling 46 documents plus seven English letters and eight registers and those in O'Brien's lodgings came to six sets and a number of bound volumes of manuscript.[55] O'Brien had been chaplain to Monsieur, brother of Louis XVI and 'had disappeared since 10 August 1792'.

At the end of February Saint-Just introduced the Ventôse Decrees proposing the sequestration of the property of suspects and enemies of the revolution which was to be distributed to indigent patriots. Six popular commissions had the task of sorting suspects into three categories: those who were to be freed, deported, or sent back to the revolutionary tribunal. The property of the last two categories was subject to sequestration. As to its distribution, the Communes were charged with drawing up a list of entitled parties. The implementation of the Ventôse Decrees ran into insurmountable obstacles and in the end became a dead letter, sabotaged at Commune and district level and perverted by administrators.

NOTES

1. A.N. F 7 4774 60 doss.1, 23 May 1793.
2. A.N. F 7 4774 55 doss.3, 26 May 1793.
3. A.A.E. Corr.Pol.Angl. 587 f159, 8 June 1793.
4. A.N. F 7 4775 52 doss.2, July 1793.
5. A.N. F 7 4774 59.
6. A.N. F 7 4753, nd.
7. A.A.E. Corr.Pol.Angl. 587 fos.296-300, July 1793.
8. A.A.E. Corr.Pol.Angl. 587 fos.306-7, 4 Aug. 1793.
9. Ibid f312, 10 Aug. 1793.
10. Ibid f314, 12 Aug. 1793.

11/12. Cf ibid 587 fos.319r & v, 325, 326, 19, 21, 26 Aug. 1793.

13. Ibid 588 f14, 2 Oct. 1793.
14. *Moniteur*, p1069, 8 Sept. 1793.
15. *Moniteur*, p1069, 8 Sept. 1793.
16. Maynooth, Papers of I.C.P. Ms.60, 18 Nov. 1801.
17. Ibid cf A.N. H3 2561A, Mar. 1811, p29.
18. A.N. H3 2561A, Mar. 1811.
19. I.C.P. 3W 1. Qtd Boyle, I.E.R. May 1908, pp461-5.
20. A.N. C.271. 666, 8 Sept. 1793.
21. Tuetey, op. cit. 11, p597.
22. *Procés-verbaux de la Convention Nationale*, p32, 29 Sept. 1793.
23. Tuetey, op. cit. 9 pp443-4, 28 Sept. 1793.
24. A.N. BB 70. 320, 28 Sept., 20 Oct. 1793.
25. A.P. A A/200 *Panthéon*, 539, 7 Sept. 1793.

26. Ibid 552, 8 Sept. 1793.
27. A.N. F 7 4720 doss.5, 8 Sept. 1793.
28. A.N. T 1259, 22 Sept. 1793.
29. *Moniteur* XVIII, p88, 10 Oct. 1793.
30. A.N. F19 6237A, *Administration*, p14.
31. Ibid, pp26 & 30.
32. A.A.E. Corr.Pol.Angl. 588 f3, 23 Sept. 1793.
33. *Moniteur*, 8 Sept. 1793.
34. A.P. Register, 10 Oct. 1793. Ibid, 23 July 1794, cf Hayes, op. cit. pp144-6.
35. Hayes, op. cit. p164.
36. Ibid, pp160-2.
37. A.N. F 7 4774 28 doss.1.
38. A.N. F 7 4774 59, 23 Sept. 1793.
39. A.N. F 7 4774 50 doss.4.
40. A.P. Register, 13 Oct. 1793.
41. Ibid, 15 Feb. 1793.
42. Ibid, 13 & 11 Oct. 1793.
43. O'Reilly, op. cit. pp228-33; Byrne, op. cit. 3 pp156-8.
44. The Scots college and the English Benedictine monastery of St Edmond in rue St Jacques were also pressed into service as detention centres. Some doubt exists about the English college in rue des Postes as the records use the expression aux Anglais, which most often designates the Benedictine house. Collège des Lombards escaped this fate probably as it was already occupied by army carpenters.
45. A.N. F 7 2514 p84.
46. A.P. Register, 19 & 25 Oct. 1793.
47. A.N. F 7 4774 27, 6 Jan. 1794.
48. A.P. Register.
49. Hayes, op. cit. pp165-71.
50. Corr. Générale de Carnot, t.2. qtd Hayes, *Irish Swordsmen of France*, p184.
51. A.N. F 7 4753, nd.
52. A.N. T 1636, 3 Feb. 1794.
53. Ibid. cf A.S.P. DQ 10 b.3592, 4 Mar. 1794.
54. Ibid, 15 Feb. 1794.
55. Ibid, 4 Mar. 1794.

8
Road to Freedom

Their joy was inexpressible; they expressed such gratitude and respect for the law of the Convention, that they asserted that they had only one regret, that of not being French themselves.

–Release of Irish students in Toulouse, 30 October 1794.

On 8 September 1793 the students of the Irish college had petitioned the National Convention to except them from the law against British subjects.[1] The Convention made no reply to their request. They tried again early in 1794, sending a *mémoire* to the Minister of the Interior. In it they complained that officials had attempted to remove student property from the college and demanded that orders be given to prevent them. 'Several of the young Irish' they declared, 'intend to study medicine and were exempted from arrest in virtue of the decree of 3 November.'[2] The minister believed the students' claim to be well-founded and that the law had been abused. On 6 February he wrote to the directory of the Department of Paris enclosing the students' *mémoire*, and requested them to write to the revolutionary committee of the Observatory section instructing it 'to leave to the students whatever properties they can prove is theirs.'[3] They could well have argued that the entire college was their property as a result of the *donation entre vifs* made by the founder, Laurence Kelly on 7 May 1772 to the students and signed by each of them. The Collège des Lombards was also in origin a student foundation with all rights vested in the original student bursary-holders.

The fate of the Irish students was finally decided on 25 April when the National Convention issued a decree, following a report by the Committees of Public Safety and Finance:

> The young Irish, to the number of ten, residents of the former Irish seminary, rue du Cheval Vert will receive from the national treasury five hundred pounds each to pay their return fare. Article 2: The

> Commission of the Navy will take the necessary measures to insure their departure, as soon as possible, for Ireland, their native land.[4]

Their release was ordered within 24 hours. Two days later the Committee of Public Safety authorised the navy to execute the decree by putting them on a neutral ship bound for Hamburg.[5] They were still in Paris on 6 May when the police arrived at the Irish college to place seals on Kearney's effects, on the library and, among other things, on an antique clock and ten green velvet armchairs.[6]

Soon afterwards, armed with certificates of civism, the Irish set out for Dunkirk, unaware that the road to freedom was to prove very long indeed. While they were waiting for a boat at Dunkirk the Committee of Public Safety ordered the suspension of the decree authorising their departure,[7] giving as the reason recent despatches from the war front. They ordered that the students be transferred to Arras and imprisoned. There they were to languish until September when the representative in the north wrote to the Committee of Public Safety seeking instructions, claiming that with their certificates of civism they would be 'proscribed in their own country'. The Irish students 'believed themselves victims of the triumvirate, lack everything and demand their freedom'. The representative concluded that the matter required prompt attention. He referred only to nine students whereas the prison records at Arras have the names of Bartholomew Murry, Thomas MacKenna, Francis O'Beirne, Patrick Murphy, Bernard and John MacSheehy, Fitspatrick and MacCurtain.[8] All were subsequently released and returned to Paris and the Irish college.

For the Irish superiors, Walsh and Kearney, June and July were to prove the most dangerous time. On 10 June 1794 the Convention passed the law of 22 Prairial intended to accelerate the procedures of the revolutionary tribunal of Paris and enlarge the numbers of those who could be brought before it for judgment. One of its provisions stipulated that the only punishment for all offences would be death. The law increased the number of capital crimes for which one might be recognised as an enemy of the people and weakened the right of the accused to challenge the evidence presented against him or offer any on his own behalf.

In the hands of the public prosecutor Fouquier-Tinville this proved a most effective weapon of the Terror. Observing whatever few formalities now remaining, he produced what he knew was wanted. He prosecuted the clergy with vigour and non-juring clergy were automatically accused of being counter-revolutionaries. Robespierre defended the law, pointing out that France was full of counter-revolutionary conspirators, assassins and foreign agents and the Convention had to be defended against them. The law of 22 Prairial raised the activity of the revolutionary tribunal of Paris to its highest level in 23 months of existence. During June and July it sentenced 1,594 persons to death, almost 60 per cent of all the condemnations it ever pronounced. In the first ten days of June the average number of executions was 17 per day: for the remainder of that month it rose to 27, and for July to 30. The Terror had reached its zenith. It was an anxious time for Kearney and Walsh and the other Irish prisoners.

Reaction was bound to set in and it did with the Thermidorian revolution at the end of July when the architects of terror were to follow the multitude of their victims to the guillotine. A majority within the Convention had been disconcerted by the mass trials and executions following the law of 22 Prairial, while General Jourdain's decisive victory over the Austrians at the battle of Fleurus had ensured the reconquest of Belgium, convincing the moderate members of the Convention that terror had outlived its usefulness. The triumvirate of Couthon, Saint-Just and Robespierre were overthrown and executed on 28 July and their fate was shared, in the days which followed, by 87 members of the Commune. The guillotine was turning on its masters.

The Thermidorian reaction set in motion the dismantling of the complex of phenomena which had consituted the Terror, though another five months and more were to elapse before the prisons finally yielded up their inmates. Legislation emasculated the revolutionary tribunal by the abolition of the law of 22 Prairial and by an obligation to acquit an accused whose intentions had been pure. But old habits died hard and Nicholas Lynch, a Galway priest who had been 30 years in Paris and was now a prisoner in the Scots college approached a fellow prisoner, Charles Kearney, for an attestation. Kearney signed as 'administrator of the Irish bursaries in Paris' and it was countersigned by Lemaire, apparently also a prisoner there, as 'notary of the Irish houses of education in Paris'.[9] Both were careful to purge themselves of any religious connections.

Six Irish students had been imprisoned in the Irish college in Toulouse. Their superior, Robert MacCarthy, had escaped in disguise to Spain and from there to his native Cork. On 17 August

1794, the students petitioned the National Convention for their release, their petition being sent successively to the Committee of Public Safety and from there to the Committee of Finance. Their plight was raised by Cambon at the National Convention itself on 17 October. 'Incarcerated for a long time without help, far from their relations,' he declared, 'they have been compelled to borrow to survive; without any resources at this moment they have no other hope than the national benevolence.'[10] The Convention decided to apply the decree of 26 April regarding their Paris colleagues, apparently forgetting that it had later been suspended by the Committee of Public Safety.[11] The students were released on 30 October and each of them demanded a copy of the decree. In the minute recording their release the commissioner stated that 'their joy was inexpressible; they expressed such gratitude and respect for the law of the Convention that they asserted that they had only one regret, that of not being French themselves.'[12] The six students were Tracy, O'Meara, Cotter, Murphy and two brothers named MacCarthy. In their session on 7 November 1794, the Committee of Public Safety ordered that the navy put them on a neutral ship to Hamburg and from thence to Ireland. Presumably, the Toulouse students had more success than their Paris colleagues.

John Joseph O'Guinnivan also addressed a petition to the Convention:

> It is from the depths of the prison where he bemoans his fate for thirteen months, in total deprivation, that the Citizen John Joseph O'Ginivan raises his voice to his fellow citizens for help to secure his release.

He claimed that he was imprisoned on 20 August 1793 on the orders of the 'conspirator' Couthon alone. Born in Ireland, he had been in France for 23 years, having made his profession in the Capuchins in Bar-sur-Aube where he was superior in 1790. He took the oath of the Civil Constitution and became a curate of the parish of St Roch in Paris. He had received a certificate of civism only days before his arrest, prior to the enactment of the law against foreigners. He pointed out that 'his former priesthood had been well effaced by 13 months of detention, misery and sickness'. Liable to be put to death if he returned to Ireland and imprisoned in his adopted country France, 'he now finds himself in a class isolated from all the rest of the human race'.[13] O'Guinnivan sent his petition on 15 September and was taken on

10 November before the Committee of General Security which ordered his release on 9 January 1795.[14]

On 30 October 82-year-old Bernard O'Dunne, detained in his own home, was also released. The commissioners lifted the seals at 7pm and when they tried to get O'Dunne's signature on the release form, they 'found him in bed and in such a weak state, that he was not capable of signing.'[15]

Most of the prisoners appear to have been released in the winter of 1794-1795, those in the Irish college being among the earliest. John Pigott, Edward Hunt and the ex-Capuchin Dominick Fitzsimons were released from there on 24 September 1794,[16] 28-year-old William Martin from Luxembourg early in November and the 25-year-old medical student, William Walsh, from St Pelagie during the same month. Early in December William Robert Lyster was released as was another Irish medical student, James O'Connor. Richard Fitzpatrick was released from the Luxembourg early in January. Surprisingly, the Irish nuns were the last to regain their freedom: Thomesson O'Ryan, detained in her convent room, was released in January, while those detained in the English convent, rue des fosses St Victor, were all released on 27 February 1795. These included Elizabeth Stapleton, Anasthasia Stafford, Elise O'Keefe, Elizabeth MacDonald, Therese Hagan, and a 31-year-old novice, Elizabeth Glynn.[17] There are no records of the release of either of the Irish superiors, Walsh or Kearney. One Irish prisoner, Francis Woulfe, died during his detention.

Only one Irish priest was guillotined. He was Martin Glynn from Tuam, Co. Galway, superior of the Irish college in Bordeaux. Some 40 students managed to escape and make their way back to Ireland in the early days of the Terror. One of these was Fr Michael Murphy of Wexford '98. The 80-year-old superior Glynn stayed on and continued to minister as a priest. He was brought before the revolutionary tribunal which had established its headquarters in the Irish college, condemned to death and guillotined.[18] Ironically, Glynn would have known Dr Guillotin well as the latter taught for a while in the Irish college.

The second largest of the continental colleges after Paris was the one in Nantes. After a short period of detention, the staff and students were placed on board an Irish ship, the *Peggy*, on 8 April 1793 and conveyed to Cork.[19] They were fortunate, as during Carrier's reign of terror priests were rounded up, hustled into boats on the Loire and drowned.

The winter of 1795-95 was particularly harsh. With the collapse of the *assignats* and the abandonment of the Law of the Maximum which had fixed the price of bread, the standard of living for the ordinary people was greatly reduced. There was a steep rise in prices and famine as well as cold added to the disastrous consequences of undernourishment. The Irish students who had returned from imprisonment were reported to be 'dying of hunger.' On 24 January 1795 the national domain authorised cutting down the trees in Collège des Irlandais, the timber to be given to individuals in the section in lieu of salary. Felling began at the end of March. Citizen Poisson was employed, working seven hours a day for 18 days for a wage amounting to 126 *livres*. He produced 186 bundles of faggots which could have been sold for 216 *livres*. But the cold and starving Irish did not stand idly by: they claimed the timber as their property. Recognising their right by the law of 3 January, the national domain suggested that Poisson should send the bill to the Irish as they benefited.[20]

On 1 and 2 April food insurrections took place in Paris, the Irish colleges, whose assets had been confiscated or frozen, being particularly hard hit. Walsh petitioned the Committee of Public Assistance for help on behalf of 22 persons who now formed the community. Describing themselves as 'refugees', he pointed out that they 'were driven from their country by British despotism' —they had been deprived by the penal laws of any kind of education in Ireland. Their establishments in France were neither ecclesiastical nor state-owned. Their titles of proprietorship were deposited with the Department of Paris in conformity with the law. He pointed out that their Irish ownership was preserved by the laws of 7 November 1790, 6 April 1791, 4 February, 8 and 12 March 1793. 'Only the law of sequestration had effected their property'. The Irish were now experiencing distress 'exacerbated by a long detention ... They had only recovered their liberty so that they might better experience the cruel effects of destitution.' Apart from poverty, some of the Irish suffered from sickness and old age, 'which adds infinitely to the horror of their situation.'[21]

Walsh cleverly raised the question of the sequestration of the Irish properties while deferring to the government's right to decide the matter: if they were entitled to benefit from the law of 14 Nivôse they would not now be a burden on the state. He also pointed out that for three years the young students had been studying literature, medicine and surgery. Some were employed in hospitals and others had joined the army of the republic. 'The others are ready to leave at the first call to arms.' He ended by stating that if the sequestration were not lifted their present needs could not be postponed. The annual revenue of the Irish colleges was more than 100,000 *livres* and only 22 persons required assistance. He appealed to the 'justice and humanity which characterised the French government' and suggested that the Irish be assimilated with the refugees from invaded French colonies.

Merlino, in the name of the Committee of Public Assistance, took the floor of the National Convention to plead for the Irish and delivered a long oration, borrowing heavily from Walsh's petition:

> There are two questions to be decided at this moment. Firstly, is it a matter of justice for the National Convention to restore to the Irish the properties they acquired and preserved under the auspices and guarantee of the French people? Secondly, is it a matter of justice and humanity for the Convention to give to the Irish, from the revenues of their properties, some financial help, to deliver them from the poverty and distress to which they are reduced?

The first question was a matter for the Committee of Public Safety; the second lay within the competence of the Committee of Public Assistance. The Irish had fulfilled the two conditions necessary for French benevolence; they were refugees from royal despotism and they contributed to the public good of their adopted country. 'Several of them are at this moment at the frontiers' he declared, 'where they stand side by side with our brave brothers in arms.' Arguing that it was by acts of justice and humanity that the republican government would become cherished, it was more desirable in the case of the Irish as it would give the lie to the calumnies against the republic circulating in 'that part of Great Britain'.[22]

Merlino's advocacy of Walsh's petition was successful and they were provisionally assimilated with the refugees from the colonies until the Convention decided definitely on the question of the sequestration of their properties.[23] The list of Irish to be assisted was headed by 80-year-old Charles O'Neill, who had preceded Walsh as superior of Collège des Lombards and had since been committed to Hôpital-Cochin, where, Lally Tollendal later wrote, he died of poverty. Two other names among the administrators not met elsewhere are 75-year-old Thady O'Sullivan and 37-year-old Glennan. Like the Kerry priest, John Leyne, they were probably Irish priests caught in France during the Terror and now experiencing need. The other three were John Baptist Walsh, whose age was given as 53, Charles Kearney and Patrick Murphy, the former prefect of Collège des Lombards.

Fourteen were listed as students: the two MacSheehys, MacCurtain, Moriarty, O'Beirne, Delaney, MacKenna, Murry, Foley, Cruise, Walsh, Fitzpatrick, Jean O'Neill and Jerome MacMahon. Two were listed as serving in the army: O'Molony and Jean MacMahon.[24] Jerome MacMahon was one of the O'Molony bursary-holders at Collège Louis-le-Grand. He had opted for the ecclesiastical state and Walsh had sent him to Langres to avoid arrest. Young O'Molony was the other bursary-holder. He joined a regiment of dragoons and went off to fight the war in La Vendée. An armistice had been declared there in February but O'Molony had returned seriously wounded for life. Walsh later gave both of them 500 *livres* to get them as far as London where their relations could help them continue to Ireland. Among the students there were a few of the original rebels—the two MacSheehys and Murry—and whether he was aware of it or not, Walsh was now seeking financial help for Bernard MacSheehy, who had denounced him to the Convention. Three of the Champ de Mars six, O'Beirne, Delany and MacKenna, were still in the college, the latter having now spent ten years there. William Walsh and Jean O'Neill were medical students, as was probably Richard Fitzpatrick.

The year 1795 was crucial for the future of the college. Walsh later wrote: 'I can say truthfully, that it was to my efforts all during the course of Year 3 (1795) that I owe largely the conservation of the establishment.'[25] A decree of 12 May ordered the sale of national property deposited and Walsh, fearing the loss of his books which had been confiscated the previous year, delegated Bernard MacSheehy to approach the arts committee to request their return. They were now in 'a depot of national literature' at the Cordeliers, but the committee ordered their delivery to MacSheehy.[26] And not a moment too soon. Three days later the furniture of Collège des Lombards came under the auctioneer's hammer in Navarre college where it had been deposited. There was not much on offer—nine chairs, a straw-upholstered armchair, a screen and six curtains. Kitchen utensils consisted of two tumbler-stands, one sauce tureen, 36 tumblers, five salt-cellars, 35 damaged plates, four soup tureens and one spirit-lamp. The sale realised 141 *livres.*[27] The amount may have been insignificant but the event was ominous.

During the whole course of the revolution Walsh had retained the services of a legal expert whom he had payed generously.[28]

Now more than ever he was going to need his assistance in having the sequestration lifted and the properties restored. The law of 14 Nivôse (3 January 1795) provided the first faint glimmer of hope. It distinguished between governments and princes of countries with whom France was at war and mere passive citizens. To the latter it restored their property, insisting that 'the reign of liberty and equality for which the French nation was fighting, should be based on inviolable justice. Consequently, monies invested in the public treasury will be reembursed to the depositors. Properties will be restored to their owners.' However, article 2 of the same law revoked none of the previous sequestration decrees 'concerning ecclesiastical bodies, communities or benefices'.

'All I could do at this unhappy time,' Walsh wrote, 'was to solicit these revenues with a persistence which cost a world of trouble and much expense'. He petitioned the national domain for the return of the Irish title-deeds. Its director wished to know whether the Irish houses were acquired originally with Irish or French money.[29] By 15 May he had concluded that the law of 3 January 'on raising sequestration on foreign property, required no further formality, beyond justifying their proprietorship.' To achieve this a considerable number of documents had to be assembled. A dossier of 12, including Archbishop Troy's nomination of Walsh and Kearney of 21 February 1791, was lodged, though the task had been rendered almost impossible by the seizure of all Kearney's and Walsh's papers the previous year.

Irish persistence paid off. On 18 September 1795, the national domain issued a decree reinstating Walsh and Kearney, 'purely and simply' in possession of the Irish properties and revenues, including revenue owed them by the republic. Tenants were obliged to pay what they owed. All belongings removed from both colleges, religious ornaments and furniture were to be returned. Even what had been handed in to the National Mint, described by Lally Tollendal as 'the widow's mite' could be solicited. Lastly, and most importantly, the title-deeds, 'not only authentic copies but the originals' were to be restored. Walsh had provisionally recovered his apartment in Collège des Lombards in June. Before that he had stayed with his friends, the Montesquiou-Fézensac family, in place des Cinq Cents.[30] Anne-Pierre Montesquiou-Fézensac had been commander of the army of the south in 1792 but later fell foul of the Convention and took refuge in Zurich to avoid arrest. In 1795, however, his name was struck off the list of *émigrés*. With the exception of Walsh's apartment Collège des Lombards was let out to tenants and never re-opened as an educational establishment. For over a hundred years it had served the Irish Church as a national seminary, a kind of pre-Maynooth Maynooth. Maynooth itself, founded in 1795, was to become politically linked with the decline of the Irish colleges in France.

Having succeeded in the legal battle for the restoration of the colleges, albeit with the proviso, 'until the matter be decided definitively', a huge task lay ahead of the superiors physically to restore and refurnish the premises. Walsh later wrote:

> In October 1793, there wasn't a nail missing in this building, completely new and carefully built ... Soon afterwards, it was converted into a house of detention and the government was charged with its upkeep. ... The prisoners themselves did not leave a pane of glass intact.[31]

It was not a very pleasant prospect for the winter of 1795-96, which was once more extremely severe. The collapse of money, following the catastrophic devaluation of the *assignats* under the Convention, immediately ruined all salaried people as well as those living on investments. Poverty was rampant and the Department of the Seine reported an excess of 10,000 deaths over births that winter. Creditors also reappeared once word got out that the sequestration had been lifted from the Irish establishments. Citizens Gallet and Lelong, drapers, put in a hefty bill for cloth provided to students for suits and soutanes. Money was still owed to the architect, François-Joseph Bélanger. To add to this litany of problems, Charles Kearney was still having trouble with the police. He was again denounced and picked up for questioning a few months after his release. However, this time the police were quick to 'recognise the falsity of the charges made against him.'[32]

NOTES

1. A.N. C 271 666, 8 Sept. 1793.
2. A.N. F 17 2500, 6 Feb. 1794.
3. Ibid.
4. *Procés-verbeaux de la Convention Nationale*, p141, 25 April 1794.
5. Aulard, *Recueil des actes du Comité de Salut Public*, XIII, p94.
6. A.P. A A/198, *Observatoire*, 275, 6 May 1794.
7. Aulard, op. cit. XIII, p586.
8. Hayes, op. cit. p186.

9. A.N. F 7 4774 27, 26 Aug. 1794.
10. *Moniteur* XXII, p273, 21 Oct. 1794.
11. A.N. BB 3 54, 17 Oct. 1794.
12. Ibid, 30 Oct. 1794.
13. A.N. F 7 4474 59, 15 Sept. 1794.
14. Ibid, 14 Jan. 1795.
15. A.N. F 7 4774 59, 29 Oct. 1794.
16. A.P. Register, 24 Sept. 1794.
17. Ibid.
18. Hayes, op. cit. pp70-1.
19. Hayes, op. cit. pp66-8.
20. A.S.P. DQ 10, 5 doss.3222, 24-5 April 1795.
21. A.N. F 17 14764, 4 April 1795.
22. *Moniteur* XXIV p148, 4 April 1795.
23. A.N. F 19 6237C; F 17 14764; *Collection Baudouin*, 54 p85, 4 April 1795.
24. A.N. F 17 14764, 4 April 1795.
25. A.N. F 19 6237A, *Administration*, p30.
26. Guillaume, M.G. *Collection des document inédits*, VI p235.
27. A.S.P. DQ 10. 131. 3577.
28. A.N. F 19 6237A.
29. A.S.P. DQ 10 b.3592, 2, 10, 13, 15 May & 19 Sept. 1795.
30. A.N. F 19 6237A, p13n.
31. Maynooth, Papers of I.C.P., *Mémoire à consulter*, nd. p11.
32. Ibid, Ms. 60, 18 Nov. 1801.

9
'Vile and Detestable Profession'

Living in honourable independence, I would blush to eat a morsel that contained either shame or remorse. I have nothing to expect, I ask nothing from an English ministry, who could never employ me under a Protestant government.

–Nicholas Madgett, from prison in Paris, 1795.

After his expulsion from his illegally-assumed post as superior of the Irish college Nicholas Madgett, ex-curé of Blaignon, continued to frequent the milieu of Duckett and his little coterie of Irish republicans. His motive may have been to infiltrate Jacobin circles as a preparation for the career he was about to follow. His older cousin, of the same name, at Foreign Affairs chose him to go with Duckett, Sidderson and Edward Ferris on the abortive secret mission to Ireland in March 1793.[1] Informed by the English secret agent–the ex-priest, Charles Somers from Wexford–the English authorities arrested all four. Madgett, however, was in Ireland by June of that year and had become attached to the English secret service. The Chief Secretary at Dublin Castle wrote to Whitehall: 'A Mr Madgett, a French clergyman of a Kerry family has been employed by the government here privately ... Madgett might be of use if anything is on foot ...'[2] Later that year the other three also made their way to Ireland. Edward Ferris went in the company of Edward Lewins at the request of the diplomatic committee of the Convention and settled in his native Tralee as 'an apostle of liberty'. His fellow Tralee-man now assumed his true colours as a vehement anti-revolutionary.

On 4 August 1794 Madgett left London on *The Belmont*, bound for Jamaica. Eight days later the vessel was captured by three French frigates off the coast of France and Madgett was taken as a prisoner-of-war to Brest, where for four weeks he was detained in a ship at anchor in the bay. On 7 January 1795 he was transferred to the hospital at Brest, from where he escaped with four English detainees and made his way back to England. He later claimed that while in prison he wrote a *mémoire* in which he presented a plan for importing boots, shoes, harnesses and blankets for the army in France. The merchandise was to be brought out of England on a neutral ship and transferred to a French ship on the high seas.[3]

Back in England Madgett immediately prepared to make another attempt to enter France. In May the dispenser of secret service money, Huskisson, gave him £100 sterling 'for a journey to Paris.'[4] At the end of that month he acquired a passport made out in the name of William S. Burns, an American businessman, and signed by the US chargé d'affaires in London.[5] The date on the false passport is difficult to reconcile with the police records in Paris. According to the latter, Madgett was again in prison in France, this time at Orties, from 24 May until his release on 12 June.[6] He himself claimed that he left London on 5 June for Dover, where he remained until 22 of the month when he crossed over to Calais. But then Madgett belonged to what he described himself as a 'vile and detestable profession'. In any event, on 23 June he had his passport signed by the municipality at Calais with an attestation by the mayor who was also the US vice-consul. Four days later he arrived in Paris. When he tried to get his passport visaed he was told that he required a witness to identify him. Returning the next day, he was recognised as 'a dangerous intriguer' and immediately arrested and detained at Quatre Nations prison.[7]

On 8 July Delaunay raised the activities of Madgett on the floor of the Convention, claiming that 'the English government were using their latest means to stop the march of the French revolution'. Her emissaries had penetrated the republic's territory. 'These foreigners are watched by your Committee of General Security', he declared. 'It follows them step by step, knows them and is quick to foil their manoeuvres.' He then went on to recount the history of Madgett from his arrival in Paris in 1770 as a student in Collège de Ste Barbe until he left France: 'Sold to the English ministry, Madgett went to Ireland, spied on and persecuted the patriots in Dublin, who, jealous of our revolution, wish also to become free.'

Delaunay proposed to the Convention that they should make an example of Madgett 'which would teach the traitors and spies of England what they can expect of us.' He brought forward a decree which was adopted. Madgett, alias William S. Burns,

American businessman, was charged with espionage, to be tried by the military commission. Thus, 'the soil of the republic would be purged of these perverse men who try to destroy it'.[8] Oddly enough, the Convention then went on to decree that place de la Révolution would no longer be used as a place of execution. Luck might still be running on Madgett's side.

He was held in Quatre Nations to await his trial by the military commission which consisted of five members: a brigade general, a chief of brigade, with the rank of captain, a cavalry captain, an infantry captain and a recruit. The trial took place on 22 July in public. Madgett was subject to a rigorous examination. There were no grounds for an indictment on the charge of espionage, but as Madgett admitted under cross-examination to escaping from Brest where he had been detained as a prisoner-of-war the Commission returned him to prison until the government committee should decide on appropriate measures. They ordered that their judgement be printed and posted wherever necessary.[9]

From prison Madgett dispatched a number of letters attempting to prove his innocence. In a covering note he wrote 'the monotonous life of a priest during his stay in France was not interesting enough to bore you with the details.' Instead he concocted the story of how he came to France to provision her army posing as an American businessman. He claimed, in what must be judged a highly detailed piece of fiction, that he had been in Ireland–in Cork, Kerry and Dublin–from the beginning of the French revolution until January 1794. In Cork he rescued a French captain and his vessel 'from the fury of the people, who wanted to murder the captain and burn his boat, for some views he expressed about Jesus Christ and religion.' He rendered a similar service to another French sea-captain in Dublin who was carrying whiskey in smaller measures than permitted by the law. His boat was confiscated but Madgett helped him to buy it back. The vessel belonged to Citizen Delamain from Libourne. In Dover on his way to France in June, he helped a Captain Petit of the 4th battalion, a prisoner-of-war and destitute. He ends this letter on a high rhetorical note:

> I have been subjected to the shame and humiliation of a criminal trial, the purity of my intentions has been recognised by my judges. They saw that it required someone completely different to me to be a spy. Vile and detestable profession! and it is not at a time when the infernal policy of the English cabinet has the Catholics of Ireland massacred by her paid satellites, to bend them under an iron yoke,

that she would seek to hire a priest of that communion to practice the profession of a spy. Living in honourable independence, I would blush to eat a morsel that contained either shame or remorse. I have nothing to expect, I ask nothing from an English ministry, who could never employ me under a Protestant government. I am, thank God, independent and without ambition. All its rhetoric and all the wealth of the exchequer could not entice me to dishonour myself.[10]

After his release on 25 November and once safely back in London Madgett put in a bill for £100, 'to repay the expenses of his trial and escape from prison in Paris.'[11] The English government decided that Madgett would be more efficient and less expensive if he stayed out of France and out of prison for the future. They posted him to Ireland in 1796 to report on the activities of the United Irishmen and French emissaries there. In one of his reports he complained that he was not being adequately remunerated: 'After hazarding my existence in the proof of my loyalty, I may have perhaps been entitled to a return more than I have met with ...' In another, he refers to the 'traitorous correspondence' being carried on by William Duckett, his fellow conspirator in the Irish college takeover bid in the autumn of 1792. 'It was no secret in my relation's [Nicholas Madgett Sr] house' he wrote, 'that Mr Duckett was a violent republican and that the object of his mission was to prepare the minds of the people for insurrection.'[12] It would seem that Nicholas Madgett Sr, in spite of his astuteness in such matters, too readily accepted his clerical cousin's republicanism.

Madgett also denounced Richard Ferris as in the pay of the French government.[13] The latter had indeed set out for London as their emissary in October 1793 and before he left met Madame du Barry who gave him some letters for her friend the Duchesse de Mortemart in hiding in Calais. Madame du Barry, a former mistress of Louis XV, was soon after imprisoned in Sainte-Pélagie together with Marie Louise O'Murphy, another mistress of the king. Later she was charged with depravity and licentiousness as mistress of the beheaded king's grandfather, indicating the puritanical side of the revolution, and was guillotined. In Calais, Ferris offered to help Duchesse de Mortemart to escape. Bluffing his way past the various checkpoints as a functionary on an important government mission, with the duchess travelling as his sister, he finally reached Ostend where he embarked for England.

He made his way immediately to Walmar Castle, where the Foreign Secretary, Lord Grenville, was staying, with the intention of offering his services to British intelligence. Grenville did not receive him but instructed his secretary, Goddard, to conduct him to London to be interviewed by the under-secretary, Bland Burges. The interview began at 9am on 13 October and Burges made a detailed and lengthy minute of it.[14] The conversation was general in Goddard's presence. Ferris had brought some letters from 'his friend' Somers for Grenville and Burges and they were examined. Then they talked about the queen, Brissot, shortage of bread, La Vendée, Toulon etc. At this point, Goddard discreetly left to dress for dinner.

Ferris pulled up his chair close to Burges and continued the conversation in French. He gave him a brief résumé of his life to show that he had always been a royalist. He had returned to France after serving in the army of the princes to try and save whatever remained of his fortune. He was closely linked with Somers, and well-informed by him, even on his correspondence with Burges. He was well-known to the French Foreign Minister Des Forges: they had been at school together. Through that connection he had managed to rescue Somers from prison where he had been detained the previous August. Des Forgues sent him on this secret mission to England to infiltrate the ministry, gather news and information about armaments and prepare the way 'for introducing people to assassinate the king and some of the ministers'. On Somers' advice, Ferris had accepted the mission 'as a sure way of aborting the plans of the Jacobins'.

At this point Ferris produced the French secret code. Somers was to act as the agent in Paris to communicate with the French Foreign Affairs and Ferris would correspond directly with him. He then went on to tell Burges that Isabeau, first under-secretary of state had informed him that the French had somebody working for them in the foreign office in London but he refused to divulge the name to Ferris, in spite of his repeated demands. Possibly here, Ferris over-played his hand as Burges quickly pointed out that it was strange that they trusted him with such an important mission and yet withheld such a vital piece of information.

Burges then cross-examined Ferris on his connections with Somers. The latter explained how Somers communicated by writing on the borders of newspapers with vitriol and the network he used for their delivery and that he had just drawn on Burges' bank for £200. Ferris urged that a system of communication be established immediately between London and Paris and that Burges and Lord Grenville should write in vitriol to

Somers. He left a parcel of French newspapers that Somers had sent, giving his address in London as Golden Cross, Charing Cross and assuring Burges that he was always at his disposal.

On the same day Burges wrote to Lord Grenville summarising the interview and informing him that Ferris had left him the cipher which he said he believed to be the same that was used by the other agents in Germany and elsewhere. Burges insisted that one item deserved special attention: Ferris' commission 'to prepare things for the safe reception of certain persons who might be sent over to assassinate the king and those of his servants, who are more particularly obnoxious to the Jacobin party.' Burges went on to observe: 'He appears to be a very sensible discreet man, and to know fully the importance of keeping the secret; and I therefore think it will be safe in his hand.'[15]

On the following day Ferris himself wrote to Grenville in French. As with Burges the day before he began with a résumé of his career up to the outbreak of the revolution. 'He enjoyed a fortune beyond his hopes' he wrote, 'when the revolution began to ravage that beautiful country.' Minister Lebrun had suggested that he become a French secret agent in England and made him 'pecuniary offers capable of tempting a man whose only goal was his own personal interest'. It was then that Somers 'a friend for twenty years' confessed to him that he was a British secret agent. Lebrun's successor renewed the offer to Ferris and after consulting Somers he finally yielded.[16]

He believed that it was his duty for the good of humanity and the peace of England to accept and that his stay in England could be useful from different points of view. England would have nothing to fear from individuals sent to commit crimes as he would guarantee the safety of the king and his ministers by informing them of the arrival of such persons as well as the names of persons planted by the Convention in English government offices and those in receipt of money to stir up trouble in the three kingdoms. He could communicate to the French false information. Grenville could monitor his correspondence with Somers, a correspondence now more necessary than ever with the beginning of the siege of Toulon and the trial of the queen.

Ferris then made a number of propositions to the Foreign Secretary. He should be mandated in France to acquire all public news either from newspapers or taverns. Further, that the minister should have communicated to Ferris all inconsequential news relative to the movements of troops etc. which would enable him to continue to enjoy the confidence of the French government. Ferris undertook to receive nothing from France or to send anything there without it being examined by Burges. Lastly, he offered to travel to France whenever required.

Ferris concluded his letter by offering to provide in England 'persons of the highest distinction who would answer for his honour and his principles'; giving the names of the Duke and Duchess d'Harcourt, the Duke and Duchess de Mortemart and the two princesses de Craon 'and a host of other persons of quality'. During his time as administrator of Collège de Montaigu, Ferris had made many important connections. He became tutor to Prince de Craon, now living in England with the family of Lord Harcourt, their relations. While waiting for a reply from Lord Grenville Ferris called several times on the Duc d'Harcourt.

On 17 October Grenville replied to Burges about Ferris that his seeing him was obviously out of the question. However, he suggested that Ferris' statement be shown to Pitt, the Prime Minister, also insisting that Ferris be shadowed constantly.[17] M. Duban, whom the Foreign Office believed to be a French gentleman (though Ferris claimed he was the son of a Paris delph-seller), was given the assignment.

According to Duban Ferris usually rose between 9 and 10 and made a number of visits, returning at 4pm and dining in his room; When he dined out he always returned reasonably early. He lodged in the house of a restaraunteur called Pippin at the corner of Sherrard Street. London in late 1793 was teeming with French *émigrés*: there were over 5,000 priest-refugees alone. Many of them supported themselves by giving French lessons. Ferris called on Abbé Germain, a former professor at Collège de Montaigu and now teaching French to the children of a rich Englishman called Huddlaston. Abbé Germain described Ferris to Duban as a 'respectable priest, an excellent royalist and a brave soldier during his campaign'. He also visited Madame de Cocheret, a creole from St Domingue whose husband had represented the colony in the National Assembly, and another creole, Madame Digneron. He was visited by the bishop of Périgueux and also saw the bishop of Limoges. Duban reported that Ferris 'spoke often of his desire to go and join the royalists in La Vendée.'[18]

Among the numerous French *émigrés* then in England were Talleyrand and Lally Tollendal. Ferris may have met the latter as they both lodged at the same address in London on occasion. Much later Lally wrote that he had not met Ferris ten times in his whole life. In any event a Dr MacCarthy spoke to him several times in England about him and 'always with the highest praise.' Lally Tollendal was later to describe Ferris as 'enlightened, educated, incisive, wise, capable, and precise'.[19] He had several meetings with M. Ozée (Hussey), chaplain at the Spanish embassy. This was probably Thomas Hussey, a close friend of Edmund Burke, who suggested to Ferris that he write to the latter as someone who carried considerable weight with the British government. He did so but Grenville replied to Burke about the 'necessity caution and reserve, in such times and on such an occasion'.[20] Burges had already informed Grenville that he had received reliable information that Ferris was 'a dangerous agent of the Jacobins.' In November Ferris called again on Burges and asked him to forward a letter to France which he had sealed with the seal which belonged to Somers. This made Burges suspect that Ferris was opening and resealing the reports sent by Somers to him. In spite of all his efforts Grenville remained unimpressed.

In London Ferris sought out some of his old army comrades. Moves were then afoot to form a new Irish brigade in the British army from the royalist remnants of the Irish regiments in France, and a scheme devised by Count Charles Daniel O'Connell was submitted to Pitt. It was planned to raise six regiments. O'Connell was among a group of senior army officers, headed by Duc de FitzJames, who signed an attestation for Ferris, declaring 'that in all circumstances he has given unequivocal proof of the most steadfast conduct and zeal and attachment to the royal cause.'[21] Ferris then offered to join Lord Moira's expedition to La Vendée, but Grenville made sure that he was detained at Portsmouth from where he wrote to Edmund Burke: 'I fear neither the sea nor the French, and I will not refuse ... to embark on the smallest cutter in a cause such as ours.'[22] By January the revolt in La Vendée had collapsed.

By July Ferris was running out of money and wrote again to Grenville: 'as you seem determined not to favour me and as I am penniless, I beg in your goodness to grant me a gratuity.'[23] There was no reply and a month later Ferris wrote another much longer letter. He had even been refused a commission in the new Irish brigade, having been listed as suspect. 'I cannot bear the shame of being suspected' he declared, 'I would sooner die in fetters rather than live with that'. Ferris believed that part of his trouble resulted from a confusion in British intelligence circles between himself and his cousin Edward Ferris in Tralee. 'Someone must have mistaken me for a disloyal subject of the same name sent to spread sedition in Ireland,' he wrote to Grenville. In any case Madgett continuously warned the Foreign Office that Richard Ferris was 'the secret agent of Charles de la Croix, French Minister of Foreign Affairs and in his pay.'[24]

Charles Somers, whom Ferris claimed as a friend of 20 years, had been educated and ordained a priest in Paris,[25] beginning his studies there about 1775, when Ferris also began his. Unlike Ferris, he took the oath to the Civil Constitution of the clergy. Soon afterwards he abandoned the priesthood and married the widow of a shoemaker. Moving among the lower orders of the *sans-culottes* he passed for an extreme Jacobin. From 1792 he was a paid secret agent of the English government and sent regular despatches to London, including a detailed account of the meeting in White's Hotel when a group of Irish and English residents sent in a congratulatory address to the National Assembly, with the complete list of signatories. He also warned the official English agent, George Munro, that his name figured on a list of those suspected of being spies. Munro left France and Somers succeeded him. He visited Peltier, a well-known royalist journalist in hiding during the week of the September Massacres, to check on his safety. Peltier described him as 'a brave Englishman, the loyal Somers'. He reported Arthur Dillon's speech at the Convention asking for 10,000 men and arms for a military expedition to Ireland. His report on the mission of four Irish students to Ireland in March 1793 led directly to their arrest on arrival in England and suspicion being thrown on the superiors of the Irish colleges as the informers.[26]

In a letter to Lord Grenville early in 1793 Somers claimed to be acting from the purest of motives:

> ... the most ardent and disinterested love for the sacred person of my king and for the constitution of my country, which I have seen indignantly outraged, has forced me to break silence and to denounce the conspiracies of a horde of scoundrels, who are conspiring against both one and the other.[27]

However, a mere four days later he wrote to Wickham, who dispensed the secret service money:

> Dare I take the liberty, dear Sir, of applying to you for a trifling sum of money–twenty or thirty pounds only. I have been at some expense to get at information here. A thousand pardons for the liberty I take ...[28]

In August 1793 the National Convention solemnly pronounced the English Prime Minister, 'the enemy of the human race'. In a dispatch to the Foreign Office, Somers wrote, 'there is an Irishman in Paris ... this monster has offered to kill Pitt and the king of England'.[29] This was the information that Richard Ferris had passed on to Burges in his first interview and which Burges had warned Grenville should be taken seriously. Ferris claimed that Somers had been arrested in August 1793 and that Ferris had been instrumental in securing his release.

Somers continued to provide intelligence to the English government almost to the end of the Napoleonic era. It would appear that he was well remunerated and 'carried on ... from his appearance and expenses, a profitable business.' By 1812, he and Ferris 'still continued on amicable if not intimate terms'.[30] That year, Somers delivered a letter at a dinner to celebrate the departure of an Irish captain of an American ship about to sail for New York. On the way he was due to call at one of the Channel ports where he had promised to post the letter for Somers. Richard Ferris was one of the guests at the party. Later that night the letter was opened. Somers was denounced to the police as a spy, court-martialled and executed the following day. His widow received a large sum in compensation from the English government.[31]

Probably the most reliable secret agent to emerge from among the former students of the Irish college was William Duckett. He had finished his studies there and left a week after the fall of the Bastille, returning briefly in the autumn of 1792 when he was elected administrator by the rebel students under the aegis of the Paris Commune. A close associate of Nicholas Madgett of Foreign Affairs, he was assigned by the latter to lead the first French mission to Ireland in March 1793 which ended with their capture in England. On his release, Duckett continued in his chosen profession of espionage. Going and coming between England and Ireland, he made contact with the local radicals. Ordered to preach revolution in Ireland he wrote articles for the *Morning Chronicle* and the *Northern Star* under the pseudonym 'Junius Redivivus' attacking the British government.[32] On returning to France Duckett continued as a French secret agent, becoming one of the most reliable and professional in that service.

NOTES

1. A.A.E. Corr.Pol.Angl. 587 f45, 22 Mar. 1793.
2. P.R.O. London FO. v43, June 1793 qtd Hayes, op. cit. p206n.
3. A.N. F 7 4774 28.
4. Brit.Mus. Huskisson Ms.38769 qtd Hayes, op. cit. p207n.
5. *Moniteur*, p187, *Séance* of 8 July 1795.
6. A.P. Register.
7. *Moniteur*, p187, 8 July 1795.
8. Ibid pp187-8.
9. A.N. BB 3 56, 22 July 1795.
10. A.N. F 7 4774 28.
11. Brit.Mus. Huskisson Ms.38769, qtd Hayes, op. cit. p207n.
12. Ibid pp285-6.
13. Hayes, op. cit. p285.
14. Bodleian Library Oxford, Bland Burges Papers, 13 Oct. 1793: I am indebted to Marianne Elliot for this information.
15. Dropmore Papers, 11, 445 qtd Purcell, *Richard Ferris*, p29.
16. Bland Burges Papers, 14 Oct. 1793. Ferris to Grenville, pp183-7.
17. Bland Burges Papers, p188. Grenville to Burgess, 17 Oct. 1793.
18. Ibid, 26 Oct. 1793, p188-92.
19. A.N. H 3 2561A, pp21-2.
20. *Corr. of Edmund Burke*, VII, pp464-5, qtd Purcell, op. cit. p31.
21. P.R.O. FO. 27, 43, qtd Purcell, op. cit. p34.
22. Qtd Purcell, op. cit. pp34-7.
23. P.R.O. FO. 27, 45 ERD/2354, qtd Purcell, op. cit. pp39-40.
24. Ibid.
25. On Somers see Hayes, op. cit. pp14, 62, 101, 121-2, & *Biog. Dict.* pp289-90.
26. P.R.O. FO. 41, 42.
27. Ibid.
28. Ibid.
29. Ibid.
30. O'Reilly, op. cit. pp240-2.
31. Ibid.
32. Others also followed a roving mission in Ireland, according to their instructions to lead 'a wandering life, in order to encrease their contacts and enable them to exert the greatest influence on popular thinking.'

10
The Wolf in Mr Tone

I objected all along to priests as the worst of all possible agents and here is one who is the worst of all possible priests.

–Wolfe Tone on Fitzsimons, Paris, 1796.

According to Nicholas Madgett, the English spy and his former fellow-conspirator in the Irish college, Duckett was sent to Ireland with 14,000 *livres* to assist the defence at the trial[1] of William Jackson, a protestant clergyman from Dublin who had been living in Paris since the early days of the revolution. Like Duckett he had signed the famous address from White's Hotel in the autumn of 1792. Early in 1794 the French government sent Jackson to Ireland to sound out opinion on the feasibility of a French invasion, but betrayed by a friend who shadowed him all the way, he was arrested.

He had sent Wolfe Tone's memoir on the subject through the open post and it was intercepted, unfortunately for Tone. Jackson's trial took place 12 months later: he was convicted but robbed the executioner of his prey by taking poison. Deeply compromised, Tone had little alternative but to flee the country. In May he took ship for America with the intention of returning from there to France to act as delegate for the United Irishmen. He arrived in France from Philadelphia on 1 February 1796.

Duckett, too, returned to Paris in 1796 and soon their paths were to cross. In fact the only Irish Tone were to meet in France were the remnants of that 200-year-old community which made up the Irish colleges, or others who in some way had belonged to it. Like Duckett they were people who had spent most of their lives in France, spoke the language perfectly and had been schooled in the university of its revolution. The Ireland that spawned them and whose memory they cherished was a peasant Catholic country largely hidden from Tone and the Dublin ascendancy. They were the educated cousins of Tone's 'poor Pat'.

> When everything else is ready, let them send in a large quantity of wine and brandy, and some French *filles*, and then when Pat's heart is a little soft with love and wine, send in two or three proper persons in regimentals with green cockades in their hats, to speak to them, of whom I will very gladly be one.[2]

Tone never felt comfortable in the presence of the Paris Irish and would have preferred not to have had to use them as mediators with French politicians. Delacroix, Minister of Foreign Affairs, left the business of Ireland and in particular Tone's mission to a large extent in the capable hands of his subordinate, Nicholas Madgett. It was in the minister's ante-chamber on 26 February that Duckett and Tone had their first casual encounter.

> A person came in, and after reconnoitring me for some time, pulled out an English newspaper and began to read it. Looked at him with the most interesting indifference, as if he was reading a chapter in the Koran. Did the fellow think I would rise at such a bait as that?[3]

Later, Delacroix informed Tone that the person was an Irish patriot, named 'Duchet, who was persecuted into exile for some writing under the signature of Junius Redivivus.' He added that Duckett had presented several memorials on the state of Ireland. 'Who the devil is Junius Redivivus?' Tone wondered. 'I must talk a little to Madgett of this resurrection of Junius, of which, to speak the truth, I have no good opinion.'[4] He must not have raised the matter with Madgett as Delacroix mentioned his name again on 11 April, suggesting the advisability of sending proper persons to Ireland to give notice to the people there of what was intended. Tone replied that he knew nothing at all about him.[5]

On 14 March Tone went to the Luxembourg palace where Carnot, who was holding one of his public audiences, introduced him to General Clarke, stating: 'He has the confidence of the government; go with him and explain yourself without reserve.'[6] That evening Tone wrote in his diary: 'I would rather stick to Carnot but what can I do when he has handed me over to Clarke.'[7] Clarke was descended on both sides from a long line of military men who served in the Irish regiments. His father died when he was a boy and he was brought up by his uncle, Colonel Henry Shee, of a family with a long association with the Irish college both before and after the revolution. He began his own military career as a lieutenant in Berwick's regiment, and went on to become Minister of War under Napoleon and again under the restoration.

Clarke questioned Tone on the influence of the Catholic clergy over the minds of the people and the possibility of their warping them against France. Tone assured him:

> ... that it was much more likely that France would turn the people against the clergy; that within these last few years, that is to say since the French revolution, an astonishing change with regard to the influence of the priests had taken place in Ireland.[8]

From this first interview Tone concluded that Clarke's ideas on Ireland were 30 years out of date.[9]

Towards the end of March Tone had another interview with Clarke who was still preoccupied with finding somebody suitable to send to Ireland. He sought Tone's views on the Irish priests still remaining in France. Tone was adamantly opposed.

> I answered that he knew my opinion as to priests of all kinds; that in Ireland they had acted, all along, execrably; that they hated the very name of the French revolution, and that I feared, and indeed was sure, that if one was sent from France, he would immediately, from the ésprit de corps, get in with his brethren in Ireland, who would misrepresent every thing to him; and, of course, that any information which he might collect would not be worth a farthing.[10]

When it came to naming a general to command the French expeditionary force to Ireland the officers of the former Irish regiments fared little better in Tone's estimation than had Irish priests. His views on this matter were a little indelicate, considering Clarke's own stint in Berwick's regiment. Tone himself wanted a French general of some reputation and suggested Bournonville. Clarke suggested Jennings, 'who used to call himself Baron de Kilmaine–God knows why.' Tone replied 'that in Ireland we had no great confidence in the officers of the old Irish brigade ... and, as to Jennings ... he was at any rate not a fortunate general.' Clarke himself spoke of O'Connell 'with respect, as a good parade officer to prepare troops for service, but as having no extent of genius for command.'[11]

Delacroix had first suggested to Tone that Fitzsimons might be the right man to send to Ireland. Dominick Fitzsimons was the Capuchin priest from Bar-sur-Aube who had spent his imprisonment in the Irish college. Tone replied that he 'had strong objection to letting priests into the business at all; that most of them were enemies to the French revolution'.[12] Madgett later told Tone that Fitzsimons had been recommended by Prieur de la Marne, who had known him for 20 years and 'would stake his life on his honesty.' Under no circumstances would Tone accept Fitzsimons, adding that he 'I dare say, hates a Presbyterian like the devil.'[13] Unfortunately for Tone's blood pressure he finally met Fitzsimons in the flesh and in Madgett's office, where the latter spoke to him 'without reserve'. 'I never was more provoked in my life', Tone later wrote in his diary.[14] He was becoming obsessed by Fitzsimons after one casual meeting. 'I objected all along to priests as the worst of all possible agents,' he wrote, 'and here is one who is the worst of all possible priests.'[15] And all this because Fitzsimons made some foolish joke to Madgett's nephew, Sullivan, about the Portuguese despatches to Rio de Janeiro, written in English.

At dinner that evening Tone brought up the matter with Madgett, declaring that he would not communicate with 'such an eternal blockhead.'[16] In the face of Tone's outburst, Madgett abandoned his attempt to defend Fitzsimons. The following day Tone called on Delacroix and informed him that Fitzsimons 'was absolutely unfit for the mission'.[17] Finally, an Irish doctor called Aherne was chosen. There was a student of that name in the Irish college in August 1792. At first Tone was satisfied with Aherne and his republican sentiments but later he began to have second thoughts about him too.[18]

With Fitzsimons disposed of, Duckett became once more the target of Tone's venom. Madgett reported that he had heard from Duckett that two expeditions were planned, one from Flushing commanded by General MacDonald, the other from Brest under General Hoche. Referring to Duckett as 'a great blackguard', Tone admitted that the report could well be true 'but it is most terribly provoking to have the subject bandied about as table-talk by such a fellow as this Duckett'.[19] By this time Tone had revised his opinion of Clarke, blaming Aherne, Sullivan and even Madgett for his original prejudice:

> I would blot out all the passages which reflect upon him, but upon second thoughts, I will keep them as a memento to prevent me forming hasty judgements of people.[20]

However his purpose of amendment did not extend to Duckett. Early in July Clarke once more raised the 'boring' matter of Duckett. Tone said that he did not know him or wish to know him, because he understood from Madgett and others, that 'he was a blackguard.'[21] It seems odd that Madgett, his early mentor, would have turned against Duckett. Clarke, a little taken aback, remarked, 'Ay, but he is clever.' The matter was not pursued as Tone admitted he knew Duckett 'merely by report'.

Napoleon had taken command of the army of Italy early in March and two months later achieved a signal victory at Lodi. Soon the Pope had to sue for peace and was granted an armistice. He dispatched his ambassador to Paris. Tone commented in his diary:

> I am heartily glad that old priest is at last laid under contribution in his turn. Many a long century he and his predecessors have been fleecing all Europe, but the day of retribution is come at last.[22]

Tone was hopeful of converting the event to his advantage in Ireland. He raised the question with Clarke and suggested that Cardinal Antonelli, legate for Ireland, should be approached with the view to 'artfully get a line from him to Dr Troy, it might save us some trouble.'[23] At his first meeting with Hoche the latter questioned him on what the attitude of the priests in Ireland might be. Tone explained at some length to him that they certainly could not be relied on for assistance but neither was it likely that they would provide any effectual opposition.[24]

Two former Irish college students continued to dog Tone's steps, mostly to his displeasure. When he arrived at Rennes on 20 September to join the army of the west preparing for the invasion of Ireland, he was given as adjutant Bernard MacSheehy,[25] who had left the Irish college shortly after April 1795 and opted for a military career. Tone sent him to inform Hoche of his arrival. When he called on the general the following day, the first question Hoche put to him was about Duckett who was also in Rennes. Tone said he neither knew nor intended to know Duckett and 'mentioned his prating at Paris to all his acquaintance, about his influence with General Clarke and Hoche himself.'[26]

Two days later Duckett's name came up again, this time in conversation with Clarke's uncle, Colonel Henry Shee. Tone reiterated that 'he believed him to be a blackguard.' Then Shee struck a soft spot when he informed Tone that Duckett had told several people that he was sent here by the committee of nine, who managed the affairs of the catholics, as their plenipotentiary. Tone was furious, claiming 'that Duckett was a scoundrel and if he were to tell so outrageous a lie in my presence, I would knock him down on the spot.' He urged Shee to warn Hoche about Duckett but Shee was sure that Hoche would see through him. 'I'll Duckett him, the scoundrel, if I can catch him fairly in my grip' Tone concluded the entry in his diary, still fuming.[27]

He later told his wife about an incident which occurred during dinner conversation with Hoche. They were discussing the national funeral accorded to Lord Chatham. Duckett remarked that it was his greatest ambition to receive a national funeral to which Colonel Shee retorted that it was highly probable in his case, 'for whenever you die, the parish will surely have to bury you'. This anecdote was added in by Tone's son, probably not realising that he was unwittingly enhancing the status of Duckett by having him dine in such exalted company.[28] Shee did speak about Duckett to Hoche and 'it was decided to keep the fellow here until the last moment and then despatch him.'[29] In all of this one gets the distinct impression that Tone is being humoured; but he continued to worry, particularly when there were long periods of no communication between himself and Hoche. He confided as much to Shee, pointing out that

> as there are two Irishmen here, (M'Sheehy and Duckett) besides myself, and as the first is a blockhead and the last a scoundrel, I did not exactly know whether the general might not lump us all together, in forming his opinion.[30]

On 1 November 1796 Tone arrived at Brest, where preparations for the expeditionary force to Ireland were in an advanced state. A week later Colonel Shee informed him that Hoche wished to have last minute information on the state of Ireland. He wanted somebody to go immediately, 'as he had a safe American who would sail at a minute's warning.'[31] Tone suggested MacSheehy. Hoche was consulted and agreed that if MacSheehy had no objection he should leave the following day. Tone approached MacSheehy, speaking of it as his own idea. He 'agreed without difficulty to go, if the general desired it.' On the following day, Hoche sent for MacSheehy and gave him verbal instructions. He should contact the persons whom Tone would name:

> and learn from them as much as he could on the actual state of the country at this moment, the temper of the people, the number and disposition of the troops, whether the French were expected or desired, and if so, in what part particularly.[32]

MacSheehy was not to pass on any information except 'that

the dispositions of France were highly favourable to Ireland.' Hoche then gave MacSheehy twenty *louis*. Tone brought him to his lodgings and made him change into other clothes, 'all either Irish or made after the Irish fashion.' He gave him two addresses, those of Oliver Bond and Richard McCormick, secretary of the Catholic committee. He then walked with him down to the quay where he boarded the waiting ship, the *Washington*, at 8pm on a moonlit night. Tone estimated rather optimistically that it would take a fortnight to complete the mission. 'I hope MacSheehy will acquit himself well;' He entered that night in his diary, 'he has not much to do'.[33]

It was a gross understatement. For the 22-year-old MacSheehy, only recently released from the Irish college, it was an extremely hazardous undertaking.[34] They were scarcely clear of Brest on the following day when they were intercepted and boarded by Sir John Warren in command of a squadron of four frigates. Reilly, the American captain, was questioned about certain irregularities in the ship's register but they were allowed to continue. The same day they sailed through another English squadron which consisted of 15 sail of the line. Three days out they encountered the fleet commanded by Admiral Jervis, consisting of eight of the line, three of which were three-deckers, and were examined by two frigates which made up the van. MacSheehy later wrote in his report: 'During these examinations I always took great care to remain hidden in a corner, having someone to cover me with some of the sailors' old clothes.' The next problem they had to face was a 'violent hurricane' within five leagues of Guernsey. They stood out to sea for a day and a night to avoid being dashed against the rocks.

Eventually they sighted the Isle of Wight and were piloted into Cowes. Reilly persuaded the pilot to take some passengers, including MacSheehy, into Portsmouth, by offering to reward him suitably. 'Money' MacSheehy observed, 'is the great incentive of everything in England.' There they put up at an inn from which at 4am the next day they left on the stage-coach bound for London 'knowing that it would be much easier to remain unknown there than anywhere else.' A French *émigré* travelling on the same coach remarked to MacSheehy that he was wearing a hat and coat 'after the French fashion', which reflects unfavourably on Tone's contribution to the mission. They arrived in London at 11pm on 17 November and remained there for three or four days 'as much to await a place in the mail coach as to throw off the government spies in the event of their having learnt of my arrival.'

MacSheehy found a considerable amount of anti-government feeling among the general public. He noticed that the women had their hair cut short *à la jacobine* to display their democratic sentiments. He even managed to fit in an evening at Covent Garden theatre when the king and the royal family were present. At the suggestion that 'God Save The King' should be played, several people shouted 'God save the people.' He left London for Holyhead on the mail-coach on 22 November. The only other passenger was a king's messenger and MacSheehy quickly and cleverly wormed his way into his confidence. He was bringing instructions from the English government to the Irish viceroy to take immediate measures to arrest 'one Bryan, aged about twenty years, who had come from Brest to Portsmouth on the American ship, *Washington*.'

They spent the night in Holyhead and left on the following evening on the Dublin packet. Major-General Lake, who was about to take command of the army in the north and his aide-de-camp were the only other two passengers. Lake was not very happy with his appointment, fearing 'the wrath of an embittered and exasperated people'. MacSheehy thought him 'quite an honest man.' So well did MacSheehy play his role that the king's messenger offered to put him up at the Castle when they reached Dublin at midnight on 26 November. He opted rather to lodge at the Marine Hotel on Rogerson's Quay.

Next day he tried to get in touch with his contacts. 'I experienced more difficulty in gaining their confidence', he remarked, 'than that of the messenger.' Eventually, a rendezvous was arranged outside the Post Office in College Green and a signal agreed. As the clock finished striking, MacSheehy emerged from the shadows and gave the agreed sign to William James MacNeven, while two others stood away at some distance. They all walked towards Parliament House, informing MacSheehy of the state of the forces in the country. They met again the following day outside the Marine Hotel, where they strolled and exchanged information for about an hour. An emissary was sent north and returned two days later with the information that there were 50,000 men ready to welcome the French.

> If General Hoche lands, Ireland will be free. France has a faithful ally and her natural enemy, the enemy of all nations, will be struck off the list of nations.

With his mission completed, MacSheehy left Dublin for London, which he reached on 4 December.

Nobody could leave England without a special passport signed by the Home Secretary. 'I was now in a most critical situation,' MacSheehy observed. He decided that Guernsey was the only safe route and left on the mail for Weymouth on 8 December just in time to catch the packet. From Guernsey, with the help of some gold, he managed to persuade an American to make a run for France. He landed near Paimpol in Brittany and reached Brest on 18 December, three days after Hoche had set sail for Bantry. General Hédouville forwarded his report to the Directory, adding that 'this intelligent and educated young Irishman seems to have fulfilled his mission perfectly'.[35]

Hoche's expedition, consisting of 43 sail, had left Brest on 16 December with Tone on board, 14,450 troops, 41,644 stand of arms and a supply of green cockades. On board also was a former Irish college student, James Bartholomew Blackwell from Ennis, who had been one of the nine rebels of the autumn of 1792. He had already seen service in the early revolutionary campaigns and held the rank of colonel on this expedition. A more recent recruit from the Irish college was Thomas MacKenna, who had been nearly lynched by the Paris mob six years earlier outside Hôtel de Ville after the incident on the Champ des Mars. In spite of that and at least two bouts of internment he had managed to preserve his republican sentiment. MacKenna had been among the group of Irish students who had assured the National Convention in 1793 that they would 'yield to no citizen whatever in their republican sentiments': on this occasion they were to be tested by weather rather than war. Thick fog dispersed the fleet on the first night and Hoche's frigate was separated from the main fleet. They arrived in Bantry Bay during a snowstorm on 21 December, 16 ships entering the bay and 19 standing outside, but there was still no sign of their commander. Ravaged by storms and indecision, they finally cut their cables on the day after Christmas and sailed back to Brest. Four days later Hoche and his little flotilla returned. The expedition had been a complete fiasco.

Tone met Hoche for five minutes the day after the latter arrived in Paris on 22 January. Hoche questioned him about MacSheehy's mission and requested a copy of his report which Tone delivered the following morning.[36] A week later Hoche sent a note[37] to thank MacSheehy:

> I have received, Citizen, the journal of the journey which you recently made to Ireland. The government no longer concerns itself at this time with the resumption of the enterprise which was beset by so many misfortunes and disappointments but appreciates nonetheless all you have achieved. I am very grateful for all the trouble and care you took to carry out the mission entrusted to you.'

Hoche transferred his interest to the Rhine and kept Tone on his staff. Captain Bernard MacSheehy was reassigned as his adjutant to their mutual dissatisfaction. Referring to MacSheehy as a 'sad blockhead' he went on to complain that he 'latterly is turning out the most insufferable coxcomb I ever saw–he pesters my life out; he is the neat pattern of a vulgar, impudent, Irish dunce, with great pretensions. I will move heaven and earth to get rid of him;–confound him! I wish he was up to the neck in the Rhine; with all my heart.'[38] A year later they parted company, MacSheehy making his way to Toulon with an American called Lewis who had accompanied him to London on his Irish mission. General Chérin, Hoche's chief of staff on the Bantry expedition commending him for promotion, praised his 'talents and republican zeal'.[39] An informer described him to the Irish government as 'an officer of some merit'.[40] MacSheehy joined Bonaparte's expeditionary force to Egypt–on the way he raised a Maltese legion. He served at the siege of Cairo and had a sword of honour conferred on him by General Kléber for his part in the recapture of Suez.

Father James Coigly had left the Irish college in October of 1789 to return to the mission in his native Armagh. Though leaving Paris as a fervent anti-revolutionary he had by the end of 1796 become a sworn member of the United Irishmen. In April 1797 a warrant was issued for his arrest and he fled to England, from where he decided to go to Paris in the hope of recovering some family property–presumably the Maginn foundation about which he had taken the superior Walsh to court when he was a student. Coigly claimed a relationship to Patrick Maginn, one of the two original founders of Collège des Lombards, on his mother's side. When he put in his claim in Paris, he 'was told that everything belonging to the Irish would be restored, but not until the end of the war.'[41] At this point he was destitute, having exhausted the £20 collected by some of his political contacts in England. 'It was my good fortune' he later wrote, 'to meet an old college companion, now an officer of distinction in the regular forces.'[42] This was most likely James Bartholomew Blackwell. Writing later from his death-cell in England, Coigly acknowledged his debt to Blackwell: 'He became my security and protected me; offered likewise to procure me employment as a priest; but on application, it was absolutely necessary to take certain oaths. These I refused positively, choosing rather to return and die in any manner in my own country than swear against my conscience.' In Paris, Coigly was observed walking out '*à la militaire*'.[43]

While in London Coigly had been in communication with the 'members of the chief revolutionary committee of England' and undertook to deliver a message[44] from them to the Directory in France. The English committee undertook to seize the leading members of the privy council if France sent an expedition to Ireland. Should the French decide to invade England, the English patriots laid down certain preconditions for their support. The British Isles were to form distinct republics and they were to choose their own form of government. The message was jointly signed by Coigly and Rev. Arthur MacMahon, a Presbyterian minister who accompanied him, and they claimed that their characters would be endorsed by 'their countrymen now in Paris engaged in the cause of liberty'.

Napper Tandy had arrived in Paris from America in June and he expected to assume automatic leadership of the Irish refugees there. New arrivals like Coigly and MacMahon gravitated towards Tandy's party as did others like Madgett and Blackwell.

Tone's undisputed leadership in France was now threatened. Coigly and Tandy called a meeting[45] and summoned him and Lewins to appear before it, but Tandy failed to substantiate the charges. Coigly left Paris soon after the mock trial of Tone and Lewins, his mission apparently connected with the removal of Lewins as United Irish envoy in Paris. He went via Hamburg where William Duckett was now based as secretary to Léonard Bourdon and proving invaluable in providing help and passports for Irish patriots entering, or others, like Coigly seeking to return.

In London, Coigly met Arthur O'Connor and the newly created committee of United Britons, an alliance being formed between the United men in Ireland, England and Scotland. Coigly and O'Connor were anxious to inform France of these latest developments and a Corkman, Edward O'Finn, was chosen for the assignment. Coigly left London and reached Dublin three days later. The following day he met Lord Edward Fitzgerald and presented the two English delegates, William Bailey and Benjamin Binns, who had brought an address from the United Britons to the

United Irishmen. This was discussed at a national meeting of the United Irishmen. Coigly then left for Belfast. Early in February he again left Ireland with instructions for O'Connor to lead a new delegation to France. His departure from England was delayed by the protracted preparations of O'Connor for what he expected would be a lengthy stay in France.

Coigly left London on 27 February, posing as a Captain Jones, with two servants, Allen and O'Leary, both United men. O'Connor passed himself off as a Captain Morris with Binns as his servant. They were bound for Margate from which they hoped to get a boat to France on the following day. But warrants had already been issued in London for their arrest, and while they slept that night in the King's Head at Margate two Bow Street Runners were riding hard. The inn was surrounded and in the morning all five were arrested. A document was found in Coigly's greatcoat which purported to be an address from the London United society to the French Directory. O'Leary managed to flush O'Connor's documents down the privy of the King's Head. One of these would have been his appointment as the new United envoy in Paris.

Three weeks later Tone read an account of the arrest in the English papers which had reached Paris. He noted that O'Connor was accompanied by 'Quigley (Coigly) the priest, who was some time since in Paris, and of whom I have no great reason to be an admirer.' Commenting on the paper discovered in Coigly's coat, he wrote, 'I should not believe it possible any man living would leave a paper of such consequence in such a careless extraordinary place'.[46] Writing from his prison cell where he was awaiting his execution, Coigly stated:[47] 'None but an idiot or a madman would have kept in his pocket such a paper, under such circumstances.' And he was prepared to declare 'most solemnly in the face of his country and his God' that there was no such paper in his pocket, 'unless ... some other person unknown to me put it there.' His friend, Valentine Derry, who later published his writings from prison, stated that he was with Coigly in Dublin on the day the incriminating paper was written in London.

The trial began on 21 May. Some prominent Whig politicians such as Fox the leader of the opposition, and Sheridan and Grey, came forward to testify for O'Connor. No witnesses were called for Coigly–in fact, O'Connor himself tried repeatedly to shift all the guilt onto him. Coigly was convicted of high treason and the other four acquitted. He was sentenced to be hanged, drawn and quartered. Tone read the verdict in the French papers on

12 June and wrote in his diary: 'Quigley (Coigly) the priest, is found guilty; it seems he has behaved admirably well, which I confess was more than I expected; his death redeems him.'[48]

During the few weeks left before his execution he wrote some biographical letters which he gave his friend and now daily visitor, Valentine Derry. Derry published the text as it was written adding only his own preface. He had met Coigly shortly after he returned home from the Irish college in the autumn of 1789 and remarked that 'he certainly was not then a friend to the French revolution.'[49] He went on to describe Coigly as 'mild, liberal and charitable–abhorrent of meanness and hypocrisy–feeling indignant of injustice and cruelty.'[50] On Thursday 7 June at 11am he was chained to a hurdle and dragged to Pennington Heath about a mile outside Maidstone. He addressed a few words to the large crowd assembled round the gallows, asserting his innocence and forgiving his enemies. Then he was hanged and later beheaded. Two weeks later Tone heard the news in Paris and commented: [51] 'Quigley (Coigly) has been executed, and died like a hero! If ever I reach Ireland and we establish our liberty, I will be the first to propose a monument to his memory; his conduct at the hour of his death clears everything. "Nothing in his life became him, like the leaving of it." '

When Léonard Bourdon was appointed French agent in Hamburg in December 1796 William Duckett became his private secretary. Their acquaintanceship dated back to the student rebellion in the autumn of 1792 when Duckett, the leader, had been vigorously defended in the National Convention by Bourdon, then a Montagnard deputy. Hamburg, a neutral port, was an important transit centre for *émigrés* and soon became the preferred route for Irish republicans entering and leaving France. It was an obvious centre for British and French espionage networks. Bourdon and Duckett concentrated on establishing an intelligence network in England and Ireland and especially on infiltrating the British navy with United Irishmen. As the navy held complete mastery over the seas and as that of France served as little more than troop carriers it was imperative that efforts be made to undermine British naval supremacy. In numerous *mémoires*[52] to the French government Duckett emphasised and at times exaggerated the numbers of Irish seamen serving on British ships. His main argument for a French invasion of Ireland was that it would cut off an important source of supplies both of men and provisions to British shipping. In the early months of 1797 he worked energetically at inciting mutinies among Irish sailors in British ports.[53] A number did take place early that summer and later investigation revealed an unusually high Irish participation. In July Duckett was assigned an official mission[54] to travel to England and contact the mutinous sailors but this was abandoned when news reached Hamburg of the collapse of the mutiny.

As news of the rebellion in Ireland in the summer of 1798 began to trickle back to France the Directory's enthusiasm for a French invasion began to revive. Bruix, Minister of the Marine, sent Duckett on another secret mission[55] and allotted him 28,000 *livres* as costs. He was given a free hand, his mission directed mainly at the Irish in the British armed forces in the hope of getting them to come out in sympathy with the rebellion and thousands of addresses to Irish sailors were distributed in neutral ports. On his way, Duckett was arrested by mistake in Hanover, and when he produced his French passport Hanover's neutrality was threatened. As a result of the rumpus he created and as neither England nor France wished to compromise Hanover's neutrality Duckett was released and returned to Hamburg. His mission, however, had to be abandoned.

Preparations were made to send three expeditions to Ireland, one under General Rey from Dunkirk, another under Humbert from Rochefort and the third under General Hardy from Brest. Tone joined the latter, his brother and Bartholomew Teeling sailing with Humbert while Tandy and his supporters went to Dunkirk. Humbert's three frigates were the first to arrive, reaching Killala on 22 August. The first man to reach the shore was a former priest, Captain Henry O'Kane,[56] who had been appointed official interpreter by Humbert because of his fluency in English, Irish and French. He had been a *curé* near Nantes at the outbreak of the revolution when 'he was reduced by poverty to enlist in the French armies.'[57] Madgett's nephew, Sullivan, was also with the expedition. Among those who volunteered their services was a 36-year-old priest, Michael Gannon from Castlebar, who had been educated in France and had returned to Ireland at the beginning of the revolution. 'Those priests and students who had to leave France at the height of the revolution', Leonard MacNally informed the government, 'are the most active of the propagandists'.[58] Described as 'a tall, handsome man, with dignified agreeable manners',[59] Gannon was employed as a commissary to the French army. Michael Burke, a government informer, described him at Castlebar as 'a priest who was very superstitious –he used to be showing oils to the people, telling them that if any were wounded he would anoint them so that they would go to heaven ...'[60]

After an initial success at Castlebar, Humbert and his Irish-French contingent were annihilated at Ballinamuck some two weeks later. He and his officers were taken to Dublin where they were treated more as guests than as prisoners of war, but those Irish who landed with him, such as Mathew Tone and Bartholomew Teeling, were court-martialled and executed. Captain Henry O'Kane escaped the gallows, pleading that he had eight years' service in the French army prior to the expedition and had lived in France for 14 years.[61] Surprisingly, his claim was allowed and he was sentenced to 'banishment for life from the kingdom of Ireland'. Michael Gannon went into hiding for a year but was arrested late in 1799 and sentenced to transportation. He escaped and made his way back to the continent and by 1810 was once more resident in Collège des Irlandais in Paris.[62]

Tandy's expedition arrived at Rutland Bay in Donegal on 17 September. It consisted of one fast-sailing frigate, the *Anacréon*, with 200 officers on board, 80 of whom were French and the rest Irish. Among the latter were former Irish college students Thomas MacKenna and Bartholomew Blackwell, MacKenna acting as adjutant to Napper Tandy. Two members of the expedition, George Orr and John Murphy, tried to desert but were prevented by Blackwell who threatened to kill them. They later sold their services to the British government. Orr, in a letter to the Duke of Portland, said MacKenna was from Maghera, Co. Down and had spent ten or twelve years in the Irish college. He added: 'He has very much the air and demeanour of a Frenchman and speaks French as well as any Parisian; he is about five feet seven inches high, has a black beard and is strongly built.'[63] Blackwell came to the Irish college when he was 11 years old to take up a bursary founded by his uncle, Dr Bartholomew Murry. After a number of years he left to become a Hussar in the Esterhazy regiment. In 1784 he became a naturalised French citizen. Two years later he was raised to the rank of sub-lieutenant and remained in that regiment until it was disbanded. He joined the republican army as a captain in a cavalry corps which later became part of the army of the north under Dumouriez. He held the rank of major and his regiment formed part of the garrison of Paris when he was ordered to Dunkirk on 13 July 1798. In a secret report[64] to Dublin, he was described as thin and smart and about five feet ten high, wearing 'long whiskers of a light sandy colour and also mustachios of the same colour.' He took a lot of snuff and spoke French like a Frenchman. A spy on board reported that 'This Blackwell had Tandy like a child in leading strings ...'[65] Orr described Tandy as marching about on deck in the foppish finery of a general, looking more like a decadent politician than a rebel leader.

In Rutland Bay they were informed by the locals of Humbert's defeat. Nevertheless, many of those on board were eager to march into the hills and continue the struggle and the natives were willing to join them. Tandy and Rey felt the situation was hopeless and decided to withdraw. They sailed away on the following day, 18 September.

Two days before Tone had set out from Brest with one sail of the line and eight frigates under Admiral Bompart transporting 3,000 soldiers under the command of General Hardy. It was 12 October before they reached Lough Swilly, where they were engaged in action with a superior British force commanded by Admiral Warren and decisively defeated. Tone was arrested and taken to Dublin where he was tried and condemned to death. He cheated the gallows by cutting his own throat and died a week later on 19 November. When word reached Paris of the complete failure of all three ventures, the French became thoroughly disillusioned with the exaggerated claims of Irish patriots, particularly those of Napper Tandy. Duckett advised the Minister of the Marine to be wary in future of the views of the upper class United Irishmen who were out of touch with the mass of ordinary Irish people.[66]

The *Anacréon* reached Bergen in Norway where it disembarked its passengers. From there Tandy and Blackwell decided to return to Paris via Hamburg where they put up at the American Arms Hotel.[67] They had written to Talleyrand requesting permission to enter France. The English ambassador Craufurd forced the city magistrate to arrest them as British subjects and requested their extradition to England, the French authorities being refused permission to see the prisoners. Blackwell wrote a note in blood describing the appalling conditions of their prison. It was picked up in the street and the French compelled the city authorities to improve matters. An international tug-of-war followed, a number of powers threatening sanctions unless Hamburg's decision favoured them. France declared that the extradition of the prisoners would violate the neutrality of Hamburg. The city involved Prussia as guarantor of their neutrality and it advised the senate of Hamburg to sit out the crisis. Russia became involved on the side of Britain. Stalemate set in through spring and summer of 1799. Finally, Russia threatened to occupy the city if the prisoners were not extradited. The Hamburg senate were cowed and at the end of September handed the prisoners over to be transported to England. It was decided to convey them directly to Ireland.

The French Directory reacted[68] swiftly to what they considered was 'an attack on the rights of man, a crime against humanity and a deep insult against the French republic'. Unless the crime was punished, Europe would rapidly return to 'a state of barbarity.' They ordered that the action of Hamburg be denounced to all allied and neutral governments, that the French consular and diplomatic agents were to quit Hamburg immediately, that Hamburg agents were to leave France within 24 hours and that a general embargo was to be placed on all Hamburg ships in French ports. Tandy and Blackwell were interned in Kilmainham. Blackwell's wife, Sophie wrote[69] to the French Minister of the Marine, pointing out that her husband was a naturalised French citizen who had given 17 years' military service to France and whose case should not be confused with that of Napper Tandy who had only recently come to France. She enclosed a précis of his life, printed in French. She addressed the same précis with a similar letter to the Irish Attorney General. But both Blackwell and Tandy had to await the signing of the peace of Amiens before they were finally released.

NOTES

1. Hayes, op. cit. p285.
2. Tone, *Memoirs* 1 p30.
3. Tone, op. cit. 1 p247-8.
4. Ibid 1 p250.
5. Ibid 1 p269.
6. Ibid 1 p275.
7. Ibid 1 p281.
8. Ibid 1 p279.
9. Ibid 1 p280.
10. Ibid 1 p306.
11. Ibid 1 p309-10.
12. Ibid 1 p271.

13. Ibid 1 p284.
14. Ibid 1 p330.
15. Ibid 1 p331.
16. Ibid 1 p332.
17. Ibid 1 p333.
18. Ibid 1 p409.
19. Ibid 1 p421.
20. Ibid 2 p2.
21. Ibid 2 p14.
22. Ibid 2 p5.
23. Ibid 2 pp11-12.
24. Ibid 2 p16.
25. Ibid 2 p55.
26. Ibid 2 p56.
27. Ibid 2 p59.
28. Ibid 2 pp59-60.
29. Ibid 2 p61.
30. Ibid 2 pp76-7.
31. Ibid 2 p94.
32. Ibid 2 pp94-5.
33. Ibid 2 p97.;
34. A.N. F 111 186b. On MacSheehy Mission see F.W. Van Brock, 'Captain MacSheehy's Mission' *Irish Sword* (1972) X pp215-28 & C.J. Woods, 'The secret mission of Captain Bernard MacSheehy, an Irishman in French service, 1796' *Jnl. Cork Hist. & Arch. Society*, LXXVIII pp93-108.
35. A.N. AF 111 186b, doss.860, qtd Van Brock, op. cit. p223.
36. Tone, *Memoirs*, 2 p158.
37. A.N. AF IV, Carton 1671, f129v, qtd Woods, op. cit. p105.
38. Tone's *Journal*, 13 April 1797. Passaged suppressed from *Memoirs*, qtd Woods, op. cit. p107.
39. Qtd Van Brock, op. cit, p228.
40. Qtd Woods, op. cit. p107n.
41. Coigly, *Life*, p27.
42. Ibid.
43. Fitzpatrick, *Secret service under Pitt*, p40.
44. A.A.E. Corr.Pol.Angl. 592 43r. 14 Oct. 1797.
45. Tone, *Memoirs*, 2 p292.
46. Tone, op. cit. 2 pp283-4.
47. Coigly, *Life*, p40.
48. Tone, op. cit. 2 p312.
49. Coigly, op. cit. iv.
50. Ibid, v.
51. Tone, op. cit. 2 p324.
52. Cf. A.A.E. Corr.Pol. Ham. 111 fos.311-12; A.A.E. Corr.Pol.Angl. 592 fos.80, 84-5, 129-130.
53. Cf Marianne Elliot, *Partners in Revolution*, pp140-2.
54. Ibid, p142.
55. A.N. BB4 123 fos.193-8; A.N. AF 111 149 doss.701, fos.67, 71. cf. Elliot, op. cit. pp218-9.

56. Hayes, *Last invasion of Ireland*, p17.
57. Qtd ibid, p206.
58. Qtd ibid, p191.
59. Byrne, op. cit. 3 p62.
60. Qtd Hayes, *Last invasion of Ireland*, p66.
61. Ibid, pp206-7.
62. *La Montagne Sainte-Geneviève et ses abords*, no 192, p56 (Oct. 1976).
63. Qtd Hayes, *Biog. Dict*. p183.
64. Qtd Hayes, *Ireland and Irishmen in the French Revolution*, p31n.
65. Ibid, p32.
66. Cf Marianne Elliot, op. cit. p235.
67. Ibid, pp261-265. *Moniteur* XXIX, p598 *bis* 3 Jan. 1799.
68. *Moniteur* XXIX, p856, 19 Oct. 1799.
69. A.A.E. 592 f288r; 593 fos.451rv, 452rv.

11
School for Dandies

It was a jolly time that could not last for ever.

–O'Reilly on MacDermot's Academy

The main problem facing Kearney and Walsh after the restoration –albeit provisional–of their colleges in 1795 was to find students for them. Even if they were willing to come from Ireland the war made it almost impossible for them to do so. In any case, the British government, anxious to lure the Catholic church away from its French connection, founded the national seminary of Maynooth in 1795 endowing it as a royal college. Thomas Hussey, chaplain to the Spanish Embassy in London, became its first president. He had studied for seven years in Seville and later in Paris where he completed his theology. Maynooth's academic staff consisted of a number of French *émigré* ecclesiastics and former professors from the Irish colleges in France. The bishops led by Troy of Dublin were quite happy to see Paris languish in return for continuing government subsidies for the new foundation. Their only interest in Paris now was the possibility of transferring its funds to Ireland when peace was re-established.

In this situation Kearney and Walsh had no option but to lease out their respective colleges as advantageously as possible. Collège des Lombards, no longer in a fit condition to serve as an academic centre, was let to tenants and Kearney let Collège des Irlandais for six years to two booksellers, Citizens Nyon and Onfroy. By the summer of 1797 a more attractive offer presented itself and with a little persuasion and the provision of alternative accommodation in Collège de Navarre, the booksellers were willing to allow their lease to expire.

With the suppression of religious houses in the early years of the revolution France had been left virtually without a system of education. A whole generation of the children of the revolution were condemned to illiteracy. On 25 October 1796 the Directory decreed the establishment of primary, secondary and central schools in each Department but the decree remained very much a dead letter. People of means did as best they could to find tutors for their children and Irish priests like Charles Kearney and Dominick Fitzsimmons with their command of languages were very much in demand. Others, like Abbé Patrick MacDermott, enterprising enough to establish their own schools had a monopoly of the market and were cultivated by some of the best families in France. MacDermott, who had come to the rescue of Kearney and Collège des Irlandais in the summer of 1792, with the offer of a substantial loan,[1] now kept a prestigious boarding school in St Germain-en-Laye and was anxious to transfer his school and its 40 pupils into the chic Latin Quarter and the spacious new Irish college. Kearney was eager to oblige his old friend, particularly as there was no possibility of ever reimbursing MacDermott for his original loan since money had suffered several depreciations. The Irish colleges had suffered enormous financial losses during the revolution. Most of their property consisted in investments on the public funds, and all payments were suspended during 1793, 1794, 1795, and the first half of 1796. For the next few years the royal treasury paid nothing at all or paid in bonds. In 1800 the *rentes*, or state investments, were reduced to one-third consolidated. Thus in addition to the loss of annual revenue for a number of years, two-thirds of the capital of the Irish foundations were lost forever.

MacDermott had made a loan of 27,000 *livres* and had deposited a further 38,000 with a notary with the view to establishing bursaries on the five per cent annual interest. Agreement was reached between Kearney and MacDermott giving the latter a nine-year lease on the college at an attractively modest rent,[2] MacDermott undertaking to pay an indemnity and carry out reparations to the tune of 32,283 *livres*. MacDermott's school was operational by the autumn of 1797. M. de Mautort later declared it to be 'the most advantageous contract imaginable'[3] for the Irish college.

Lally Tollendal described the school as 'perhaps the best house of education then in France' as testified to by the top university people.[4] It also apparently attracted the children of the new rising stars: Napoleon's youngest brother, Jerome, was a student.[5] Jerome was 13 in 1797 and as he joined the navy in 1800 his stay in the Irish college could only have been of a fairly short duration. He was a pupil in the Collège du Juilly from 1796-

1798 and must have come to MacDermott's institution a short time after it moved. Jerome, who all his life had a reputation for wildness, was not noted for his scholarship, and it is recounted that Napoleon was displeased with his progress and sent for Abbé MacDermott who admitted his inability to discipline him. The result of the interview was that Jerome was sent to sea. He seemed to have retained some affection for his former teacher, for when he became king of Westphalia in 1807 he fixed an annual pension of 6,000 *livres* on MacDermott and sent a number of pages from the court to be educated by him. One of the last letters[6] MacDermott wrote, a month before he died in November 1812, was to the king of Westphalia urging him to continue to show his favour to Dr MacMahon, who had been MacDermott's associate in the school for 15 years and was 'known to your Majesty'. He assured the king that MacMahon 'would devote himself entirely to the care and supervision of the young students, your subjects, that your Majesty would condescend to entrust to him.' MacMahon was one of the medical students who had taken part in the student election in the autumn of 1792.

'The college was the centre of elegance and gaiety' a former student later recounted.[7] 'Twice a week we gave balls at which we were honoured with the presence of the highest and the most beautiful women of the day. Our festivities were graced by Josephine, the good, the amiable, the excellent, the kindhearted; by Madame Récamier; by the still more lovely Madame Tallien, afterwards Princess of Chimay and other celebrities; as well as by the pupils of Madame Lemoine, whose establishment for the education of young women was the most distinguished in Paris.' He ended his account with the observation: 'It was a jolly time that could not last forever.' Besides Jerome Bonaparte, other students included Eugène de Beauharnais, Champagny, later Duc de Cadore and one of the family of Périgaux.

But MacDermott had other students of a completely different calibre, such as Charles Forbin Janson, afterwards bishop of Toul and Nancy and founder of the Society of the Holy Childhood. In 1803 MacDermott's became one of three Paris houses of education whose pupils were admitted from the first year to compete for free places in the lycées, set up on 1 May 1802.[8] The establishment of MacDermott's academy in the Irish college at this juncture was timely.

With the signing of the treaty of Amiens on 27 March 1802 peace was established between France and Britain for the first time since 1793. Up to that normal communication between France and Ireland was virtually impossible. In a letter to Talleyrand,[9] now Minister for Foreign Affairs, in December 1797, Walsh stated that he had made several vain attempts to contact his superiors in Ireland. The matter was now urgent as he and his colleague had been reimbursed to the tune of almost 150,000 francs, two-thirds of the capital invested by the Irish establishments, and it was now imperative that his powers be renewed from Ireland. Without an extension of his mandate Ireland stood to suffer considerable losses. Recalling with gratitude former favours which Talleyrand had done him in 1791, he hoped the minister would find a solution to the present problem. In his reply on 13 January 1798 Talleyrand offered to provide Walsh with a passport to Hamburg.[10] Walsh had toyed with the idea of going to England with Citizen Gallois who was charged with supervising the exchange of prisoners-of-war but he had been dissuaded by informed people who assured him 'that an Irishman arriving from France at this moment would be arrested.' He decided instead to write to the archbishop of Dublin and await his reply 'if it could escape the jealous surveillance of the British government'.

The elections of April 1797 revealed a decided swing to the right with a massive influx of royalists into the Assembly, which now had its first royalist majority since the beginning of the revolution. Royalists were elected presidents of the Council of Five Hundred and the Council of the Ancients. The near-royalist Carnot was joined by Barthélémy, a convinced monarchist, on the Directory: the monarchy could now easily be restored by constitutional means. The other three republican Directors, however, decided to take strong action to preserve the republic. A direct appeal to the people conjured up all the horrors of 1793, but their only alternative was to call in the generals. Bonaparte, fresh from his victories in Italy, and Hoche, now commander of the army of Sambre-et-Meuse promised their support and both sent contingents of their troops to march on the capital. The coup d'état of Fructidor took place on 4 September 1797. Barthélémy was arrested and imprisoned in the Temple. Carnot succeeded in escaping. The Councils were purged of huge numbers of royalist deputies, some of whom were deported to Guiana. Returned *émigrés* were once again forced to leave while hundreds of priests were deported and others compelled to take new oaths of loyalty.

Charles Kearney was arrested on the following day. He later stated[11] that the pretext for his arrest was an 'alleged letter said to have been found in that famous collection of documents which sent so many to the Temple'. He was taken to the Mairie and kept in a dungeon for 36 days. From here he was transferred to the Temple where, according to himself, he remained a further seven months. He was accused of taking part in a royalist conspiracy and interrogated on 27 October.[12] His release was ordered after he had 'completely disproved the indictment and the examination of his documents revealed nothing which was against public order'.[13] The prison records indicate that he spent almost two months in prison, not eight as he himself claimed some years later. They describe Kearney as a language teacher and give his address as 293 rue de Doyenné.

Another Irish priest was detained at the same time: Patrick Murphy of Dublin, formerly prefect of studies in Collège des Lombards and now residing at Courseille in the Department of Séuze. He was brought to the Temple[14] with a group of 42 on 16 October and was taken out for interrogation on 7 November and returned to prison where he remained until 9 May 1798. The English spy, ex-priest Charles Somers was also arrested and detained in the Temple.[15] He was described as a native of Jamaica now residing in Versailles on a state pension as a former ecclesiastic. He was charged with plotting against the internal security of the state. Interrogated on 26 and 27 October he was released a few days later with Charles Kearney.

Perhaps the most notorious prisoner detained at the Temple at that time was Commodore Sir William Sidney-Smith. In 1793 he had destroyed the French fleet in Toulon by setting fire to it and continued to harass French shipping, making lightning raids deep into French ports. In 1796 he was captured and held under tight security in Rouen, from where he was moved to the Temple in Paris where the French considered him one of their prize hostages.

On 25 April 1798 two officers presented themselves at the Temple tower.[16] One was an adjutant-general and the other was a captain. They demanded to speak to Antoine Boniface, Temple concièrge. Written orders were produced from the Minister of the Navy to have Sidney-Smith transferred to Fontainbleau where other English prisoners-of-war were held. Smith was informed and agreed with great reluctance to leave, exclaiming with tears in his eyes that the French government was planning to execute him. He was taken away, escorted by the two officers, after formalities were completed. A week later, the French learnt of the daring escape of Commodore Sir William Sidney-Smith when they read in the London papers an account of the magnificent fireworks display on the Thames which greeted the returning hero.[17]

Suspects were immediately rounded up including, once more, Charles Kearney who was denounced to the police as an accessory after the fact 'and even as having contributed to it'. Kearney made no other comment on it other than 'it was used as a new pretext for tormenting him'. Could he have been mistaken for the English spy Somers who was far more likely to have been involved, possibly as one of the two counterfeit French officers? From the police records such a confusion was easily possible. Both were released from the Temple on the same day, both had the same first name, Charles, were both aged 47, had chestnut brown hair, blue eyes, round chin and oval face. There was, however, a difference in height–three inches–between the two men. Kearney may have been picked up because of his well-known royalist past. The temple concièrge was arrested and imprisoned and found guilty not of complicity but of negligence.

Sidney-Smith's escape had its own historical repercussions. He was sent to Egypt in 1799 and successfully defended Saint-Jean d'Acre against Napoleon. 'This man has caused me to lose my fortune' exclaimed the future emperor: 'Had Saint Jean d'Acre fallen I would have become emperor of the entire East'. Nearer home, the British government might have been very tempted to exchange Wolfe Tone for him had his escape been foiled or even postponed for another six months.

As early as the summer of 1798 Irish political refugees were beginning to arrive in Paris, many of them in straitened circumstances. Wolfe Tone raised their plight with General Kilmaine who was not overly sympathetic. 'The conduct of many of the Irish in Paris' he declared, 'was such as to reflect credit neither on themselves nor on their country. There was nothing to be heard amongst them but denunciations and if every one of them separately spoke truth, all the rest were rascals.'[18] Tone himself had been one of their favourite targets for denunciation. Kilmaine admitted there was one thing in their favour–they asked for nothing for themselves, with the exception of O'Finn 'who appeared in the light of a mere adventurer.' Edward O'Finn had been sent by Coigly and Arthur O'Connor to France with information about the alliance between the United men of England, Ireland and Scotland. Later refugees were to be far more demanding, having been through the campaigns in Ireland and lost everything.

The Paris society of United Irishmen held its meetings in rue de l'Ecole de Médicine, a few minutes' walk from the two Irish colleges, and it was not surprising that they turned their attention to what were still well-endowed establishments though in 1799 totally bereft of students. On 4 February the society submitted a project to the Directory which would give them possession of the properties and revenues under state supervision. According to Walsh,[19] some 30 so-called Irish insurgents approached Talleyrand for the use of Collège des Lombards and its revenues, 'as an asylum and indemnity for the losses they claimed to have sustained by espousing the interests of France'. On the point of consenting to their request, Talleyrand decided to consult Walsh who 'had the honour of being personally known to him.' To hand over the college, Walsh argued, would not only be contrary to justice and existing law, but also politically dangerous. What would stop the British government sending over agents and spies, 'in the guise of insurgents, assured of a refuge and an income.' Talleyrand was impressed by the observantion according to Walsh, but one cannot help feeling that it was a clever piece of footwork by the master who then suggested that Walsh might subsidise them out of college funds until a more permanent arrangement had been worked out with the Minister of the Interior.[20] Early in November the Minister of Finance wrote to Talleyrand suggesting the sale of the Irish colleges to provide money to support Irish patriots.[21] The O'Finn brothers, Edward and John, had already entered their claims as indeed had the Scotsman, Dr Robert Watson.[22] The O'Finns had written to the Minister of the Navy who passed on their request to the Minister of the Interior.

After his interview with Talleyrand Walsh paid 600 francs to the 'diplomatic agent': presumably Edward Lewins. However, the arrangement alluded to by Talleyrand was not speedily implemented and Walsh had to disburse further sums to needy individuals.[23] An undated document[24] gives a list of individuals in receipt of monies from college revenues: Bernard MacSheehy, then serving in Egypt, who was given over 2,000 francs; Ahearne, secretary to General Daendels in Holland; and 600 francs each to Captain Corbet, Lieutenant St Leger (in order to join his regiment), Lieutenant Wall, for the same reason, Major Blackwell, the widow of Captain Forbes, and the widow of Captain Hamilton. There is also a list of students destined for the army who were educated with college funds and including Healy, O'Shea, James O'Hegarty, O'Farrell, St Leger, John O'Meara, Edward O'Meara, Barker, Smith and Laurence and Hypolyte Lewins, sons of Edward, Glashins, one of whose brothers was killed in Bonaparte's service and another also in the army.

NOTES

1. Maynooth, Papers of the Irish College, Paris. Ms.60, 18 Nov. 1801.
2. Ibid, Ms.60, 18 Nov. 1801.
3. A.N. H3 2561A, Mar. 1811.
4. Ibid.
5. O'Reilly, A. *The Irish Abroad and at Home*, pp236-8.
6. I.C.P. qtd Boyle, op. cit. pp68-9n.
7. O'Reilly, op. cit. p237.
8. Aulard, *Paris sous le consulat. Recueil des documents*, Tome IV, p193, 25 June 1803.
9. A.A.E. Corr.Pol.Angl. v592. 128r, 14 Dec. 1797.
10. Ibid. f152rv, 17 Jan. 1798.
11. Maynooth, Papers of Irish College, Paris, Ms.60, 18 Nov. 1801.
12. A.P. A B/330 f88, 27 Oct. 1797.
13. Ibid. 31 Oct. 1797.
14. A.P. A B/330 f79, 16 Oct. 1797.
15. Ibid. f83 & 87, 21 Oct. 1797.
16. *Moniteur* 29, p258, 21 April 1798.
17. Ibid. pp273 & 278.
18. Tone, *Memoirs* 2 pp317-18, 16 June 1798.
19. A.N. F 19 6237A. *Administration*, p39, 8 & 10 Feb. 1812.
20. Ibid.
21. A.A.E. Corr.Pol.Angl. 593, 5 Nov. 1799.
22. Ibid. 20rv, 25 Oct. 1799.
23. A.N. F19 6237A, pp39-40.
24. D.D.A. 121/9. nd.

12
Prey to Predators

Age, infirmity and every other human consideration keeps silent when duty calls.

—Walsh, 19 December 1799.

The French government, alarmed at the consequences of the absence of an educational system, appointed Fourcroy Minister of Public Instruction and established four grades of schools throughout France with a national institution in Paris called the *Prytanée français*. The latter set up its headquarters in the former Collège Louis-le-Grand. A newly-built, unoccupied college as well-situated as the Irish college with what still remained of its endowments was bound to attract attention. Its existence was precarious to say the least, and Walsh was compelled to ward off predators from all sides—not only from the refugee United Irishmen but now from the newly-established Prytanée.

A decree[1] issued on 25 May 1798 declared that foreign property should be sold like the rest of the national property; this was followed by a further decree[2] stating that 'the bursaries founded in the former colleges in France are to be annexed to the central bursary institute, viz., the Prytanée'. A year later another decree[3] ordered the sale of one of the houses belonging to Collège des Lombards. The following day, 24 June 1799, Walsh, fearing that his college would be next on the list, wrote to the Minister of Foreign Affairs protesting strongly. 'I can add to a possession of thirty years,' he stated, 'private titles, giving me the right to live in my own house till my death.' If necessary he was prepared to squat. He pointed out that any interference with Irish funds would cause alarm among Irish catholics and considerable satisfaction to the English government.

Notwithstanding, a decree a month later ordered the confiscation and sale of all that remained of the foreign establishments.

Vultures were circling over what now appeared to be the decomposing carcass of the Irish colleges. The O'Finn brothers, United Irish expatriates, put in their claim to the Minister of the Navy assuring him that the revenue of the Irish college had been put at the disposition of the Minister of the Interior for distribution among needy Irish patriots.[4] That autumn, the Minister of Finance wrote to his colleague in Foreign Affairs suggesting the sale of the Irish establishments to subsidise exiled patriots.[5]

At this point the Prytanée entered the fray,[6] arguing that the two Irish colleges should not be sold as they did not fall within the terms of the law, urging the Minister of Finance to have the sales notices provisionally removed from the properties. A notice was nevertheless printed setting the date of sale for 30 August 1799. With the arrival of this unexpected ally at the battle-front, Walsh wisely decided to cease fire, keeping his powder dry and his guns well primed. The Prytanée carried the fight to the legislative body, the Council of Five Hundred and finally to the Seine Department to have the sale suspended, their main argument being that they should be preserved as the patrimony of Irish and Scots patriots whom the Prytanée would accept when circumstances allowed. And then they produced their trump card. They had already accepted the sons of Wolfe Tone 'who died a martyr in the cause of liberty.' The proposed sale was postponed.

The matter came up for discussion at the Council of Five Hundred on 4 November 1799.[7] A commission which had been set up to examine the question had delivered its report, as a result of which it was decreed that the Irish and Scots colleges be included in the law of 13 July 1797 which restored their bursaries to the bursary-holders of the former colleges and also in that of 1 July 1798 which annexed these bursary-holders to the Prytanée. The Prytanée had won and had acquired the Irish colleges. Later Walsh implied that the whole operation had been master-minded by him: 'I could only save the properties from the sale decreed by the Directory in the year VII' he wrote to the Archbishop of Paris, 'by getting the Prytanée to intervene.'[8] The Irish colleges had at least been spared the irrevocable and sordid fate of a public auction though they had now become part and parcel of the French educational system. The Prytanée wrote to the Minister of Finance asking him to notify the Seine Department so that it could 'arrange for the property and papers to be handed over' as soon as possible.[9] On the same day, 9 November, a new era began in France with the coup d'état of 18 Brumaire.

Napoleon had returned from Egypt, arriving in Paris on 16 October: the Directory was overthrown and the Consulate inaugurated. On 12 December the constitution of the year VIII was introduced establishing Bonaparte as First Consul and effective master of France. Later the same month the Council of State and the Senate were installed.

Meanwhile, Walsh had been preparing for a protracted paper war against the Prytanée. On 19 December he sent in a petition[10] to the Ministers of Finance and Foreign Affairs. Four million Irish catholics, he declared, were awaiting the re-establishment of peace to re-open communication with France and inaugurate a new life for the Irish colleges. Paris housed the masterpieces of painting and sculpture. All the nations of Europe would send their students there 'and Ireland was longing for the moment to send hers'. Those without artistic talent could study medicine, surgery, mathematics or literature. Walsh proposed that the Irish colleges would serve ideally this new *foyer culturel*. Those requiring ecclesiastical studies were now provided for in the college of Maynooth, endowed by the British government. He further proposed that, now that catholic relief legislation had been passed in Ireland, the new regime in the Irish colleges would be ecumenical, 'based on tolerance and fraternity.'

Walsh attacked the claims of the Prytanée to the Irish properties, stating that 'the Irish bursaries always were and still are, in law and in fact distinct from French bursaries'. Two questions must be resolved, one of law and the other of fact. Can the Irish properties be alienated as national property? The Prytanée resolved that question by having their sale suppressed. The second question was: have the Irish properties been given to the Prytanée by the laws of 25 Messidor of the year V and the decree of the Directory of 13 Messidor of the year VI? Walsh went on to argue from the text of these laws that the colleges had been restored to their Irish proprietors. Turning to the claim of the Prytanée that they have already received Irish students, notably the sons of Wolfe Tone, Walsh declared: 'Yes, France has always offered an asylum to the unfortunate. The Irish houses had been sequestrated. At that point, the houses were being repaired and the administrators were waiting to receive their revenues. They propose now to discharge the Prytanée of these students and to place them in the Irish college where education is established on a firm footing.'

The last remark referred, presumably, to MacDermott's academy. 'The Irish have accepted with resignation the devaluation of their investments to two-thirds, to despoil them of the rest would be a gross injustice.' In what by now had become a feature of Walsh's style he ended on a high note:

> The offer of personal subsistence makes no impression on him ... Age, infirmity and every other human consideration keeps silent when duty calls. If credit and influence could triumph over justice, the struggle of a foreigner against the Prytanée would be unequal. But equity and impartiality will preside at the judgement and his case is incontestable according to the sacred rights of property.

He later claimed that the Prytanée tried to buy him by making him certain 'seductive offers'.

Walsh followed his petition with a commentary on it by his two legal experts. He had demanded the return of his documents and papers and that the two ministers in question, in the event of further difficulties, report to the government with a view to preserving the properties of which he was the administrator. They concurred with these demands.

The war continued, Walsh and the Prytanée writing alternately to ministers and the ministers exchanging views on the matter between themselves. At the end of December the Prytanée pointed out to Lucien Bonaparte, Minister of the Interior, that 'these colleges did not belong to the Irish and Scots nations since they were not founded by former kings of Ireland and Scotland'. They resulted from the legacies of certain individuals. Why should these legacies, they asked, have privileges that similar French ones did not have? They pointed out further that the colleges had not existed as such for eight years and had no students. Yet the superiors had continued to receive the revenues without accounting to anyone for them.[11]

Early in January both Walsh and the Prytanée wrote[12] to the Minister of Finance, who in turn wrote to the Minister of the Interior suggesting that he decide together with the Minister of Foreign Affairs.[13] Both Walsh and Innis of the Scots college also wrote[14] to Lucien Bonaparte stating that they awaited his decision with confidence. Receiving no reply they wrote again five days later. 'Foreigners would have no hope' they said, 'against the power of the Prytanée ... but we are dealing with Napoleon's tribunal and the name reassures us in face of the powerful coalition.' On 7 April a report[15] was presented by Duquesnoy to the minister, providing a resumé of the Irish and Prytanée arguments on which he was expected to make a final decision. The report came down heavily in favour of the legal claims of the Prytanée and expressed concern about the administration of the revenues by Walsh. It did, however, concede that some consideration be shown for their past services in the form of pensions from the college property.

A Consular decree[16] was issued on 24 May 1800 which placed the properties of the Irish and Scots colleges provisionally under the control of the Prytanée. A number of places were to be reserved there for Irish and Scots students, to be chosen exclusively by the First Consul. The present administrators were to render up-to-date accounts and might be accorded an annual grant by the minister from the college property.

Far from being vanquished by the decree Walsh launched himself once more into the attack. The word 'provisional' left the door sufficiently ajar for him to continue the controversy. On 15 July he wrote[17] again to Lucien Bonaparte at the Ministry of the Interior protesting against the decree as irregular and in formal contradiction to all previous laws. He reminded the minister that the future use of the college would be as a 'centre for commercial transactions between Ireland and France', and that an accredited agent would act as an interpreter for the businessmen. He went on: 'You like the truth, Citizen Minister, I will put it frankly. The plan to join the foreign establishments to the Prytanée is inoperable and you will be well-advised to follow the voice of experience rather than the theories of your employees.' Walsh resented the one-sided report presented by the civil servant, Duquesnoy. Calling for a new report and for the matter to be sent for resolution to the Council of State, he launched into his customary peroration:

> It is a sign of sound policy and a mark of the honour and dignity of the great nation of which you are an instrument to respect the few foreign properties that have escaped the revolutionary storm ... Every act of conservation will be both just and profitable and will give a lofty notion of the present government and will avoid all discussion of these properties at the peace negotiations.

Walsh received a reply[18] from Duquesnoy of the Interior Ministry at the end of July, acknowledging receipt of his arguments and his intention to raise the matter at the Council of State. He suggested to Walsh that he could receive an 'indemnity' from the college revenues without prejudice to the matter in dispute. If this was an attempt to buy off Walsh it failed badly. 'Far be it from an honest man', Walsh retorted disdainfully, 'any indemnity that would make him blush, any arrangement incompatible with his duty!' There were no punches pulled now. 'Property is sacred' he declared, 'and the Consuls have no right to give the Prytanée even provisional possession of Irish property.' And he added that even the Committee of Public Safety had respected it. 'In my view,' he observed, 'there is only one step between provisional and definitive possession.'[19]

Towards the end of August he wrote directly to Napoleon, the First Consul:[20]

> We were quietly waiting your return from the glorious expedition when Citizen Duquesnoy, ... profiting from your absence, surprised ... the second Consul into issuing the decree ... Under your auspices, Citizen First Consul, we will not be afraid to defend Irish interests which are supported by positive laws and the sacred rights of property and hospitality.

Shortly afterwards, a *mémoire*[21] was sent to Napoleon signed by Innis, Kearney and Walsh, which cleverly tried to distance the First Consul from the petty and partisan mentality of his subordinates. 'Citizen First Consul,' they declared loftily, 'your personal character, your well-known political principles are for us a sure guarantee that you will spurn an association which, we dare say, would be a blot on your civil and political administration were you to allow it to stand.' With regard to the pensions they were offered they commented disdainfully: 'They speak to us of personal indemnities: honour spurns the very idea'. They expressed the hope that he would send the matter back to the Council of State with a view to their preparing a new report. Early in September Walsh informed the Council that he was contesting the decree.

Finally, Walsh sent to the Consuls a nine-page printed pamphlet[22] entitled *Claim of the provisional-commissioner of the Irish house and of his colleagues in Paris against the planned amalgamation with the Prytanée.* Stating that, 'private property is respected in all policed states,' he claimed that Lucien Bonaparte had promised him at a meeting on 14 August that he would concert with Talleyrand to preserve 'at least the properties belonging to individuals.' From the beginning of the dispute Walsh had strongly insisted that the Irish funds invested in France were the property of private individuals and that they constituted seven-eighths of the total Irish college investment. Now he claimed that 'all these fine promises had in the end degenerated into a proposal of a personal indemnity for the administrators'. Turning to the claim of the Prytanée that they had saved the college from being sold, Walsh commented: 'Decent citizens who in the name of humanity help a traveller assaulted on his journey cannot claim his property as a reward for their service.' But he reserved his strongest vitriol for the civil-servants 'all powerful in their offices, putting forward proposals for the signatures of ministers ... Foreigners reduced to sterile petitions, unanswered and often unread, are denied all access.' Walsh claimed that he had been refused access to the Minister of Finance and to Lucien Bonaparte at Interior until 18 days after the decree was issued.

He now disputed the decree article by article. The first ran counter to the laws of 7 November 1790 and those of 12 February and 8 and 12 March 1793, all of which had assigned the administration to the Irish superior. The second, providing a number of places for Irish students at the Prytanée to be chosen by the First Consul, was in Walsh's view, 'as much contrary to the rights of property as to the reciprocal respect governments owe each other.' He pointed out the marked contrast with the behaviour of Spain 'who showered with benevolence the Irish establishments on its territory'. Walsh then proceeded to his customary peroration: 'Intrigue or force can wrest from us our properties ... but to ravage our honour by making us accomplices in a shameful transaction! We love France ... A forced departure will cost us dear ... But we have a homeland which is generous to foreigners; it will be just to its own children'. Walsh's outspokenness amazed his counterpart in Douai. 'You would be astonished at the boldness of the remonstrances presented to government by our superiors in Paris,' Luke Bellew wrote[23] from Douai to James Cowan in Louvain, adding that he would have been arrested had he addressed the local prefect in similar terms. In a scribbled covering note to Napoleon, Walsh wrote: 'God listens to the prayers of his creatures. Governments who represent him on earth are only men who should hear their fellow-men whose demands are based on justice'.[24] But Napoleon was then preoccupied with settling his accounts, if not with God directly, at least indirectly with his vicar on earth.

Negotiations for the concordat with the Papacy opened on 5 November 1800 and were to drag on for more than another six months, when Pius VII sent Cardinal Consalvi to Paris. In his first interview with Napoleon, the First Consul gave him five days to complete the negotiations, but Consalvi was not so easily intimidated. The concordat, which was finally signed on 15 July, by Consalvi for the Papacy and Joseph Bonaparte on the French side, revolutionised and reorganised the church in France and above all healed the division in French society caused by the Civil Constitution of the clergy.

Lurking somewhere in the shadow of the clerical negotiators, though not playing any active role, was an Irish bishop, Thomas Hussey of Waterford. A contemporary of Walsh and Abbé MacDermott in his student days in Paris, he had become senior chaplain to the Spanish embassy in London and had played a diplomatic role in Spanish-British negotations over the future of Gibraltar. In 1795 he returned to Ireland as first president of Maynooth, becoming bishop of Waterford two years later without resigning his Maynooth appointment. Neither had he resigned his office as senior chaplain to the Spanish embassy in London. In Waterford he issued a pastoral strongly criticising military regulations which insisted on catholic soldiers attending protestant services and made a *cause célèbre* out of the whipping of a catholic soldier who had refused. His pastoral caused a furore not only in government circles but also among many of his episcopal colleagues, and he was forced to leave the country. Arriving in Berlin from England in July 1800 he came from there to Paris to visit his friend M. de Muzquiz, the Spanish ambassador to France. In a dispatch to the Spanish government notifying the arrival of the Vatican negotiators de Muzquiz added: 'Bishop Hussey may be useful for the Roman negotiation and hence it will be fitting that he act as your Excellency has already directed.'[25] The Spanish ambassador was consulted by Cardinal Consalvi and it is possible that he was advised by Hussey. Be that as it may, he certainly played an active role in negotiations over the Irish college.

Walsh, with whom he lodged in rue de Lille, briefed him on his confrontation with the French government. Through the influence of the Spanish ambassador in Paris Hussey was presented to Lucien Bonaparte and Talleyrand, whom he acquainted with Walsh's demands. These views were accepted by the ministers, and Walsh immediately wrote to inform the Council of State and suggesting that a new consular decree be issued. He even presented them with an outline draft, the first article dealing with the restoration of all the unsold property to the Irish, all contrary decrees being annulled; the second proposing the amalgamation of the two Irish colleges under one administration subject to the Minister of the Interior and the third proposing that the bishop of Waterford and the minister would together draw up rules for the new establishment which would be submitted to Napoleon for approval. From that and as a result of the cajoling, persuasion, flattery and threats of Walsh over the period a new decree[26] was issued on 6 September 1801. Like the Concordat which had pre-dated it by a few months, it did not satisfy all the Irish demands but it did restore the properties to Irish administration. The decree of 24 May 1800 conveying the Irish properties to the Prytanée was abrogated.

This new decree of 19 Fructidor of Year IX–and the first relative to the Irish colleges signed by Napoleon–re-established the Irish and Scots colleges and restored whatever remained unsold of their property. It also introduced for the first time a *bureau gratuit* to administer the properties consisting of the prefect of the Seine Department, the president and government commissioner of the court of appeal, and two nominees of the First Consul. The bureau was to meet at least once a month and examine the accounts once a year and was commissioned to draw up rules for the future administration of the establishments, the number and salary of the administrators, professors and others. Professors were to be nominated by the Minister of the Interior on the presentation of the bureau. In all the decree consisted of ten articles not one of which referred to or indicated any role for the Irish bishops. 'This objectionable part, owing to the difficulty of the times,' Hussey commented[27] to Walsh, 'may at more favourable ones, be easily ameliorated.'

Hussey attributed the decree entirely to the 'persevering exertions' of Walsh, who had 'defeated the schemes of some of Ireland's unnatural children who had plotted to turn the funds of this college from their original spiritual purposes to answer their own views of selfish and profane ends.' While Hussey accepted that the establishment of Maynooth was 'undoubtably a munificent foundation' it did not possess the advantages of colleges situated on the continent which imbibed their theology from the great European universities and had easy access to Rome. 'A sister house in Paris' he contended, 'fully answers the purpose of communication.' He saw an important future for the college in relation to the Irish church, which if dependent solely on Maynooth for its theology might face the prospect of 'the national faith dwindling into a sect.' With the concordat would come the re-establishment of a catholic university in France. 'It is no small honour to Ireland,' he informed Walsh, 'that her national house should be the first licensed school of ecclesiastical instruction and it would be an additional satisfaction that the remaining doctors of the sacred faculty should meet within its walls until they are more conveniently provided for'.[28]

Hussey considered the Consular decree a remarkable achievement, considering the 'pressure of the Prytanée demanding the Irish funds, on the one side, and on the other the unblushing memorial presented to government as well by former bursars as by ... Irish immigrants, calling for a life rent for each of them of twelve hundred *livres* per year on the remaining funds.' This referred to the petition[29] addressed to the Consuls on 12 July 1800 by the central committee of the United Irish refugees in Paris and signed by their president James J. McDonnell and secretary, James Blackburn. Claiming that most of them 'were compelled to flee their country for having taken part in the insurrections there ... while others suffered the same fate for having joined the French troops who disembarked in Ireland under General Humbert,' they believed that the revenues of the Irish properties, either in whole or in part, should be devoted to their relief. They specified that each individual should be awarded a bursary of 100 francs a month or 1,200 francs a year. The present administrators should be ordered to render an account of the sums they had received since the revolution and what use they had made of them. Article three of the Consular decree did in fact require that accounts be submitted as soon as possible.

While in Paris, Hussey took the opportunity to write[30] to Cardinal Gerdil, the cardinal-prefect of propaganda in Rome, proposing Walsh as his co-adjutor in Waterford. The letter, giving a resumé of Walsh's life and achievements, bears all the marks of having been virtually dictated by Walsh himself. All the other Irish superiors in Nantes, Toulouse, Bordeaux, Lille, Douai, Antwerp and Louvain had 'abandoned their posts and these valuable houses were confiscated.' Walsh alone, exposing himself to all possible risks, had saved the two houses in Paris. The papal brief of Pius VI of 17 March 1792 had acknowledged the important role played by Walsh in the local church. All the Paris clergy paid tribute to his work 'in the co-administration of that great diocese.' 'He would be lacking in respect for the Holy See,' Hussey concluded, 'if he pretended to dictate to it the reformation of a hierarchy who more and more allowed itself become dependent on a Protestant government.' Furthermore, to complete the important work of re-organising the Irish college, Walsh's task would be rendered easier if he was given an episcopal title.

When word of Hussey's request to the Holy See reached Ireland it caused something of a flurry in episcopal circles. Rome consulted Archbishop Bray of Cashel who wrote[31] immediately to his agent Dr Connolly in Rome to inform the Holy See that he 'considered the appointment of [Walsh] ... to be Dr Hussey's coadjutor or successor, if recommended and protected by Dr Hussey, very impolitic and dangerous. That it would not fail to give great offence to our Rulers here and in England; to whom Dr Hussey had made himself so odious and disagreeable by his rash and fatal pastoral letter.' He urged the Sacred Congregation to require Hussey to resign his diocese into the hands of his Holiness in the interest of religion. 'I entertained the most favourable opinion of Dr Walsh,' he wrote to Moylan of Cork on 22 February 1802, adding, 'his having been at Paris the whole time of the French revolution and known perhaps to some of its authors and abettors, would give an opportunity to our enemies of indulging reflexions unfavourable to Dr Walsh and very injurious to our sacred character and history.' Besides, he concluded, it would be 'not only unwise but cruel to withdraw him from Paris in so critical and momentous a juncture, when his services had been so successful in recovering some remnants of our foreign Establishments and where they may be still indispensably necessary to preserve them to some advantage to this country.'

NOTES

1. A.N. F 17 2500, 25 May 1798.
2. Ibid. 1 July, 1798.
3. A.N. H 3 2561A, 23 July 1799.
4. A.A.E. Corr.Pol.Angl. 593. 20rv, 25 Oct. 1799.
5. Ibid. 5 Nov. 1799.
6. A.N. H 3 2561A, 29 & 30 Aug., 29 Sept., 16 Oct., 2, 4, 9, 12 Nov. 1799.
7. A.N. F 17 2500, 4 Nov. 1799.
8. A.N. F 19 6237A, p40, 8-10 Feb. 1812.
9. A.N. H 3 2561A, 9 Nov. 1799.
10. I.C.P. 3L3 *Petition*, 19 Dec. 1799; cf. A.S. DQ 10 117.
11. A.N. H 3 2561A. 8 Nivôse VIII.
12. A.N. F 17 2500, 11 & 13 Jan. 1800.
13. Ibid. 29 Jan. 1800.

14. Ibid. 12 Feb. 1800, 14 Feb. 1800.
15. Ibid. 7 April 1800.
16. Ibid. 24 May 1800.
17. A.N. F 17 2500 doss.2, 80r & v.
18. A.N. H 3 2561A, 29 July 1800.
19. A.N. Walsh au premier consul, 26 Aug. 1800.
20. Ibid.
21. A.N. T1259, 12 Sept. 1800.
22. I.C.P. 3L4, 12 Sept. 1800. cf A.N. T1259.
23. Jennings, *Louvain Papers, 1606-1827*, Art. 727, p520.
24. I.C.P. 3L4, 12 Sept. 1800. cf A.N. T1259.
25. Boulay de la Meurthe, *Documents sur la negotiation du concordat*, qtd Boyle, 'Dr Hussey and the Concordat of 1801' I.E.R. April 1915.
26. I.C.P. 3L2, 6 Sept. 1801.
27. Prop.Fid. 'Irlanda' 1788-1801, f417, qtd Boyle, *Arch.Hib*. VII, p.18.
28. In a letter from Pius VII, dated slightly prematurely, 5 September, the Pope commended Hussey for 'what you have recently achieved in France, where aided by the influence of the Catholic King you have once more secured to your nation the colleges established in that country for the education of Irish ecclesiastics.' Qtd Boyle, I.E.R. XV (1904) p72.
29. A.N. F 17 2500, 12 July 1800.
30. Prop.Fid. SC Irlanda 1788-1801, 10 Oct. 1801, f580rv.
31. *Collectanea Hibernica*, 14, p122, 20 Feb. 1802.

13
Imperial Solution

The first college inaugurated by Napoleon the Great ought to measure up to the genius of its august creator.

–Walsh, 10 March 1807.

On Christmas Eve 1800 Napoleon decided to spend an evening at the Opera. En route the First Consul narrowly escaped death when a barrel filled with powder–the 'infernal machine'–exploded a few seconds after his carriage had passed. Royalist tactics were now centred on eliminating Bonaparte. Fouché, the Minister of General Police, immediately ordered the arrest of all known suspects, Charles Kearney, who figured high among them, being taken into custody as a matter of course. A later published account quotes him as follows:[1]

> I was on my way to my old quarters in the Temple, accompanied by two police agents in coloured clothes, who allowed me to walk before free. On crossing the Pont Neuf, I saw approaching a former friend and pupil, Mathieu de Montmorency. He drew up, and as I passed close to him said, in an undertone in English (a language I had taught him): 'unhappy man! I know whither you are going. Will they never allow you to be quiet?' Now I had no knowledge of–nothing whatever to do with–the Infernal Machine.

The author adds: 'He did not remain long in prison on this charge.' However, the Temple register does not record Kearney's name for this period, neither does he himself mention it in a resumé of his encounters with the police which he compiled about 11 months later. The most probable explanation is that he was taken to police headquarters for questioning and later released.

The Temple prison register does contain an Irish entry[2] from about six months previously. Richard Ferris, who had returned from England in 1799, was interned there, accused of 'passing intelligence to enemies of the state'. He was described as a '45-

year-old native of Ireland, without profession, one metre 74cms tall, fair hair, low forehead, blue eyes, long sharp nose, average mouth, round chin and oval pockmarked face'. He was brought to the Temple from police headquarters on 15 April 1800 but his release was ordered on 20 of the same month and he left the following day.

Kearney was to continue to be harassed, not by the police but by the new *bureau gratuit* and his old colleague, Walsh. The bureau, following article three of the Consular decree, ordered both Walsh and Kearney to submit accounts. 'What kind of accounts could they have been,' Kearney later exclaimed,[3] 'as I had no registers, not a single paper to help my memory ... all my papers were burnt.' On 18 November 1801, he addressed to the members of the bureau a 15-page *mémoire*[4] to 'enlighten' them as to the real situation in Collège des Irlandais during the period he had been superior. Before he had assumed that responsibility at the end of 1782 three of his predecessors had died within the short space of six years. It did not take him long to realise that the debts still outstanding from the construction of the college, completed in 1776, together with the daily expenses of running it, were in no way proportionate to its income.

He pointed out the complete difference between the administration of Collège des Lombards and that of Collège des Irlandais. Both had their bursaries but in the case of Lombard's administering them was merely 'a hand-to-hand transaction', the priest-student was simply given his bursary and looked after himself. Kearney, however, was bound by the acts of foundation to provide his student-bursars with their complete maintenance regardless of the income from the bursary. In addition he was bound to pay their travelling expenses to and from Ireland. The college normally consisted of 70 to 80 students and Kearney had scarcely 30,000 *livres* to provide complete maintenance and food. His situation became well-nigh impossible with the rapid rise in prices and the suspension of payments by Hôtel de Ville for the years 1786 and 1787. He thus found himself 'several times in the cruel necessity of raising loans.'

He rejected vigorously Walsh's claim to be the principal administrator of Collège des Irlandais and that all Kearney's legal undertakings for ten years were null without Walsh's approbation. This latter claim was directed mainly at Kearney having accepted a loan from MacDermott in 1792 and subsequently giving him a lease of the college for his academy. Finally, he listed the different incidents in which he was involved since the beginning of the revolution 'not to distract them from the examination of his accounts but to prove to them by public and incontestable facts how he had always been surrounded by trouble and difficulty.' He made one request, that the members of the bureau would use their influence with the government to have restored the sum of 108,000 *livres*, the estate of one of his friends for whom he was acting as executor. The government had seized it ten years previously and placed in the national treasury money which had been intended for his friend's poor relations in Ireland.

It was a dignified and in places moving petition but it carried no weight with his inquisitors, who suggested that he 'used the political troubles as a pretext to disguise is maladministration.' Their verdict[5] on his accounts was extremely harsh. They found 'omissions impossible to excuse, and undocumented payments.' Although he had received considerable sums he had left a shortfall of 16,025 *livres*. He had acquired debts to the tune of 50,800 *livres* and could not account for the expenditure of these funds. They contended that his office did not legally entitle him to receive loans. Yet it appeared that MacDermott 'had placed all his wealth in the establishment as well as that of two women, one over eighty years old, who are now in a most terribly distressed state'. They recommended that the minister refuse all responsibility for these debts, in spite of the hardship it would cause to the individuals concerned. As to Kearney himself, they cut him off without any pension or salary. Kearney blamed Walsh for it: 'Far from calling for a pension for me;' he later wrote, 'he did everything in his power to prevent me obtaining one.'[6]

Their verdict[7] on Walsh's administration, on the contrary, was complimentary almost without reserve:

> M. Walsh, in the midst of the persecutions he experienced, never ceased to support the interests of his house. He had deployed much resoluteness in the difficult circumstances he was in; and it is perhaps to him that the conservation of the Irish colleges is due.

His accounts presented 'a fairly favourable impression of his conduct.' There was only one item they faulted him on. During his detention Collège des Lombards had fallen into ruin through the neglect of the keeper left in charge. Subsequently, Walsh leased out the building on condition that the tenant would undertake the cost of the repairs. However, he failed to present to the bureau any evidence of the state of the college before its lease or of the repairs carried out before the lease expired. This was their 'only reproach.'

They congratulated him on his firmness in rejecting the claims of certain Irish who wished to continue receiving their bursaries after they had completed their studies. One of these was Dr MacMahon, medical advisor in MacDermott's academy, who had laid claim to the MacMahon bursary and Walsh wrote[8] to the Minister of the Interior on 13 May 1801 rejecting the claim, pointing out that MacMahon was one of the rebel students who had tried to get control of the college in 1792 and had only failed by one vote to be elected on that occasion. 'This faction still exists,' he informed the minister, 'and pursues me with bitterness because I defend the properties of my *commetans* against their aggression.' He alleged that the former superior Charles O'Neill still bore him a grudge and was a relative of MacMahon's. 'There is no public man,' he added philosophically, 'without those who envy him and it would not help his job if he were to enter the lists against each of his detractors.'

Former Irish students had presented a printed petition[9] to the bureau demanding to be present at the sessions at which Walsh's accounts were examined. Otherwise, they claimed, 'Walsh would be judge and accused in his own case'. Their petition was not allowed.

At their meeting of 15 May 1802,[10] the bureau was presented with a *mémoire* by Peter Flood on behalf of the Irish bishops. Flood had returned to Ireland ten years previously after narrowly escaping the September Massacres. In 1797 he was appointed president of Maynooth in succession to Hussey. The bishops had become alarmed now that Hussey was meddling in the affairs of the Irish colleges in France and had successfully passed himself off as their representative: following his anti-English pastoral his standing with his fellow-bishops had been low. MacDermott wrote[11] to Troy informing him of the disagreeable situation that had arisen following interference by 'a former colleague of mine but now of your lordship's', in college affairs, nullifying all Dr Kearney's efforts to get the college out of debt. Hussey's interference gave the government 'a fair opportunity of wresting the properties and their administration out of Irish hands ... and in all probability will imitate Dame Justice, swallowing the oyster, while giving the two shells to the contending parties.'

The bishops were particularly anxious that Hussey stay clear of any sensitive area that could threaten their new entente with the British government and France was high on that list. This probably explains the haste with which they commissioned Flood to go to Paris and act as their attorney with the new bureau. The attestation[12] was signed by the four archbishops on 15 March 1802, but it was another ten days before the treaty of Amiens allowed normal communication to be resumed between France and Ireland after almost ten years of war. Flood was appointed agent and attorney-general of the bishops, 'with full powers to reclaim and recover all properties, movables and immovables, at present or formerly belonging to ... the Irish ecclesiastical establishments throughout the whole of the present territory of the French republic,' and to seek indemnities should any part of the said properties be alienated.

In his *mémoire*,[13] Flood proposed that all the revenues and properties of the Irish colleges in France that had survived the revolution should now be united to Paris which would henceforth be Ireland's only institution there. The bureau collected what information they could find on what still remained of the Irish colleges in Toulouse, Bordeaux, Nantes, Douai, Antwerp and Louvain. A few days later a similar proposal was made about the Scots college by Alexander Cameron, bishop of Edinburgh. The Scots had only one other college, at Douai. The bureau went one step further and proposed to the minister that 'it was impossible to reorganise the houses in Paris with the modest revenues that remained' and that the Irish and Scots houses should be amalgamated–which was precisely what neither the Irish nor the Scots wanted. The bureau argued that the rights of each nation could be guaranteed by alternating the head of the college and dismissed the Irish and Scots claim that 'national prejudices' would give rise to internal dissensions 'always fatal for study and discipline'.[14]

The bureau saw no point in proposing a regime for the united houses as required by article seven of the Consular decree. 'The extreme modesty of their resources,' they stated, 'made it impossible to make these colleges operational and to bring in students.' In the meantime, they suggested that the 'modest revenues' should be used to support young Irish and Scots students at the Prytanée which, since the signing of the concordat, had introduced religious instruction. They submitted their report to the Minister of the Interior on 15 July 1802 asking that it be presented to the Consuls with a view to issuing a decree for its execution. They also requested that the Minister of Finance issue an order suspending the sale of Irish and Scots properties 'where they were on the point of being alienated'. Chaptal proposed the amalgamation of the Irish and Scots properties to the First Consul and he approved it on 14 October 1802.

Walsh immediately took issue with some of the proposals and wrote[15] to the Minister of the Interior to acquaint him with his objections. Both the Irish and Scots considered the proposed amalgamation equally repugnant. Irish catholics numbered four million, while there were scarcely twenty thousand Scots. There would therefore be a 'total disproportion' between the number of students of each nation. He advised the minister 'to leave these two nations in the state that nature and history had placed them.' He was even more adamant in his opposition to the proposed transfer, albeit provisional, of the Irish bursaries to the Prytanée, which was a military school and its education not at all suitable for students destined for the ecclesiastical state. Furthermore, students could not remain there after they had completed their 18th year but the Irish bishops intended to send 'rather the elite of their students, already advanced in the national college in Ireland to perfect themselves under the great masters in Paris.' Finally, the British government would not permit their subjects to be educated by the French Prytanée though they could not prevent them studying in their own houses. He also impressed on the minister that the Irish bishops were unanimous in designating Walsh, with the minister's agreement, as the president of the new establishment.

On 17 December 1802 Walsh wrote[16] to Archbishop Troy informing him 'of a wide breach in the article relative to the Prytanée.' This information appears to be premature. His expectation 'to do away with the other noxious article and to defeat local intrigues' seemed at the very least optimistic. All this arose from an interesting interview Walsh had with the minister but he was wisely 'waiting for facts to confirm his promises.' He stated that he had 40,000 francs 'clear of all encumbrances.' Referring to Kearney's administration 'which is daily more and more criticised on proofs of malversation' he claimed that if he had not suspended him 'the house would have been utterly ruined many months ago'. Far from doing away with the noxious article, the French added an even more noxious one. On 22 June 1803 the English establishments were united to those of the Irish and the Scots.[17] It was a providential decree for the English properties as it just saved them from alienation. A few days later, Walsh stated 'a host of men would have been in possession of their Paris houses and those in the other departments.' In fact, in December they had to have recourse to the civil authorities to gain possession of the English seminary and similarly the Benedictine house in rue Saint Jacques a few months later. Both were in an advanced state of dilapidation, the Benedictine house requiring the expenditure of more than 12,000 francs to make it fit for leasing. To mark the occasion a special medal was struck with the legend in Latin on one side, stating that the Irish, English and Scots were guests in France *pro fide et litteris*, and Napoleon's head on the reverse.[18]

One of the reasons for amalgamating the properties was to avoid the cost of a triple administration. The minister consulted the bureau on the choice of an administrator and they unhesitatingly recommended Walsh, then on leave of absence. In their recommendation they stated: 'The proven talents of this administrator, the rigorous exactitude of his previous accounts and his firm behaviour during the stormiest period of the revolution decided us to put his name forward.'[19] He was appointed on 11 February 1803.

The first problem he was faced with was the presence of MacDermott's academy in Collège des Irlandais. The lease had still three years to run, but Walsh hoped that MacDermott, a former student of Collège des Lombards, would allow it to expire, 'with good grace.'[20] He was invited to a meeting of the bureau on 8 March when it was proposed to him that the ministry would make a 'proportionate indemnity' and allow him time to find another house for his academy. MacDermott insisted on the full extension of his lease and Walsh had no alternative but to seek redress in the courts. He based his case on Kearney having acted ultra-vires in granting the lease to MacDermott and that it fell within the competence of Walsh alone as principal administrator of Collège des Lombards, of which Collège des Irlandais was simply a daughter-house. He had not raised the matter earlier as he was involved in a struggle against the Directory on one side and the Prytanée on the other and he considered that it would 'have been imprudent to take on at the same time an internal quarrel.' He had protested to the Minister of the Interior on 10 October 1801 and immediately afterwards notified by process-server his opposition to Kearney.

Walsh now not only asked the court to nullify MacDermott's lease but also to determine a rent proportional to the value of the property for the six years that had elapsed. The court of first instance handed down a judgment in favour of MacDermott. Walsh then took the case to the court of appeal, where it appears, he acted as his own lawyer. He opened his defence[21] with the words 'A fifty-nine year old debutant begs the indulgence of the court'. When Delamalle, counsel for MacDermott expressed his astonishment at the 'audacity' of Walsh to act on his own behalf, Walsh turned to the judges and said, 'With judges like you, Gentlemen, I have the firm hope that truth will triumph over eloquence.' Walsh won but he was compelled to pay MacDermott an indemnity of 10,000 francs. MacDermott transferred his school to the former seminary of Saint-Esprit close by in rue des Postes where it continued to thrive.

Walsh set out to recover what still remained of the continental colleges in the Netherlands, now under French control. In the autumn of 1804, he undertook a journey of 250 leagues lasting 34 days and visited Douai, Saint-Omer, Tournai, Louvain and Liège.[22] He made his headquarters at Douai, where there were no less than five colleges: the English, Irish and Scots as well as the houses of the English Benedictines and Franciscans. All that remained of the latter was the church which served now as the parish church of St James. The Irish college had been alienated together with its gardens and dependencies. The external houses and rural lands of the Scots college had been sold. He estimated that the English and Scots colleges and the Benedictine house would be worth about 3,000 francs to Paris from lease. He considered the offers made too ridiculous to be entertained. 'They probably thought that I was in a hurry to conclude the business' he remarked. He expelled the tenants in the English and Scots colleges to facilitate a new lease by his attorney 'who had not the courage to expel these people.' The Benedictine house was occupied by the local commandant of the engineer corps, who refused to evacuate it. Walsh reported him to his superior officer at Tournai and to the Minister of War who despatched a letter ordering the building to be returned. He even demanded the return of the parish church of St James, 'alone against the affected indifference of the prefect, the partiality and arbitrary interpretations of the sub-prefect and of the mayor and the prejudices of the parish priest and churchwardens.' The result was indecisive but Walsh had the pleasure of selling, 'under the very noses of these gentlemen', materials from the former cloister and leased a house in the enclosure.

The English college in St Omer, where Daniel O'Connell had been a student, had been converted into a military hospital and had been well repaired by the war department. Walsh, despite the 'intrigues and threats' of the occupant, succeeded in re-possessing it. The Irish college in Tournai was beyond repair and Walsh recommended selling it. It had been a source of contention between Walsh and the bishop of Tournai who claimed it. The tenants and debtors in general refused to pay until Walsh could produce his title-deeds. These had been transferred across the Rhine and Walsh later made an effort to employ a researcher to find them in Vienna.

In Louvain, his attorney, M. Peronne, 'left nothing to be desired.' The Irish Pastoral college had been greatly improved by the freemasons who occupied it and had completely replaced stairs, doors, floors, ceilings etc; and Walsh estimated that the lease would triple on renewal. He expected an increase also in the rent of the college of the English Dominicans, though he was strangely silent concerning the fate of the house of the Irish Dominicans and, more importantly, the famous college of St Anthony of the Irish Franciscans. A representative of the English Jesuits had made 'some futile attempts' to regain possession of the English college in Liège, but his powers were limited and Walsh had little problem in disposing of him. He concluded his report to the bureau on 16 October 1804 stating that 'he believed he had carried out their intentions. By not appearing as a hard and demanding rent-collector, by settling matters justly and with moderation he had left everywhere favourable impressions of the benevolence of the administration'.

Napoleon now turned his attention to re-organising the other traditional wing of the Irish-French connection, the military. The old Irish brigade had been disbanded at the beginning of the revolution, some of the officers, such as Kilmaine, Harty, Arthur and Theobald Dillon joining the republican army while royalists like O'Connell had joined the army of the Princes. With the failure of the latter, O'Connell offered the services of the Irish brigade to England, an unnatural marriage which was destined to early failure. Numerous Irish had taken refuge in France after the failure of the French expeditions. General Humbert, then commandant at Brest, in a *mémoire* to the Minister of War on 8 October 1800 estimated their number at between 1,000 and 1,500 and proposed their absorption into an Irish legion.[23]

On 16 May 1803 war was resumed with Britain and projects of new expeditions to Ireland were re-activated in which the Irish refugees would have an important role to play. On 13 August Napoleon signed a decree[24] at Saint-Cloud for the formation of Irish battalions. On 21 November Berthier, Minister of War, gave the order for the formation of the first battalion at Morlaix, chosen because it was the usual place where English deserters disembarked. The organisation of the battalion was confided to adjutant-commandant Bernard MacSheehy who had recently returned from Napoleon's Egyptian campaign where he had distinguished himself and had become one of the government's chief advisors on Irish affairs. On 20 January 1804 Berthier wrote to MacSheehy that 'the grades conferred on the Irish legion will be provisional.' The formation of the battalion took place at Morlaix on the same day. It seemed clear that Bonaparte's intention was that it would remain a corps of officers until an expedition to Ireland was planned. In his first report[25] MacSheehy observed that 'the training of officers demands that there be some soldiers under their orders'. He claimed that over 4,000 Irish soldiers had been forced into the army of the king of Prussia after the 1798 insurrection. 'Would it not be possible' he asked, 'to negotiate their exchange perhaps for Hanoverians?'

The battalion consisted of an *état-major* and nine companies: in all there were 49 officers and one soldier. The colonel of the battalion, 'named by the first consul', was James Bartholomew Blackwell. Now 43, he had been released from Kilmainham after the signing of the treaty of Amiens. Besides Bernard MacSheehy, there was also a Patrick MacSheehy and two brothers Thomas and William Corbett. A Lacy joined from the Irish regiment, Ultonia, in Spain and a William O'Meara, formerly an officer in Clare's regiment, later served in the British army and had now returned to France. He ended up as a general and his two sons, John and Edward, were educated in the reorganised Irish college. There were a number of former Irish insurgents, like William Barker, who had distinguished himself at Vinegar Hill and lost an arm in Enniscorthy who were given inferior ranks by the war office. MacSheehy began judiciously by succeeding in obtaining commissions as captains for them. In the 5th company was a young sub-lieutenant, Miles Byrne.

Byrne, from Monaseed, Co. Wexford, took part as an 18-year-old in the insurrection in that county in 1798 and later escaped the reprisals by joining Holt and Dwyer in the Wicklow mountains.

He became one of Robert Emmet's main helpers and after the abortive rising of 1803 managed to escape to France and brought the sad news of Robert's execution to his brother, Thomas Addis, then acting as Irish agent to the Consular government. Here he met another Irish refugee, this time from Humbert's expedition, Fr Michael Gannon from Castlebar. After hiding out for a time in the Connemara mountains, Gannon had managed to get a passage on a boat bound for Lisbon, from where he wrote to Lucien Bonaparte, then French ambassador in Madrid, who arranged his passage to Paris. He was ministering as a priest in a village near Saint-Germain-en-Laye in 1803 when Miles Byrne first met him. They were both invited to tea by Thomas Addis Emmet who lived in the neighbourhood. Byrne recounts that Mrs Emmet was always glad to see Fr Gannon, 'for her husband's spirits were always cheered by his visits and conversation, as he was never desponding about Ireland.'[26]

In Paris Byrne also met frequently General O'Neill, an octogenarian and brother of Charles, former superior of Collège des Lombards. Byrne and the general strolled together in Jardin du Luxembourg while the general recounted some of his exploits in the old Irish brigade. Remarkably, Byrne, who himself lived to be an octogenarian, was to meet and befriend another Irishman in Paris 60 years later—John Mitchel, the Young Irelander. Byrne, together with Thomas Addis Emmet, Dr MacNevin, Arthur O'Connor and others presented a petition to Napoleon, seeking French aid for Ireland.

Arthur O'Connor, a trial mate of Fr James Coigly in Maidstone, had been acquitted but immediately re-arrested and imprisoned in Scotland until June 1802, when he went to Paris. In February 1804 Napoleon appointed him general of division. MacSheehy apparently resented the French government conferring such high rank on persons who had not earned their stripes like himself on the field of battle. Similar grades had been conferred likewise on his former superior officer, Wolfe Tone and also on Napper Tandy. Friction developed between MacSheehy and the Corbetts, whom he suspected were intimates of O'Connor. On 3 June 1804 when he assembled the Irish legion to take the new oath to Napoleon who had been proclaimed emperor on 10 May trouble was provoked by Captain Sweeney who questioned whether the oath lessened in any way their Irish loyalty.[27] MacSheehy succeeded in having the oath taken by the legion but on the following day the two Corbetts refused to sign the forms. In this they were supported by Blackwell, once a fellow-conspirator of MacSheehy in the Irish college. A duel took place between Sweeney and Thomas Corbett which MacSheehy was supposed to have caused. It had disastrous effects on the corp's morale as it was considered politically motivated by the swearing of allegiance to Napoleon. MacSheehy reported Blackwell and the other officers involved and it cost Blackwell his command. As a result of this incident MacSheehy left the Irish legion and returned to the main French army where he held the rank of colonel until killed by a cannon ball at the battle of Eylau in 1807. He was succeeded by an Italian who adversely influenced the future development of the Irish legion.

Notwithstanding its internal dissensions the Irish legion was invited to send two officers to attend the coronation of Napoleon as emperor in Notre Dame on 5 December 1804. To mark the occasion it was given an eagle by the emperor, the only foreign regiment in the French army to be accorded this privilege. The flag of the legion was now entirely green, with the legend: 'The Emperor of the French to the Irish Legion' on one side and on the reverse a great golden harp with the words, 'Independence of Ireland.' The legion saw little or no action until Henry Clarke became Minister of War in 1807. He retained a sentimental attachment for the old Irish brigade in which he himself had begun his military career and kept a benevolent eye on the Irish legion. Their fight was to become less and less for the independence of Ireland and more and more for the glory of Bonaparte.

Pius VII was brought to Paris to preside at the coronation and Walsh took the opportunity to present His Holiness with an address[28] in Latin outlining the new developments in the Irish college and seeking his blessing on the new merger in Paris 'where we hope, with the help of your holiness, for a resurrection of the famous Sorbonne, to which young students of sacred doctrine will flock from all regions.' He impressed on the Pope the necessity for Ireland to continue to send students to Paris to study theology if only to ensure a supply of qualified professors for Maynooth. The Pope on this occasion offered 'his most paternal wishes for the success of this establishment'.

A final decree[29] regulating the life of the united colleges in some detail was signed on 18 May 1805 by Napoleon in his palace in Milan, where he had gone to be crowned king of Italy. The decree was divided into eight titles or headings containing no less than 57 articles ranging from the relationship between the three establishments to the punishment of recalcitrant students. The Minister of the Interior was charged with its execution. The amalgamation comprised all male institutions founded in France or in its occupied territories which were now to be centred in the building which housed Collège des Irlandais in rue du Cheval Vert.

As kingdoms toppled in the wake of Napoleon's victorious armies, continental colleges of various sizes and denominations were showered into the lap of Collège des Irlandais. Walsh was given the title of administrator-general and the complete internal running of the establishment as well as the management of the properties, subject to the authority of the Minister of the Interior and the surveillance of the *bureau gratuit*. The administrator-general had to be a priest of one of the three countries, over 30 years of age and as far as possible a graduate of a Catholic university. He had to become a naturalised French citizen within a year of his nomination 'or declare, in writing, his intention to live and die in France'. Appointment to the post was reserved to the emperor, following the proposal of the minister and the advice of the bureau. The administrator-general was to invite 'the chief catholic' of each nation to send students in proportion to the monies available. If on account of a *force majeure* it was not possible to send students, the revenue was to be used for children of parents of Irish or British extraction.

The decree gave statutory and definitive recognition to the *bureau de surveillance* which was to play a paramount role in the history of the college for the next 200 years. The bureau now consisted of the Archbishop of Paris, the prefect of the Seine Department, the first president of the court of appeal of Paris, the *procureur-général* of the same court, a member of the general council of the Department and an administrator of the *lycées*. It was to supervise the management of the properties and the foundations which depended on them and the employment of capital. In this latter connection, it was especially bound to prevent the expenditure of any of the revenue 'outside the territory of the French empire'. Dr Flood was said to have been sent to Paris in 1805 and presented to the bureau a few days before the decree was issued a *mémoire*[30] in the name of the Irish bishops demanding that the revenues of the Irish foundations be repatriated annually to Ireland, presumably to Maynooth. This was the advice that Abbé MacDermott gave to Archbishop Troy in 1802 when he wrote suggesting that 'all the connected efforts and influence of the Irish bishops be used in soliciting the British government in order to obtain the properties of the nation in France and to have them at home.'

Despite the fact that there were as yet no students and the prospects of their arriving in the near future were not particularly bright, the decree dealt in very fine detail with their education and discipline. The revenues of the Irish section were to be applied to the Irish families and dioceses who had a right to it from the acts of foundation. Other young Irish could be admitted as boarders who were certified by their bishops and could show proof of their parents' solvency. Students were admitted from the end of their 11th year and could stay until the age of 21, with the exception of ecclesiastical students who could remain until they had completed their studies. Students already ordained could be sent by their respective bishops and could remain for up to five years. With regard to discipline, the rule of the establishment was that of the metropolitan seminary, with morning and night prayer, community mass, annual retreats and spiritual exercises. Punishment consisted of the punishment room, the penance table and detentions. Expulsions had to be confirmed by the Minister of the Interior. Women were forbidden to enter the interior of the college.

It was decided to re-open the following September. On 1 August Walsh issued a prospectus[31] for the new institution which was to open its doors to students on the feast of Saint Remy, traditional commencement day in the old university of Paris. The Collège des Irlandais, it stated, had, in addition to exercise halls, class halls, refectory etc., 108 student rooms as well as a 'spacious and sheltered courtyard for recreation'. The English seminary in rue des Postes would be used for retired professors and for the infirmary. Medical students would be lodged there and look after the sick under the supervision of a qualified doctor. Private tutors who could be provided by parents would also stay there.

Education would be based on the principles of the former university of Paris. Qualified teachers—doctors, licenciates or bachelors of theology—would teach dogma and philosophy in Latin and moral theology and ecclesiastical history, as well as mathematics, astronomy and geography, in English and French. There would be a class in advanced literature which would follow that of philosophy so that the students 'could combine the gracefulness of an oratorical style with the precision of ideas and the strength of reason'. The food would be healthy and plentiful and professors and students would eat together in the same refectory. In a word, the college would seek to inculcate in its students 'that amenity, that considerateness, those attitudes that well-bred people ought to have in society.'

NOTES

1. O'Reilly, op. cit. p226.
2. A.P. A B/334 f.25, 15 April 1800.
3. D.D.A. 121/9, 29 Jan. 1816.
4. Maynooth, Papers from the Irish College Paris, 18 Nov. 1801.
5. I.C.P. 3J, 18 July 1802.
6. D.D.A. 121/9, 29 Jan. 1816.
7. I.C.P. 3J, 18 July 1802.
8. A.N. F 17 2500, 13 May 1801.
9. I.C.P. 3L, 15 Dec. 1801.
10. I.C.P. 3U1, 15 May 1802.
11. D.D.A. Troy (1802-3), 17 April 1802.
12. D.D.A. 121/9, 15 Mar. 1802.
13. I.C.P. 3U1, 15 May 1802.
14. I.C.P. 3J, 18 July 1802.
15. A.N. F 17 14761.
16. D.D.A. 121/9, 17 Dec. 1802.
17. A.N. F 19 6237C, 22 June 1803.
18. A.N. F 17 14761, 22 June 1803.
19. I.C.P. 3J, 18 July 1802.
20. Maynooth, Papers from Irish College Paris, *Mémoire à consulter*, nd.
21. I.C.P. 3V1. cf A.N. H 3 2561A. pp10, 11, 24.
22. I.C.P. 3U4, 16 Oct. 1804.
23. Carles, Lt. Col. Pierre, 'Le corps irlandais au service de la France sous le Consulat et l'Empire.' *Revue historique des Armées*, No 2 (1976) pp24-48.
24. Ibid. p28.
25. Ibid. p31.
26. Byrne, op. cit. 3 p63.
27. Carles, op. cit. pp31-32; Byrne, op. cit. 3 pp110-13.
28. A.N. F 17 14764, 24 Dec. 1804.
29. A.N. F 19 6237A, 18 May 1805.
30. I.C.P. 3L, 18 May 1805.
31. I.C.P. 3L5, 1 Aug. 1805.

14
Pursuit of Purple

The college in Paris created by Napoleon the Great should receive from him all the lustre it was capable of by having at its head a bishop in partibus.

—Walsh, 4 May 1807.

There was only one problem left to be resolved and that the most important of all—where to find students for this enlightened institution. For ten years Walsh had been telling all and sundry that students would flock to Paris from Ireland once its college was restored. Lally Tollendal accused him of using this argument to evict Abbé MacDermott and his academy. 'He had lied audaciously,' he wrote later,[1] 'repeating *ad nauseam* that all the English ports would be thronged with young catholic students waiting to embark as soon as they learned that the Irish house in Paris was ready to receive them.' The truth, according to Tollendal, was that there was not 'a single one in a single port'. In fact and worse still the Irish bishops, anxious not to offend the British government, were threatening to excommunicate any clerics who went to Paris.

In desperation Walsh attempted to seduce a number of Irish clerics who had disembarked at Lisbon, offering them places in Paris. This occasioned an extremely strong condemnation[2] of Walsh by the Irish bishops dated 24 January 1807 and sent to the president of the Irish college in Lisbon: 'We ... have lately been acquainted with an extraordinary proposal of the Reverend Walsh of Paris to the young men at present under your care and guidance in Lisbon inviting them to abandon that establishment and repair to the seminary established by the head of the French nation, under his direction in that city'. The episcopal anger was almost palpable. 'You may easily conceive the degree of indignation we felt at such a proposal' they continued, 'nor can we believe that it proceeded from any but very sinister motives.' The bishops refrained from making any further comments 'on the general conduct of Mr Walsh since the period of the French revolution'. However, the great inducements held out to the Lisbon students 'seemed calculated to inspire them with veneration for and attachment to the present French government which is at the same time actuated by a desire to alienate them from that allegiance which they owe to the government of their own country.' Pointing out to the Lisbon superior 'that one of the principal duties of a clergyman is to inculcate subordination to the law and allegiance to the established authorities under which he lives,' they declared that 'an education received under such a hostile and revolutionary government as Bonaparte's' was hardly calculated to inculcate these virtues. 'Bound as we are' they continued, 'by every tie of gratitude to the government for the very liberal support of our ecclesiastical establishment at Maynooth (and which under the auspices of the present administration we hope will very shortly be considerably enlarged)', they declared in the most unequivocal terms their 'reprobation of such attempts to seduce the youth' of the Lisbon college and that they would deal severely with any students who dared accept 'that insidious offer'.

The bishops' condemnation was a severe blow to Walsh. 'If the signatories of the letter' he wrote,[3] 'had notified to him not to receive their subjects he would have acted in conformity with their instructions.' Referring to the Lisbon students, he claimed that the peninsular war had forced them to take refuge in Spain, 'where soon after they found neither refuge nor means of education.' He justified his offer to them on humanitarian grounds. 'In this state of distress' he remarked, 'he felt it his duty to listen to the voice of humanity ... to repeat the sweet invitation of his Divine Master: *Venite ad me omnes, et ego reficiam vos.*'

Up to this Walsh had argued to the French government that the failure of students to arrive from Ireland was due to 'the English government, who missing no opportunity to tyrannise the poor Irish, had put so many obstacles to prevent them leaving, that several had been arrested and others obliged to return from Lisbon even after they had disembarked.' Now, in February 1807, he decided to come clean with the Minister of the Interior.[4] 'It is due to an entirely different cause' he wrote, 'which I can no longer hide from you.' The Irish bishops had managed to send students during previous wars. Their failure now was due to their opposition to the united colleges in Paris which they had declared the previous October. He enclosed a report on the three Irish students who had arrived in Lisbon, 'destined for Paris.'

In spite of the total absence of communication with the Irish bishops caused by the war, Walsh managed to keep himself abreast of political news from Ireland by scouring the English newspapers in the French Department of Foreign Affairs where he was becoming a familiar figure. Here, he read in *The London Evening Post*, under the date of 5 March 1807, an extract from the house of commons debate on the supplementary grant to Maynooth college.[5] It was already receiving an annual grant of £8,000 and had petitioned for an additional £5,000. Grattan made the point that if their clergy leave the kingdom, 'to learn foreign politics, Irish priests must become pensioners of the king of England or the emperor of the French'. They should be educated in their own kingdom where they can swear allegiance to their sovereign. That was the purpose of the parliament voting an annual grant to Maynooth. Mr Wilberforce drew attention to the existence on the continent of 'a great seminary under the patronage of an extraordinary man [the Emperor Napoleon] on whom it was most undesirable that this establishment should depend'. These students might one day become the bishops of Ireland.

The Secretary of State, Lord Howick, stated in his reply that refusal of the grant would take on the character of persecution. He instanced a fact which proved the necessity of home education for the Irish clergy. 'Dr Walsh, a priest of talent, who was appointed head of the college established in Paris for the education of catholic priests, had used all the means in his power to induce such of the Irish catholics as were for their education in Lisbon, to go to his college. He had offered them not only education, but every temptation that he thought likely to withdraw them from their king and their country.' Howick reassured the house of commons that 'on representation of the matter to the catholic bishops in Ireland, they treated it as it deserved.' The politics of encouraging the seminary in Ireland was obvious. Maynooth could not cater for the number of students demanding places. Several were embarking for Spain, Portugal and France. Walsh noted in the margin here: 'some of these students who were in Spain as well as in Portugal made their way to France.' The only way to prevent this emigration was to enlarge Maynooth. The supplementary grant was voted.

Walsh made maximum capital of this newspaper extract, waving it under the noses of French government ministers on all possible occasions. He pointed out that the English were alarmed at the potential development of the Paris establishment. 'They spend their gold', he said, 'to prevent the emigration of Irish Catholics to France.' Once returned to Ireland, they feared their influence on the catholic masses there.

Realising that he was now contending with the violent opposition of the Irish bishops in whose name he continued to act and that without their support there was little hope for the survival of the college, he now attempted his most daring stroke to date: to become a bishop himself. Only a bishop could authorise clerics to attend his seminary and provide them with the necessary canonical permissions to allow them proceed to ordination. He was too intelligent and too well-informed an ecclesiastic not to realise the immense odds against his entering what must be one of the most exclusive clubs in the world. He had already failed once when he was promoted by Hussey as his coadjutor in Waterford. That had been due to the strength of the opposition of the local bishops. Such opposition had apparently intensified considerably since then but Walsh was seeking to become not an Irish diocesan bishop but a bishop *in partibus*. He now claimed that he himself had declined the coadjutorship of Waterford at the request of the bishop of Orléans who believed he could serve the Irish and French churches more usefully as head of the united colleges with the title of bishop *in partibus*. For that, he required French rather than Irish backing. He had lived long enough in Napoleonic France to realise this was possible. He had seen the Pope dance too often to Napoleon's tune, from the organic articles to the coronation, to be discouraged at the prospects.

Besides, he had all the requisite qualifications and more. He was a doctor of theology of the Sorbonne. He had served as superior in three seminaries, Nantes, Collège des Lombards, and now the seminary of the united colleges of Ireland, England and Scotland. He had remained a priest, refusing all oaths during the most violent period of the French revolution and had been imprisoned for it. More, he had contributed outstanding and courageous service to the French underground church during its persecution, for which he was commended in a papal brief. More recently, as vicar-general of the diocese of Clermont, he had been instrumental in reconciling some former Constitutional clergy with their canonical authorities, and succeeded in persuading the Constitutional bishop Dupoux to resign. He was a man of irreproachable virtue. He could easily be forgiven the delusion that he was *episcopabilis*, at least *in partibus*.

Walsh had launched his campaign as early as December 1804 when the Pope was in Paris for the occasion of the coronation.[6] He had raised the matter then with the Cardinal Prefect of propaganda and Cardinal Fesch, Napoleon's uncle. They advised him that his demand should not be made in France but in Rome itself. All the documents were left with Monseigneur Mazzio, attached to the legation, who promised to pursue the matter when he returned to Rome. Walsh wrote to the Minister of Religion on 22 June 1806 to inform him that he had heard nothing about it since, pointing out that it was of the greatest importance to the college that its superior possess the title of bishop. He enclosed a *mémoire* detailing the reasons. The imperial government, following the sound policy of keeping the British government in a state of 'perpetual alarm', had created the Irish legion. The same legion could not survive without the support of the Irish seminary in Paris, because the corps of officers was recruited from the non-ecclesiastical students of the college. The ecclesiastics themselves would propagandise for the legion on their return to Ireland and encourage emigration to France. He pointed out that the present commander, Bernard MacSheehy, had been educated in the Irish college. It was well-known that the British government used all possible means to thwart the continental education of their catholic subjects. They opposed the cohabitation of English and Scots students with those from Ireland because they feared that this would destroy the 'anti-Gallic sentiment' normally associated with the English and Scots establishments. The Irish would always be in a majority and inculcate in the others attitudes more favourable to France.

He pointed out that the needs of catholics in England and Scotland were met by six bishops *in partibus* who had only provisional jurisdiction which could be revoked at will. They were sanctioned by the government and devoted to its desires. The Irish colleges in Paris were always independent of the Irish bishops. He enclosed the papal brief which authorised the superior to promote to sacred orders without demissorial letters. An episcopal superior would attract far more students from the United Kingdom and would enhance the establishment enormously. Above all, he would thus be able to deal with the insular bishops 'as equal to equal': the means employed by the British government to prevent students coming would be nullified. He enclosed a document attesting his contribution as a member of the administrative council of the diocese of Paris, prior to the nomination of Monsignor de Belloy, and others detailing his services as vicar-general of the diocese of Clermont, in particular a letter from the prefect of Puy de Dôme to the minister stating that Walsh 'had put an end to all the theological quarrels which had agitated his Department for far too long.'

Walsh now initiated proceedings in Rome, placing the business in the capable hands of the Irish Dominican, Luke Concannon, who was later to become the first bishop of New York. Tactically this may have been a mistake as Concannon was the official agent of the Irish hierarchy in Rome and particularly close to his fellow Dominican, Archbishop Troy of Dublin. However, Concannon in his letter[7] to Walsh on 25 March 1807 showed nothing but enthusiasm for the project. He enclosed a memorial in Italian to be presented to the Pope through the mediation of Cardinal di Pietro and requested Walsh to correct any part of it 'that may not be to your liking.' The memorial summarised the career and virtues of Walsh, highlighting his contribution during the French revolution 'when his church became the centre of catholicism in Paris and when his college became a refuge for a great number of ecclesiastics from various parts of France.' Concannon proposed giving the document to Monsignor Isoard to peruse, 'who promised to recommend it.' Isoard suggested getting a letter from the Archbishop of Paris and the Minister of Religion giving their consent. Without their signatures, 'Mr Isoard imagines it would not be prudent to risk or urge the business.'

On 4 May Walsh wrote[8] to the minister enclosing an extract from the history of Ireland. He pointed out that Maynooth would be tolerated for a certain time but that its future was in no way assured due to the 'changing policy of the British government which held the Irish bishops in its hands.' The college in Paris created by 'Napoleon the Great' should receive from him all the lustre it was capable of by having at its head a bishop *in partibus*. This was sound policy as this prelate could then act as a 'counter-weight' to the insular bishops 'and undo the influence they exercise at the dictates of the British government.'

He followed this with another letter[9] to the minister enclosing a copy of the proposed re-organisation of the college approved by the bureau. 'I am convinced' he declared, 'that [the Irish] cannot conserve their religion in its purity, without, after God, the human means that only France can provide them.' He referred to the three Irish students who had arrived in Lisbon on their way to Paris and were deterred by a letter signed by the four archbishops, 'forced, no doubt, by the British government, who compels them to say yes or no depending on its whims.' Hence, the necessity of a 'counter-weight to the actions forced from these prelates.' He pointed out that his proposed bishopric *in partibus* was 'not without interest to the Minister of Religion. Already, priests who had escaped from the recent troubles in Ireland and were condemned to perpetual exile in Botany Bay had sought refuge in France and were ministering in the dioceses of Versailles and Meaux. Former students of the Irish college in Bordeaux, naturalised by the original act of foundation, were working on both sides of the Loire and aboard French ships. Walsh went on to describe Ireland 'as in some way a levitical country' providing priests for the mission in England and America. Irish students would form a nursery for supplementing the French clergy which was declining daily. Protesting his disinterest 'in any personal elevation', he maintained that a bishop *in partibus* at the head of his establishment 'would contribute powerfully to the good of religion.'

Walsh followed this the next day with yet another letter, pointing out that his appointment as bishop *in partibus* would not involve any additional expense. The Roman agent, Concannon, could attest that he had 'a fortune superior to that usually demanded in similar cases.' Walsh's persistence finally paid off. The minister wrote [10] to Napoleon seeking imperial approval. Pointing out that if Walsh were promoted to the episcopacy the students who came to study in his establishment would no longer have to seek dimissorial letters from the Irish bishops in order to be ordained, he added 'this measure seemed especially useful at a time when the catholics of Ireland groan under oppression and tyranny'. The solution would be for Walsh to be named bishop *in partibus* by the Pope. Walsh had assured him that 'he would easily obtain this favour from the court of Rome.' Having been nominated by the emperor as director of the establishment in Paris, he could not without his consent solicit the favour of being promoted to the episcopacy. Napoleon granted his assent [11] to Walsh's petition in his palace at St Cloud on 4 August. It would appear that the imperial approval was caught between changes at the Department of Religion. Walsh wrote [12] in February 1808 explaining to the new minister that his predecessor, Portalis, had not signed the official notification of the emperor's approval because of the state of his health. The matter apparently was quickly rectified as he wrote again on 8 March asking the minister to recommend him to the French ambassador in Rome.

While Rome deliberated on his future status, Walsh had other pressing problems to resolve. The most important, now that the Irish bishops had imposed their embargo, was where to find students for his college. As a provisional measure he installed Abbé Fontanel as prefect of studies together with his little French boarding school from rue des Postes. He had received authorisation for this from the Minister of Home Affairs on 5 December 1805. Considering his expulsion of MacDermott and his academy this represented nothing less than a U-turn in his attitude but the circumstances demanded drastic action. Among the students in Fontanel's school were children from some of the finest families in France, such as the four de la Rochefoucauld brothers, one of whom later became Duc de Rochefoucauld. In all, French students numbered 45.

There was also a growing number of children of Irish extraction. One of them, William Shee, a relative on his mother's side to Henry Clarke, Napoleon's Minister of War, later penned a short account of his memories[13] of this school. He entered the Irish college after Easter in 1807 and left in January 1814 to enter the Ecole Militaire. It had its own professors who held class within the college and in each hall there was a pulpit from which the lectures were given. The large hall (the present refectory) was called *la salle du tombeau* because it had 'a monument of black marble with an inscription to the memory of James II'. Religious services were performed in the college chapel, with the superiors acting as officiating priests and the students as choristers. On certain occasions during the year processions were held in the courtyard while 'the windows of all the houses which could look into our court were fully occupied by a great many people, who took part in the service.' St Patrick's Day every year was the main festival 'when the council board gave a large banquet to the friends of the college'. Though education in Napoleonic France had decidedly military features the Irish college was an exception. As Shee commented: 'We never wore a uniform or regimentals like the other schools or colleges; we never used drum.'

Another Irish student who arrived about the same time was Arthur Barker, then only nine years old. His father, Captain William Barker, was marching with his regiment to Germany and tried to have his son placed in the Irish college. Captain Barker had lost an arm in the battle of Vinegar Hill in 1798 and later escaped to France where he joined the Irish legion. Walsh, 'with every wish to oblige,' could not receive his son without a ministerial order and the Captain was pressed for time. He left little Arthur with Wolfe Tone's widow until the minister's consent came through a month later.[14] Arthur was to remain in the college until after the battle of Waterloo. The two sons of Edward Lewins, the United Irish agent in France and close collaborator of Wolfe Tone, were also pupils. They Francofied their name to an aristocratic de Luynes and one of them, Hippolyte, later became a priest in France. Among the families of the older Irish represented in the college were Louis and Theobald Walsh de Serrant, to whom the superior was alleged to have been related.

Walsh had always declared 'his tender attachment to the bursars who really serve the republic', that is those who adopted the military profession. Those preparing for a military career predominated among the Irish students of this period. 'Several of our officers finished their studies there' Miles Byrne recorded;[15] 'The three brothers Saint-Leger, Wall, Swanton, the youngest Glashan, O'Brien, etc., got their commissions as sub-lieutenants for the Irish regiment, on leaving the college.' Others remembered by Colonel William Shee as fellow students included Walsh, Corbett, O'Heguerty, John, Edward and Daniel O'Meara and Maurice O'Farrell, all of whom joined the French army. Walsh maintained that he deliberately restricted the number of *originaires*, i.e., students of Irish extraction so as not to deprive the *indigènes*, i.e., the native Irish who might present themselves. In all, there were 13 of Irish origin: Green, Butler, Saint-Leger, Walsh (Olivier, Antoine Théobald), de Luynes, Barker, O'Shee, Spring, Walsh de Serrant (Theobald), Walsh de Serrant (Louis), O'Heguerty, Wall and one student in the Scots section. Twenty-five external students followed the philosophy course in Latin and they debated in public every fortnight.

By February 1808, the college had a complete list[16] of professors drawn from Ireland, England and France. Walsh justified the presence of Frenchmen on the staff by referring to de la Hogue, last chancellor of the university of Paris, and Anglade, professor of philosophy, who taught in Maynooth from its inception. Reciprocity in education had always been a feature of the liaison between Ireland and France since the time of Charlemagne. The presence of French students would facilitate the exchange of languages. The 62-year-old Walsh headed the list as administrator-general and principal. He was assisted by Dom Henry Parker, former prior of the Benedictine house of St Edmond in rue St Jacques, who filled the roles of bursar and professor of English. The treasurer was MacNulty from Dublin and a former Irish Capuchin from Bar-sur-Aube. Abbé Burnier Fontanel was prefect of studies and professor of philosophy and mathematics. The humanities section comprised mostly French priests as well as a professor from Lycée Napoléon. All the professors were priests with the exception of the professor of Greek who was a layman. Michaël Gannon, who had played an active role with the French expeditionary force in Killala was in charge of fifth years. He was a licentiate in theology and his age was given as 63. Two young Irishmen, Joseph and James Kennedy, were employed as doctor and surgeon respectively and resided in the English seminary. They were assisted by Nicolas Carrew(?), an English Benedictine brother, who carried out the duties of nurse.

Parker, MacNulty and Fontanel wrote a joint letter[17] to the minister informing him that education in the college was based on religion without prejudice to the sciences. The number of native students was not considerable at the moment due to the problems caused by the war. However, they claimed that students of Irish origin were increasing daily and together with natives of the United Kingdom they now made up almost one half of the total. They enclosed an extract from *Journal de Paris* which stated that both the families and the public were happy with the results obtained in the examinations at the end of 1807. The administrator and his cooperators worked assiduously and in harmony for the good of religion and society. 'Religious services' they observed, 'are celebrated worthily, even majestically in one of the most beautiful chapels of the capital.' Students from Ireland and Britain would be received 'with open arms' whenever they came. In the meantime, the will of the founders would be observed by admitting catholics from all nations. They supported strongly Walsh's contention that the British government had endowed the college of Maynooth expressly to lure catholics away from France, adding that Maynooth's future depended on the Paris college for two reasons. Once the British government had achieved its purpose of stopping the flow of students to Paris, 'they will not hesitate to suppress Maynooth'. Secondly, Maynooth cannot be erected into a university as it would require an agreement between the Pope and the king of England as head of the Anglican church. As a result the Catholic bishops will be obliged to send 'the élite of their ecclesiastical students to the Imperial University of Paris'.

In spite of his preoccupations Walsh managed to find time officially to request the municipality to change the name of the street where the Irish college stood. His petition was granted and by a prefectoral decree of 6 February 1807 rue du Cheval Vert became rue des Irlandais.[18] In August of that year Walsh was approached by someone who by now had almost become a ghost from the past, the former superior Charles Kearney, who had been cut off without a penny by the bureau in 1801 and since then had managed to eke out a frugal existence by giving lessons in English. He may not have been all that seriously deprived as Lally Tollendal stated[19] that he had 'found consolation in the generous goodness of the Queen of Holland.' She was Hortense de Beauharnais, Josephine's beautiful daughter, who had married Louis Bonaparte and had accompanied him to Holland where he had become king in 1806. Kearney could not have been benefiting very long, if at all, from her generosity. He now wrote a letter[20] to Walsh, oddly enough in French, asking him to use his influence to obtain a pension. Walsh was about to present a financial statement to the bureau. 'Your report will contribute, according to its tone,' Kearney told him, 'either to strengthen or diminish the very unfavourable impression already entertained regarding me.' He still claimed that he had been judged unfairly. The bureau only had access to the book of receipts. The book of expenditure was a casualty of the revolution as Kearney had 'neither register nor receipts nor note of hand.' To have condemned him for not having kept an account of his expenditures is to have forgotten the events which deprived him of these documents. 'It is to accuse one who has suffered shipwreck,' he said, 'of not having preserved what he possessed when the weather was calm and serene.'

In time, Kearney had hoped to make good the deficit:

> That time has come and has led you to become the instrument of that interesting operation. The house has risen from its ruins. The establishment has been placed on a firm basis. I rejoice in the good I see done, though I have not been able to share in it. But I ask not to remain buried beneath the old ruins, which it has been impossible to avoid, and not to be obliged to live the victim of unjust accusation. This would be to treat me with greater severity after the revolution than did, at its commencement, the revolutionary committee, which pursued me with a violence of which there ought not to be another example.

All Kearney now pleaded for in his retirement was a modest pension. 'Nowhere could I have so strong a claim to a pension' he concluded his letter, 'as from the funds of a house of which I was the head for several years, and of which I am today, perhaps, the oldest pupil.' Walsh remained deaf to Kearney's plea and he was obliged to wait some years more before his claim to a pension was sympathetically received.

NOTES

1. A.N. H 3 2561A, Mar. 1811.
2. D.D.A. 121/9, 24 Jan. 1807.
3. I.C.P. 14A, 30 Dec. 1814.
4. A.N. F 17 14764, 6 Feb. 1807.
5. Ibid. 5 Mar. 1807.
6. A.N. F 19 6237A, 22 June 1806.
7. A.N. F 19 6237A, 25 Mar. 1807.
8. A.N. F 19 6237C, 4 May 1807.
9. A.N. F 17 14764, 14 May 1807.
19. A.N. F 19 6237A, 15 July 1807.
11. Ibid. 4 Aug. 1807.
12. Ibid. 18 Feb. 1808.
13. I.C.P. 23B, 7 Jan. 1866. qtd. Boyle, 'The Abbe John Baptist Walsh D.D.', I.E.R. XVIII (July-Dec. 1905) pp441-3.
14. Byrne, op. cit. 3. pp261-2.
15. Ibid. 3. p193.
16. A.N. F 17 14764, *Etat de Situation*, 19 Feb. 1808.
17. Ibid. 4 Feb. 1808.
18. Cf. I.C.P. 3W2, 9 Aug. 1807.
19. A.N. H 3 2561A, Mar. 1811, p32.
20. I.C.P. 3W1, 5 Aug. 1807, qtd. Boyle, I.E.R. (May 1908) pp461-5.

15
Decline and Fall of an Accountant

Whatever wrong M. Walsh may have done, I have never concealed the fact that it was largely due to his care, skill, and courage that the property composing the British establishment today was preserved.

–Minister of Interior to Napoleon, 13 September 1809.

Little is known of the activities of Richard Ferris after his release in April 1800 from prison in Paris. One thing is certain: he was not wasting his time, which he spent renewing old acquaintances among the returned *émigrés* and cultivating new ones among the rising stars of the Napoleonic administration. He succeeded so well that by 1806 'powerful men in government were loudly recommending M. Ferris as a great administrator.'[1] They went so far as to suggest to Walsh that Ferris would be a very useful acquisition on the *bureau de surveillance*. In this context Ferris' name was coupled with that of another former spy and priest, Nicholas Madgett, who had also returned to France and by 1805 was ministering as curé in Civray, a town in Vienne. It was an odd coupling, considering that Madgett had ten years earlier sent in reports to Dublin Castle denouncing Ferris. Nothing prevented the accession of Ferris and Madgett to the bureau except the presence there of the aged Cardinal du Belloy who acted as president and 'would never consent to sit beside two such notorious ex-priests'.[2] In June 1808 the cardinal died, aged 99, and shortly afterwards Ferris and Madgett were co-opted to the bureau. No sooner installed they began to undermine Walsh to such an extent that one of the French members described Ferris as behaving like a 'prosecuting attorney'.[3] According to Walsh they were intent on settling old scores, as they were 'the principal dancers' in the student takeover of 1792 which Walsh had successfully overturned.

The threat posed by the presence of Ferris and Madgett was overshadowed by the larger one of a new takeover, this time by the

Imperial University which Napoleon had established to replace the Sorbonne, suppressed in 1793. Soon the new university began to cast covetous eyes in the direction of the united colleges in the Irish college. Using the pretext that most of the students there were French, it sought to have it placed under its jurisdiction. Walsh moved swiftly to counteract this threat, proposing[4] to the bureau that Fontanel be given a year from 1 April to wind up his boarding school in the Irish college. He would be given preference for the post of professor of philosophy and later of theology as soon as such a class was formed. On 16 August Fontanel agreed to abandon his boarding school and remain on in the college as prefect of studies. The bureau agreed to pay him an indemnity of 16,000 francs.

On 6 April 1808 Walsh wrote directly to the grand-master himself outlining a somewhat different proposal for linking the college to the university. He offered him what he described as 'the widow's mite': the Irish college as a provisional location for the university's faculty of theology. Pointing to its central location close to the Panthéon and its fine large hall 'almost comparable to that of the former Sorbonne', he added that its 'beautiful chapel could be used for the assembly of the doctors each *prima mensis*.' On 14 April[6] the grand-master sent a note to Walsh agreeing to meet him for discussion and the following day Walsh sent him a *mémoire* which could be discussed at their meeting. Apologising for his presumption in meddling in the affairs of the Imperial University, Walsh explained that his 'age and character freed him from all personal ambition' and as a doctor of theology of the former faculty of the university of Paris he was entitled to be concerned with 'sound doctrine.' It was, indeed, his duty as administrator of an establishment catering for the needs of catholics of the United Kingdom who had now lost their former colleges in Italy, Spain and Portugal as well. The grand-master decided to postpone his meeting with Walsh and there were no further developments during the rest of the summer.

By August Walsh decided to go over the head of the grand-master. He wrote directly to the Empress Josephine.[7] 'Ireland has the honour to be the land of your ancestors;' Walsh informed her, 'she confidently claims your majesty's protection.' He informed her that the grand-master of the Imperial University was under great pressure from several interested parties to seize the Irish college. Such a measure would violate the sacred rights of property and hospitality and alienate several million catholics in England, Ireland and Scotland from the present government. Two days later he wrote almost an identical letter[8] to Napoleon himself. Referring to his establishment as a 'seminary-college' he informed the emperor that seven ecclesiastics had recently arrived to continue their theological studies. He reminded him that article 42 of his decree gave the bishops of the three nations power to send such students and that article 47 made the rule of the archiepiscopal seminary obligatory for the establishment.

Writing at the same time to the Minister of Religion,[9] Walsh underlined the fact that his house was a seminary and as such fell more properly within the competence of the ministry than that of the grand-master. In fact, the Irish college bore the title inscribed in marble *Seminarium Clericorum Hibernorum*. All the foundations were dedicated to the teaching of philosophy and theology. Moral theology, sermons and controversies were always taught through the medium of the English, Irish and Scots languages. Bishops and heads of families with claims to the foundations would only confide their subjects to their compatriots who were familiar with their 'temperaments, customs, language and spiritual direction.' Walsh pointed out to the minister that had his ministry existed when the definitive decree regulating the college had been promulgated, it would have been confided to his ministry rather than to that of Interior. This was to become a familiar theme in the future correspondence of Walsh. He had reverted to 'chanting the Psalms' as Lally Tollendal put it in his confidential report[10] to the Minister of the Interior, adding rather acidly that 'no-one other than he could move more easily and with less embarrassment from black to white and back again to black.' In fact, by invoking the intervention of the Minister of Religion, Walsh was 'stirring it up' in inter-ministerial politics. It was a good tactical move—at least in the short-term. The minister wrote to Napoleon supporting Walsh's views. On 10 September, Walsh was again in communication with him,[11] raising the matter of the oath of fidelity to the reigning dynasty required from all the students and professors in the Imperial University and pointing out that foreigners could not take this oath as it would deprive them of their civil rights in their home countries.

In spite of all his efforts the Irish college property was handed over to the administratorship of the university by a decree of Napoleon on 16 September 1808. Notwithstanding, Walsh continued the fight, writing again to the minister on 13 October.[12] The grand-master had placed a petition before the council of state demanding the annexation of the Irish college while maintaining the original Irish foundations in the new university. Walsh argued that the Irish college itself was the chief foundation, adding 'If one touches the root, the tree necessarily perishes.' Together with Parker and MacNulty and six other Irish priest-students he sent a memorandum[13] to the council of state suggesting that the proposed annexation of the college to the university was contrary to right principles and sound politics. It would estrange several million catholics in the United Kingdom from Napoleonic France and assist the attempts of the British government to close the Irish college. It was unthinkable that Napoleon's government would consider destroying a college which had escaped the revolution itself. Foreign students could not be required to take the oath of fidelity to the ruling dynasty which was obligatory on the French. 'However unreasonable the refusal of the British government to grant emancipation to Irish catholics may be,' they observed, 'nevertheless the administrator and professors of the Paris establishment will not diverge from pure principles and will constantly teach that catholic subjects of the United Kingdom owe allegiance and fidelity to a protestant prince as long as Providence keeps him on the throne.' They were careful however to point out that they would inculcate in their students obedience and eternal gratitude to the host country and its government 'which authorises and protects its establishment.' Besides, the college was in reality a seminary which bore the same relationship to the university as foreign mission congregations, over whom the grand-master had no jurisdiction.

The question was discussed at the council of state on 15 November.[14] It was decided to replace the bureau by the grand-master and council of the Imperial University. The students were to be subject to French educational regulations. The administrator, professors and other employees would be admitted as members of the university by simply applying. The college was to remain subject to the Minister of the Interior. The decision was approved by Napoleon in Madrid on 11 December 1808.[15] Still Walsh persisted. He wrote to the vicars-general[16] of the diocese of Paris urging them to press the claim of the archbishop to a place on the supervisory body of the college which he had had from time immemorial. They complied with his request and wrote to the grand-master on 23 January 1809.[17] They sketched out for him the 'former connections' which existed between the Irish college and the Archbishop of Paris which had ceased at the beginning of the revolution but had been restored by the imperial decree in 1805. This rapprochement would have enormous prestige in the eyes of the clergy of the United Kingdom.

Walsh was accused by Ferris and Madgett of engineering the annexation by the university expressly to get rid of the bureau because they were now members. They launched their attack at a stormy meeting of the bureau early in December. Walsh was staunchly defended by the French members and particularly by the acting president, M. Séguier, who informed them that the bureau was now only provisional pending the takeover by the Imperial University on 1 January. Walsh wrote immediately to the grand-master. He advised him to open a secret file because it would deal with matters 'ecclesiastical, foreign and sometimes political'. Explaining that ordinarily the bureau consisted of five members, he added: 'I do not know by what means and for what purpose two priests, natives of Ireland, were recently added to it.'[18] He informed him that Ferris and Madgett had declared their intention to ask the prefect of the Seine to convoke an extraordinary meeting of the bureau for reasons unknown to him.

Writing again a week later[19] Walsh informed the grand-master that he was 'perfectly calm in the face of the rage shown by certain members of the bureau' because he felt assured of the protection of the grand-master against their malevolence. His adversaries had no other resource than to impose, if that were possible, upon the goodwill of the sovereign. He understood that they were planning this at the regular meetings they held at the préfecture. As an academic, Walsh concluded his letter, 'he would yield to no-one in faithfully observing the university laws'. On 5 January 1809 the bureau ceased to function. Three members signed the act of cessation but Ferris and Madgett declined, preferring to retire from the meeting. Walsh urged the grand-master to accelerate the inauguration of the new supervisory body, obviously fearing the machinations of Ferris and Madgett more than he was prepared to admit in public. The tone of his letter is uncharacteristically ingratiating. 'I will always conform' he assured the grand-master, 'with truly sacerdotal docility.'

The grand-master was to suffer the brunt of Walsh's docility when he began by delegating his functions to his vice-rector, M. Emery, on 24 January.[20] Walsh was not going to be fobbed off with underlings and informed the grand-master that the decree of 11 December required the presence of the grand-master and two of his council on the supervisory body. When the grand-master and his council issued a decree regulating the administration of the college, Walsh immediately drew attention to a number of errors they had made. Article 4 stated that the administrator-general and the professors would remain provisionally in office. Walsh replied by quoting article 3 of the imperial decree of 1805 which stated that 'in case of death, resignation or dismissal he could only be replaced by His Majesty.' He also pointed out that the *bureau de surveillance* was not charged with the administration of the college, as the grand-master's decree implied, but only with supervising the administrator. Finally, he invited the grand-master to retain the title of Seminary-College which was its official designation in the imperial decree. The grand-master, like a wayward pupil, must have felt thoroughly rebuked. But Walsh was shooting himself in the foot. He was going to need all the allies he could find.

When the bureau met in the Irish college on 9 February a letter was read from the Minister of the Interior requesting them to nominate three commissioners to examine Walsh's accounts for the years 1807 and 1808. On 20 April the prefect of the Seine, president of the bureau informed[21] the Minister that Walsh had just deposited his accounts, that commissioners had been chosen from among the members of the bureau and that they were proceeding without delay to examine them. Ferris and Madgett, to Walsh's obvious chagrin were among those chosen. A month later the prefect announced that Walsh's accounts were not properly presented and in fact were 'disgraceful, defective and without receipts.'[22] Furthermore, he stated that Walsh seemed disinclined to accept the jurisdiction of the bureau 'because he knew that the members had acquired, by means of the two Irishmen who had been co-opted, information hitherto unknown which would necessarily lead the bureau to judge his recent accounts with greater severity and might perhaps demand a revision of his earlier accounts.' After a detailed report from his department the minister instructed the bureau[23] to examine all Walsh's accounts since 1801.[24] At first Walsh was willing to comply but on 22 July the prefect informed the minister that Walsh had protested against this decision and 'that he had declared that the revision of his former accounts would never be executed because no authority had the right to make such a revision'.[25] Former pupils of the Irish college presented a petition[26] on 15 July, denouncing the administration of Walsh. 'The head of that establishment,' they declared, 'formerly so renowned for its studies, discipline and high standards, is unfit to direct it.' They proposed the rather drastic solution of suppressing the college, leasing the building and creating within the university a bureau for foreign establishments, financed from the proceeds. The students would fare better dispersed in the *lycées* of the Department and the ecclesiastics in the diocesan seminary.

Walsh deposited his accounts for 1807 and 1808 with a solicitor, refusing to hand them over to the bureau. He had finally overstepped the mark. Ferris and Madgett had manoeuvred him into a corner from which he could not extract himself. The prefeet called in the name of the bureau for Walsh's suspension.[27] After a further report from his department, the interim minister suspended Walsh on 28 July, replacing him with Henry Parker, the English Benedictine, as provisional administrator.[28] He informed Napoleon,[29] claiming that Walsh had behaved with such 'discourtesy and insubordination' that he felt it his duty to suspend him. He told the emperor that Walsh no longer possessed 'either the bearing or strength of character which should distinguish the superior of an educational establishment and yielding unrestrainedly to his natural vivacity he had compromised the dignity of his establishment by behaving in a manner which he would not have done had he listened to the voice of reason.'

The minister submitted to Napoleon a draft decree proposing Richard Ferris as the new administrator-general. He was the only candidate who possessed the requisite qualifications. 'I do not propose to your majesty' he added 'to employ Walsh, the present administrator, in the new administration, whose functions will cease inasmuch as serious suspicions are cast on his administration and these are confirmed by his refusal to render his accounts in spite of repeated injunctions over several months.' Because of his advanced age he proposed to Napoleon that he should be accorded a pension from the college revenues as soon as he had rendered his accounts. The minister also informed[30] the grandmaster of Walsh's suspension, instructing him to place seals, if necessary, on all Walsh's papers and documents. For Walsh it brought to an ignominious close a 22-year tenure of office as head of the Irish college in Paris. 'It was an unexpected blow, I must admit' Walsh commented, 'to find myself expelled from the establishment which owed its existence to me.'[31]

Bowed but not broken, Walsh declared that he did not deserve such treatment, and 'convinced that he could justify his administration before judges free from passion and prejudice, he appealed to the justice of the new minister nominated by His Majesty the emperor'. He now resorted to his second line of attack and here he found an unexpected ally. The grand-master and his council met on 4 August. The Irish college was discussed and it was decided that the function of the Imperial University should be to supervise the education in the college and should divest itself of any responsibility for its general administration. On 23 August Dom Parker, the provisional administrator and Abbé Fontanel had a meeting with the grand-master. Here, the latter expressed the view that a seminary ought to be placed under the direction of the Minister of Religion or under the Minister of Foreign Affairs as it was a foreign establishment. Consequently, he was sending the decree of 11 December back to the Minister of the Interior for clarification.[32]

Walsh immediately wrote to the vicars-general[33] pointing out that now was the opportunity to press the claims of the Archbishop of Paris to a say in the affairs of the Irish seminary. He even presented them with a draft of the letter to be sent to the Minister of Religion. Calling the attention of the minister to 'the sad state of the diocese which would soon lack ministers for the sacraments unless the ministry set up seminaries for the education of the young called to the ecclesiastical state,' it suggested that the Irish college would suit admirably for this purpose. Having consulted people attached to the United Kingdom mission, the latter assured him that the Irish college could be provisionally used for this purpose. Such a seminary should be placed under the Minister of Religion with the Archbishop of Paris presiding over the bureau which should consist of ecclesiastics.

Walsh himself bombarded the minister with a series of letters[34] informing him that if his ministry had existed in 1805 the Irish college would have been assigned to his direction and urging him to reclaim the principal direction of what in fact was a seminary. This would involve no charge on his ministry as it had sufficient funds to support 60 students at least. Furthermore, if the British government refused to allow its subjects to come to the college it would be proper that the minister have control of the college and its revenues. Three days later he sent an historical sketch of the college to the secretary of the Department proving that it was always an ecclesiastical institution and therefore belonged properly within the competence of the Minister of Religion. He pointed out that the Archbishop of Paris had always acted as president of the supervisory body. The prefect of the Department, 'who had so many pretentions,' should not be on the bureau, which should consist of ecclesiastics and laity all nominated by the minister. The latter was taking Walsh's bait and wrote on 9 October asking him for further information. Walsh replied urging the minister to act swiftly 'as time was pressing' and a new Minister of the Interior was about to be nominated.[35]

While Walsh was busily trying to strip the Minister of the Interior of his authority over the Irish college, the latter was pleading with Napoleon for a generous pension for Walsh.[36] Even in defeat Walsh commanded respect. 'Whatever wrong M. Walsh may have done' the minister wrote to Napoleon, 'I have never concealed the fact that it was largely due to his care, skill and courage that the property composing the British establishment today was preserved and for this reason he has a right to some gratitude.' And he added in his defence:

> The peculiar circumstances in which M. Walsh found himself during the revolutionary storms, the fact that he was a foreigner and compelled to hide frequently, not allowing him to keep his papers in order or fulfil formalities which he is now accused of having neglected and that he must have lost documents which makes it impossible for him now to justify certain transactions.'

The minister positively warmed to his subject:

> If I were permitted to express my private opinion I would represent to Your Majesty that M. Walsh deserves your indulgence, both on account of the real services he has rendered to the colleges by preserving a portion of their property and because he found himself by force of revolutionary circumstances, almost outside common law and often unable to operate according to the rules. Walsh may have been guilty of administering too independently and courageously, thinking that he was acting on his own and that he would never be called upon to give an account of his actions. Still, from this flawed principle good results have come and it is only right to provide for the support of the man to whom these fortunate results are due.

It was an eloquent plea from the minister who went on to propose a pension of 2,000 francs per annum and release from the debts he had left to the college. 'His advanced age' he argued, 'would not permit him to live long enough to clear the debt.'

Walsh was then in his 68th year. But the old warrior had still plenty of fight left in him and was not yet prepared to accept retirement. Through his influential friend, Madame de Montesquieu,[37] he had a memorandum presented to the Minister of the Interior in which he presented himself as the victim of persecution at the hands of the prefect of the Seine acting in concert with Ferris and Madgett. The minister asked his Department to prepare a report. It was on his desk on 24 October,[38] was highly critical of Walsh and gives rise to the suspicion that the all-pervading influence of Ferris may have reached its author. In fact, Ferris and Madgett had sent in a memorandum to the minister accusing Walsh of a long list of improprieties and claiming that he had been lining his pockets for years from the college funds. Walsh's refusal to present his accounts gave credence to these serious accusations. The chief of the department concluded that Walsh deserved to be dismissed rather than merely suspended. He proposed that the minister send a letter to the prefect of the Seine giving Walsh a week to comply and submit his accounts. Failing this he should be taken to court.

The minister decided to follow a less drastic procedure. He summoned Walsh and persuaded him to purge his contumacy by apologising in person to the prefect of the Seine. Walsh wrote to the prefect[39] asking for a meeting to apologise for the 'hastiness' of his remarks in his reply of 1 September. He was now prepared to eat humble pie, signing off his letter by declaring that he had 'the most ardent desire to merit the good grace of the first magistrate of the capital.' He sent a copy of this letter to the Minister of the Interior assuring him also that he would try 'to merit his continuing kindness'. Nothing now remained to prevent Napoleon accepting the recommendation of the minister. Accordingly, on 15 November, 'taking account of his age and length of service ... and wishing to be indulgent towards him' the emperor decreed[40] that 'M. Walsh is exempt from the debt of 31,635 francs laid to his charge. He will cease to function as administrator, but will remain on in the college, where all his needs will be met, in consideration of his services.'

It was an honourable discharge. But the old dog refused to lie down. 'I accept [it] calmly and with resignation' he later wrote[41] about his suspension, 'since 31 July 1809, without, however, ever ceasing for a instant, to watch over the interests of the establishment.' Recalling his contemptuous rejection of the seductive offers made him by the Prytanée in 1798, Walsh declared that his sentiments in this regard would never change. 'As soon as peace dawns' he wrote,[42] 'I will hasten to invite the insular bishops to designate a successor worthy of their confidence. I will yield my place to him and help him with my advice, seasoned by over

30 years of experience. ... For as long as I have the will and strength to be useful to religion and my fatherland, I will continue ...' But peace was still a long way off.

NOTES

1. I.C.P. 3L.
2. Ibid.
3. Ibid.
4. A.N. F 17 14764.
5. A.N. F 17 2500.
6. Ibid.
7. A.N. F 17 2500, 20 Aug. 1808.
8. Ibid, 22 Aug. 1808.
9. A.N. F 19 6237C, 24 Aug. 1808.
10. A.N. H 3 2561A, Mar. 1811.
11. A.N. F 19 6237C, 10 Sept. 1808.
12. Ibid. 13 Oct. 1808.
13. A.N. F 17 14761, 18 Oct. 1808.
14. A.N. F 19 6237A, 15 Nov. 1808.
15. A.N. F 17 2500.
16. A.N. F 19 6237C, 26 Nov. 1808.
17. A.N. F 17 2500, 23 Jan. 1809.
18. Ibid. 7 Dec. 1808.
19. A.N. F 17 2500, 14 Dec. 1808.
20. Ibid. 24 Jan. 1809.
21. A.N. F 19 6237C, 24 Oct. 1809.
22. Ibid.
23. A.N. F 19 6237C, 24 Oct. 1809.
24. Ibid.
25. Ibid.
26. A.N. F 17 2500, 15 July 1809.
27. A.N. F 19 6237C, 24 Oct. 1809.
28. Ibid.
29. Ibid, nd.
30. A.N. F 17 2500, 28 July 1809.
31. I.C.P. 14A, 30 Dec. 1814.
32. A.N. F 17 2500, 4 Aug. 1809.
33. A.N. F 19 6237C, 27 Aug. 1809.
34. Ibid. 19 & 22 Sept. 1809.
35. Ibid. 12 Oct. 1809.
36. Ibid. 13 Sept. 1809.
37. A.N. F 19 6237C, 24 Oct. 1809.
38. Ibid.
39. A.N. H 3 2561A, 31 Oct. 1809.
40. A.N. F 19 6237A Report, Jan. 1812.
41. Ibid. Walsh to Cardinal Maury, 8 Feb. 1812.
42. Ibid. p43.

16
Roman Exodus

I would heartily regret that his majesty might notice the lack of agreement in this matter between two of his ministers.

–Minister of Interior, 31 July 1810.

In the meantime, while the suspended Walsh struggled to find his way out of limbo, Napoleon's successful military campaigns were having their own repercussions on the Irish college. On the last day of November 1807 General Junot and the French army occupied Lisbon. This marked the beginning of the Peninsular War which was to continue until June 1813 and become the Achilles' heel of Napoleon's military endeavours. Arthur Wellesley left his post as Chief Secretary of Ireland to take command of the British expeditionary force to the Spanish peninsula. Offers were made to Dr Crotty, the rector of the Irish college in Lisbon, of a lucrative post in Paris, but Crotty, mindful of the stern warning of the Irish bishops, prudently declined 'that insidious offer'. In the autumn of 1807 General Clarke became Minister of War and immediately issued orders for the Irish legion to take part in the Spanish campaign. Walsh suggested to the government that advantage could be taken of their presence there to entice the students in the Irish colleges to defect to Paris. Some of them at least were prepared to run the gauntlet of episcopal interdictions, as Walsh reported to Napoleon in August 1808 the arrival of seven ecclesiastics from Spain.[1]

Generally, however, the Irish student body and their superiors in the Spanish college, whether from political or pastoral considerations, tended to favour the invading British army which had a large corps of Irish conscripts and their numerous camp followers. Whatever their reasons, Miles Byrne, who fought with the Irish legion in Spain was greatly disappointed and in particular with the conduct of Dr Patrick Curtis, the rector of the Irish college in Salamanca. He even went as far as to suggest that Curtis betrayed a detachment of the Irish legion as a result of which they were ambushed and made prisoners-of-war. The Duke of Wellington was reputed to have offered Curtis a protestant bishopric as a reward for his services and was somewhat puzzled when he declined the offer. Matters however were soon put right when Armagh became available and Curtis was promoted to the catholic primacy.

Byrne had met Curtis in Salamanca in 1811 when he was 'a tall and portly man'. Seven years later he met him again in the Irish college in Paris when he was Archbishop of Armagh and described him as 'quite bent and broken' as if it was divine retribution. 'It was said of him' he commented, 'that he had rendered great service to the Duke of Wellington in Spain, and that he had gained for himself a reputation not quite in accordance with the dignity of an "Irish" catholic clergyman.'[2] The French expelled the Irish students and occupied their college in Salamanca as a hospital.[3] In the see-saw struggle of the war Curtis was driven out three times from Salamanca by the French. When Sir John Moore eventually occupied the town with a British contingent the Irish students immediately offered their services as interpreters. When Wellington won the battle of Salamanca on 22 July 1812 no further recruitment of Irish students there for Paris was possible.

Unlike Spain, the war on the Italian front produced a potential windfall both of students and properties for the Irish college in Paris. The French army entered Rome in February 1808 and immediately planted the tree of liberty in the capital, the commander-in-chief, General Berthier, declaring Rome a free and independent republic. On 16 February he issued an edict ordering the property of the church to be sold within the space of two months. In March, Fr Connolly, the Dominican prior of San Clemente, wrote to Bishop Plunkett of Meath, informing him that the French had seized and sold all belonging to the English and Scots colleges, adding: 'Commissioners were to take possession today of the Irish College and all its property. I suppose they will do the same at the Irish convents of St Mathew's, St Isidore's and St Clement's.'[4] When France annexed the papal states in May 1809 events moved rapidly. On 11 June, Pius VII excommunicated Napoleon and in July the Pope was arrested and taken to Savona. The college of cardinals was ordered to quit Rome and betake itself to Paris. The Irish Dominican, Luke

Concannon, by now consecrated first bishop of New York, wrote to Walsh, Parker and MacNulty to provide accommodation for Cardinal di Pietro, the prefect of Propaganda. The cardinal had expressed a wish to lodge in the Irish college 'from a liking of Irish hospitality' and Concannon assured Walsh and company, 'that the college will lose nothing by his boarding as His Eminence is generously and sufficiently opulent.'[5]

On 9 May 1810 the French consulate in Rome decreed that 'all ecclesiastics from France, Italy, Naples, Germany, England, Ireland, Denmark and Holland shall be sent back to their own countries.'[6] Two weeks later Irish, English and Scots clerics were ordered to repair to Paris.[7] On 4 June it was established that they were all indigent and they were accorded 150 francs each. Two difficulties were adverted to: the length of the journey for the elderly and how they were to subsist once they had arrived. In Rome they had become attached to certain churches and taught English to children which provided them with a modest income. 'Transported suddenly to a new country' the master of requests observed, 'they risked dying of poverty'.[8] He proposed therefore to raise the sum granted to 250 francs and that the Minister of Religion be requested to find occupations for them when they arrived in Paris. This should not entail great expenditure as up to that point he had discovered no English or Scots ecclesiastics and only four Irish. In all 788 religious and priests were deported from Rome. Some nationalities fared even worse than the Irish. 'What a very moving sight passed through here yesterday,' O'Ryan, a medical student wrote from Verdun to Parker in the Irish college. 'A hundred and ten Spanish clergymen and among them were two bishops and a hermit aged 109 years who had not seen, for eighteen years before he was taken, a human being. The novelty of the spectacle excited the curiosity of the inhabitants as well as that of the English to go out of town to meet them ...'[9]

On 13 June the Minister of Religion wrote[10] to Napoleon suggesting housing the British clergy in the Irish college until a more definitive solution was found. He had visited the college and found there 50 empty cells 'where as a sort of a depot they could put those who come from Rome.' By 25 June the first batch had left Rome, equipped with passports from the director-general of the police and 150 francs each. Nine of them reached Turin on 6 July in a state 'of absolute destitution'[11] and approached General Alexander Lamoth, prefect of the Po department, for help. He arranged for the mayor of Turin to give 30 francs each to two of them and sent the others to the local authorities for similar help. He wrote immediately to the minister in Paris seeking the reimbursement of his 60 francs, explaining that the 150 francs given to the Irish priests in Rome 'was scarcely sufficient to exchange their monks' habits for secular dress.' They were reduced to selling some of their personal belongings to pay their way. This Irish party, which included one Augustinian, two Dominicans and six Franciscans, arrived in Paris on 15 July and declared to Parker that their journey had cost more than 300 francs. He wrote to the minister for permission to withdraw 1,550 francs which was needed to buy them clothes.[12]

A number were allowed to stay on provisionally in Rome either because of bad health or simply to wind up their affairs. These included Paul MacPherson, rector of the Scots college 'which no longer existed' and agent of the Scottish church and Joseph Taylor OP, from Castlepollard, prior of the Irish Dominican convent of San Clemente. Another Irish Dominican, 58-year-old John Connolly of Drogheda, the agent of the Irish church, also remained. He was soon to replace Luke Concannon as bishop of New York.[13] James MacCormack OFM of Dublin and William Keating of Limerick, superiors of St Isidore's and St Mathew's respectively, also remained behind to tidy up the affairs of their convents. The Franciscan Richard Hayes of Dublin left Rome but never arrived in Paris.

A major row flared up between the Minister of the Interior and the Minister of Religion over the latter's role in this affair.[14] The former had written to his colleague on 28 June informing him that the 'British colleges in the new as well as the old France fall exclusively within my competence.' He asked him to forward as soon as possible all the information he had received from Rome on the British establishments there and urged him not to make any decision on the Roman priests staying in the Irish college without consulting him. The Minister of Religion did not reply, though early in July he had written to the grand-master of the university informing him of the arrival of 15 priests who were going to stay in the Irish college 'and be fed at the expense of that establishment.' Hearing of this indirectly, the Minister of the Interior dashed off a sharp rebuke to his ministerial colleague reminding him that 'any hastiness could compromise the execution of previous orders of His Majesty himself.' He repeated his request to have all the information forwarded to him, adding: 'I have to make a report to the emperor and I would heartily regret that His Majesty might notice the lack of agreement in this matter between two of his ministers.'

Far from yielding, the Minister of Religion took the opportunity of sending his colleague a memorandum[15] on the college which he had just received from Parker. In all likelihood it had been dictated by Walsh and was not calculated to smooth the ruffled feathers of the Minister of the Interior. It argued that everything relating to the Irish college proved that it was 'a seminary in the proper sense of the word' and as such it ought to come within the competency of the Minister of Religion. 'His Majesty the emperor' it observed, 'by charging the present minister to place in the college 15 ecclesiastics who had come from Rome, had given His Excellency a strong pretext to reclaim his rights.' For 18 months the Minister of the Interior and the grand-master had been unable to agree about their respective competencies. And it added rather ingenuously: 'It is very probable that both of them would voluntarily abandon their claims to the Minister of Religion if His Excellency was prepared to stake his claim.'

The minister went even further. On 15 August he drew up a set of rules[16] to be followed by the newly arrived priests. They were not allowed to leave the college without special permission and obliged to conform to the rules of the house. The vicar-general of the diocese of Paris was charged with the execution of this ministerial decree and in case of necessity, the police commissioner of the Observatory section. At the end of that month, Parker wrote[17] to the minister proposing Walsh as the superior of the seminary 'while waiting to return to office as administrator-general.' He went on to observe that as 'it would be extremely difficult if not impossible to maintain two sets of rules in the same house, one for ecclesiastics and the other for the young students' he proposed that the Collège des Lombards be once more revived for its original purpose of housing ecclesiastics.

By 15 September there were 16 Romans in the Irish college: one Englishman, twelve Irish and three Maltese. It had been decided that 'Greeks, Armenians, Asians, Africans and Maltese, who cannot return to their own countries, are also to be sent to Paris'. Parker wrote to the Minister of Religion on 11 September objecting to the entry of three Maltese and threatening to invoke the support of the Minister of the Interior.[18] This continued to be a sore point with the Irish administration who regarded it as a misappropriation of Irish funds. Two years later there were still four Maltese priests in the college as well as an Albanian. The latter was asked to leave when he threatened one of the students with a knife. In all 24 priests were housed in the Irish college. Five Irish Franciscans from Dublin wrote[19] almost immediately on their arrival to the minister seeking passports to return to Ireland suggesting that it was possible to obtain a passage from Morlaix where conferences were being held to arrange the exchange of prisoners-of-war. Within a year, out of a total of 24, 13 had left for Ireland, receiving 600 francs each from college funds to pay their passage.

Paul MacPherson, the agent of the Scottish church secured a passport and returned home. Here he reported to the Scottish and English vicars-general on the state of their properties abroad. Through the mediation of the Scottish and English ecclesiastical authorities he also received instructions from the Irish bishops, and was asked to return to Paris and advise the French government of their wishes. On 14 July 1812 he wrote[20] to the Minister of Religion informing him that he had been instructed to act in concert with Walsh and that they were to solicit the continuing protection of His Majesty the emperor for their institutions on the continent. While admitting that Irish catholics had recently obtained 'some relief as regards their civil rights' it was certain that restrictions on their religion would be tightened in order 'to preserve for protestantism its local ascendancy.' He cited the fact that the chancellor of the University of Dublin and the provost of Trinity College had arrogated to themselves the right of visitation of Maynooth in order to introduce changes there 'to the disgust of its president and professors.' In fact the government was planning to amalgamate it with Trinity, 'under the specious pretext of fraternising with their fellow-citizens.' All this was a preamble to demonstrating that the Paris establishment was 'of the greatest importance for the insular catholics'. Its importance was enhanced by the fact that it was 'within reach of the greatest university on the continent and because the city of Paris has been declared as the residence of the Holy Father.'

MacPherson eventually reached the point of his petition. The Irish and British bishops requested to have their institutions in Rome amalgamated with the central establishment in Paris in accordance with Napoleon's constitutive decree, and had instructed MacPherson, who knew perfectly the extent of their properties in Rome, to return there and claim them. The properties had so far only been sequestrated and MacPherson urged the minister to prevent their alienation. He ended his petition by declaring that Walsh and Parker were the only people on the continent authorised to act in the name of the bishops. Then in an obvious reference to Ferris he added that the bishops 'formally excluded any other native of the United Kingdom who sought to meddle in the administration of their properties.'

MacPherson's petition bore the attestation of Walsh and Parker and all the signs of having been authored by Walsh, who added: 'We hope His Excellency the Minister of Religion will listen to our demands in favour of the oppressed catholics, all the more so because all they ask is their own properties.' Furthermore, he suggested that those who bore the expenses should be given the benefits. The Paris college had maintained 24 priests from Rome and was still providing for 11 of them as well as the four former superiors who had remained in Rome.

There were seven Irish and British institutions in Rome: the Irish, English and Scots colleges and four Irish religious houses, San Clemente, San Sixte, St Isidore's and St Mathew's. According to the imperial decree all of them should now be amalgamated with the central establishment in Paris. Their superiors themselves favoured this as it would save them from complete alienation. On 13 January 1812, Taylor OP, Connolly OP and James MacCormack OFM wrote[21] to Parker seeking a pension of 600 francs per annum for themselves from the funds of the Irish college. As superiors, they had remained on in San Clemente and St Isidore's respectively 'in order to prevent these buildings suffering any damage'. They had not been given a pension by the French authorities as they refused to take the oath of allegiance to Napoleon because they 'considered it quite incompatible with the allegiance which we think ourselves always in duty bound to profess to the British empire only.' They asked Parker to approach the Minister of the Interior with the view to obtaining the pension without requiring the oath. If the minister's response was unfavourable they intended to arrive in Paris in May where they were assured that they 'would be kindly received and enabled to live in a decent manner.' The minister sanctioned the payment of 600 francs each from college funds.

Joseph Taylor OP, prior of the Irish Dominicans in San Clemente wrote[22] to the Minister of Religion on 1 September 1812 that for reasons he could not understand the college of San Clemente 'had been despoiled of its properties.' He asked his 'powerful intervention' to have San Clemente restored in accordance with the imperial decree. The minister referred the matter[23] to the prefect in Rome on 24 May 1813. Parker also wrote[24] to the minister in November repeating his demand to have the Roman properties amalgamated with Paris. There was a doubt as to whether the imperial decree applied to later acquisitions and Parker urged that these properties should remain unalienated provisionally until the emperor clarified this point. The minister had already taken steps to prevent their alienation, but the authorities in Rome had sold St Isidore's 'probably because it did not bear the title of college'. Parker feared that the same mistake might be made regarding the other religious houses.

By 1813 most of the Irish priests had returned to Ireland: only five still remained in Paris. The four Irish superiors who had remained in Rome were also maintained from the funds of the Irish college. Parker informed the minister that the funds of the Roman establishments were 'considerable' and it did not seem now that they were going to be united with the Paris establishment. Parker proposed that the remaining priests should be sent back to Rome. In June, the four superiors in Rome themselves wrote[25] to the minister asking him to order that their pensions be paid in Rome just as their compatriots receive theirs in Paris. The petitioners were Paul MacPherson, rector of the Scots college, Joseph Taylor OP, superior of San Clemente, James MacCormack OFM, superior of St Isidore's and John Connolly OP, agent of the Irish bishops.

Nicholas Walsh, an Irish Franciscan, had spent six months in the Irish college. In July 1811, he had tried to return to Ireland but was refused entry. Back in France, his pension was reduced to 500 francs and was stopped altogether in March 1813. He appealed to the minister to have it restored.[26] Simon Lannon, ex-religious from St Bartholomew's convent in Rome, having spent more than a year in the Irish college, had received a passport and left for Ireland. Arriving at Portsmouth in England he was held for a week as a French prisoner and then expelled back to France where he became attached to the parish of Poissy and continued to receive his pension from the college until March 1813. His parish did not provide a living and he was forced in the summer of 1813 to return to Paris and solicit the minister to order the restoration of his pension or allow him to live in the college.[27]

Lannon's petition was forwarded to Ferris, who reminded the minister that he had already sent him a copy of a letter from the bishop of Versailles, complaining that the minister had withdrawn the Irish priests from his diocese. He also pointed out that such priests followed no rule in an establishment containing a hundred students who were subject to the regulations of the *lycée* and would inevitably undermine the discipline. He also drew the minister's attention to the continuing presence in the college of the Maltese priests whom he suggested should be sent to the bishop of Versailles. They were good priests but could not make a living in the parishes of Paris. Because of them Ferris was 'obliged to leave without food several old men, bound down with age and virtue, all of whom were former superiors of our establishments in France and were now without resources after a half-century of service. And all this to provide an opulent life to foreign intruders who had no right to it, and who were in the prime of life.'[28]

NOTES

1. A.N. F 17 2500, 22 Aug. 1808.
2. Byrne, op. cit. 3. p196.
3. McDonald, Wm., I.E.R. XI, 1874, p112 'Irish colleges since the reformation', cf Henchy, Monica, *Studies*, Summer/Autumn 1981, p224, 'The Irish college at Salamanca'.
4. Cogan, op. cit. 3, p219.
5. Douai, Parker Papers, 20 Dec. 1809.
6. A.N. F 19 6237A.
7. Ibid. 21 May 1810.
8. Ibid. 4 June 1810.
9. Douai, Parker Papers, 27 Oct. 1810.
10. A.N. F 19 6237A, 13 June 1810.
11. Ibid. 7 July 1810.
12. A.N. F 19 6237A, 25 July 1810.
13. Concannon died in Italy while trying to secure a passage to New York.
14. Ibid. 31 July 1810.
15. Ibid. 4 Aug. 1810.
16. A.N. F 19 6237A, 16 Aug. 1810.
17. Ibid. 30 Aug. 1810.
18. Ibid. 11 Sept. 1810.
19. Ibid. 2 Aug. 1810.
20. Ibid. 14 July 1812.
21. Douai, Parker Papers, 13 Jan. 1812.
22. A.N. F 19 6237A, 1 Sept. 1812.
23. Ibid. 24 May 1813.
24. Ibid. 23 Nov. 1812.

25. A.N. F 19 6237A, 26 June 1813.
26. Ibid. 24 July 1813.
27. Ibid. 12 July 1813.
28. Ibid. 3 June 1813.

17
Captain Ferris rides the Green Horse

I know of no class of people in the world, more prone to calumny and more self-opinionated than Irish priests.

Hely d'Oisel, 4 April 1820

Sixteen months had elapsed since Walsh had been suspended. In January 1810 he had eventually handed in his accounts to the commission appointed to examine them. Somewhat mollified by Walsh's apology, the prefect of the Seine had written to the Minister of the Interior distancing himself from the witch-hunt of the other two commissioners, Ferris and Madgett. He told him that he had always been of the opinion that Walsh's administration was not above reproach but that whatever irregularities were in his accounts were largely due to the extraordinary circumstances of the time. 'Indeed, the truth is' he commented, 'when the superiors of the different British establishments fled and abandoned their posts, Walsh alone struggled constantly to rescue the remains of the properties of the colleges.'[1] The fact that he had now 88,000 francs remaining in liquid assets in spite of the enormous expense of the repairs he had carried out did not indicate a 'bad administration.' The commission continued to hold 'long and frequent meetings' fine-combing his accounts, in the hope of finding some proof of his corruption. They explained the delay to the minister, claiming it was due to Walsh's alleged ill-health. Walsh assured the minister that he had not required the services of a doctor for more than a year and that 'his intellectual faculties had remained sufficiently sharp to deal verbally or in writing with business which concerned him.'[2]

It was becoming increasingly clear to Walsh that Ferris' influence in the Ministry of the Interior was virtually unassailable. He now therefore concentrated his efforts on his second front and resorted once more to 'chanting the breviary'.[3] As an ex-priest

Ferris would forfeit all credibility if the college were recognised as a seminary under the patronage of the Archbishop of Paris and the authority of the Minister of Religion. It was a dangerous ploy as Cardinal Maury had just been intruded into the vacant See of Paris by Napoleon and the Pope had refused to grant him canonical institution. Maury was getting a sullen and uncooperative reception from the Paris clergy. He was more than receptive to Walsh's approach and invited him to submit a report.

This he did on 8 February 1811, urging the cardinal 'to place this establishment, essentially ecclesiastical, under the lofty and powerful protection' of the Archbishop of Paris. 'To entrust it to either laity or ecclesiastics who had abandoned their state' he argued, 'would be to pervert the nature of this establishment'.[4] He went further and offered the college and its revenues, 'at least provisionally' to the archbishop, if Irish students would not or could not return to the continent. Claiming that 'the monarch has at times condescended to cast a considerate eye even on the administrator's person' he urged him to take up his defence with the Minister of the Interior. He hoped that would suffice and that 'it will not be necessary to ask Your Eminence to bear to the foot of the throne my request to be heard by His Majesty in his council of state'.[5] But all Walsh received from the cardinal were 'fine promises' and he soon abandoned both him and his college to the prejudices of the minister. Walsh, however, did get the question raised at the council of state in the presence of the emperor. Napoleon declared that 'he intended to preserve intact the properties of the Irish bishops.' Walsh understood that to mean that he, as their legitimate representative, would be maintained in his post. The minister, however, put a different interpretation on it.

Baffled by the charges and counter-charges of the Irish and unable to reach a final decision the minister approached Comte Lally Tollendal seeking his 'complete opinion' on this affair. The latter took him literally and submitted on 12 March a tightly written 43-page manuscript,[6] entitled *confidential notes on the administration of the united Irish, English and Scots colleges in the French empire*. 'It would have been shorter' he assured the minister, 'if he had more time and less on his mind.' Almost half of it was devoted to a character assassination of Walsh which must have few parallels in any language. Two generations of his family in France had done little to dilute this peculiarly Irish talent. Describing Walsh as one 'who all his life has shown himself a being consumed with selfishness, jealousy, hatred and dissension'[7] he went on to detail his harsh treatment of all those unfortunate enough to have become his victims. Beginning with Walsh's predecessor, Charles O'Neill, 'who married 40 years of service to 80 years of virtue' and whom Walsh had left to die destitute in Hôpital-Cochin, he meted out similar treatment to 'his former teachers grown grey in the exercise of their pious ministry.' He had taken Abbé MacDermott to court and evicted him from the Irish college, causing him such pain 'that he would have put an end to his life if his religion had not prevented him'. He had expelled Charles Kearney from the college 'where he had spent 27 years of his life from student grade to that of superior'.

Lally declined the temptation to comment on Walsh's financial accounts. 'But there are other accounts to be rendered' he said, 'and I believe I have the right to inspection of those when my feelings urge me to snatch from his hatred, his hypocrisy and his cold inhumanity the victims against whom all his vices have conspired'.[8] He claimed that he had been urged by his compatriots to do what he could to save the establishment from Walsh's 'selfishness, tyranny, ineptitude and vanity and from his perverse views'. He quoted the bishop of Cloyne as stating at an episcopal meeting in Ireland that Walsh 'deserved to be driven out of the college in Paris with a horsewhip.'[9] Needless to say, Lally impressed on the minister the absolute necessity of sacking Walsh forthwith.

> There is not a day which passes that one does not discover in him some trait of character that renders him more and more unworthy of trust. I would say today that he was worthy of punishment if respect for his cloth and an automatic pity for a being with a human face did not forbid me seeking his punishment.[10]

Walsh's dismissal, he informed the minister, would be greeted like the 'cry that resounded throughout Holland at the news of Cromwell's death: "The Devil is dead." '[11]

Lally had been roused to these extremes of vindictiveness on reading the *mémoire* Walsh had written to Cardinal Maury which had just fallen into his hands. Here, in what was a thinly disguised reference to Lally himself, Walsh had referred to 'two-faced men who had one foot in Paris and the other in London.'[12] Furthermore when Lally had finally returned from London, where he had fled in 1792, he took up residence with his married daughter in the Irish college in Bordeaux, a situation that Walsh was not prepared to tolerate for long.

In his report to Cardinal Maury, Walsh himself admitted that his adversaries claimed that he was a person 'who made enemies'. He dismissed the charge by retorting: 'What public man is without them? My enemies are a handful of self-interested men who would claim to share among themselves the revenues which I have increased for the proprietors and the establishment.'[13] Lally declared that Walsh was not so much a man who made enemies as one who made himself the enemy.

Of all the charges levelled at Walsh this was the one he could least refute. For most of his life he had been involved in disputes which invariably left in their wake an ever-increasing number of injured parties. His appointment as superior of Collège des Lombards in 1786 was deeply resented not only by the replaced superiors themselves but also by a cross-section of the student body. In his Address to the People of Ireland[14] written in his death-cell in Maidstone in 1798, Fr James Coigly claimed that Walsh by starving the students had 'pocketed some hundreds per annum'. He also claimed that Walsh was acting as a spy on the French government for William Pitt. Ironically, Richard Ferris, who was then negotiating a role for himself in London as an English spy, had acquired a copy of Coigly's Address there and now published it 'in the form of a hors d'oeuvre' at the end of one of his pamphlets, to discredit Walsh. 'We would like to believe,' Walsh replied to this charge, 'that M. Coigly, a priest, made a better use of the precious moments that remained to him and forgave his enemies, among whom we have no reason to believe we were numbered'.[15]

Patrick Murphy, a former colleague of Walsh's in Collège des Lombards whom he left in charge of the college when he went into hiding in the autumn of 1792, subsequently disappeared from view apart from a brief reappearance in the records of the Temple prison in 1797-98. Twenty years later he re-emerged from obscurity. He had apparently settled in Versailles where he ministered as a priest in the intervening years. He had left his belongings in his apartment in Collège des Lombards and now wrote to Dom Parker to make arrangements about their removal to Versailles. His antagonism for Walsh was such that he refused to refer to him by name preferring instead to call him sarcastically 'our great teacher' and in terms of vilification his letter[16] has few equals, not even the confidential report of Lally Tollendal. Referring to Walsh's 'scandalous and thievish behaviour' he added, 'I fell often a victim to the roguery of our penny sharper but never was the dupe of his low and mean tricks. I can't conceive how such a despicable being was ever named to command in a regular house having no other sort of merit but that of marking up money.' He went on to express his amazement that 'this fellow being suspended from his functions would still go on and act despotically.' In a final fit of exasperation, he begged Parker to 'pay no regard to my English. I hardly know what I write, my head is broke'. As an excuse for this vicious attack, he claimed that 'if shocking proceedings madden me, fair dealing has always conquered me over.'

In his denunciation[17] of the Irish superiors to the National Convention in September 1793 Bernard MacSheehy had singled out Walsh as 'a man more adept at intrigue, more politically-minded and more counter-revolutionary' than the others. He alleged that he was 'in the pay of the cabinet of St James' and suggested that if the Convention required further proof of his conduct 'they had only to consult all of the people who lived with him in his college'. There is an impressive unanimity among the numerous character witnesses against Walsh, with almost nobody expressing a favourable opinion of him as a man. 'It would be a revealing challenge to M. Walsh' Lally Tollendal remarked,[18] 'to invite him to produce a half a dozen testimonies of friendship or even of approval'. There was, however, at least one who left on record his approbation: Miles Byrne, a frequent visitor to the college during these years described him in his *Memoirs* as 'the venerable and worthy abbé Walsh' and commented that he 'was much liked and esteemed by the students and their parents.'[19]

In Walsh's defence it might be said that a man with less steel and more humanity would not have saved the college. For most of his term of office he was assailed by wave after wave of predators, French as well as Irish, revolutionaries as well as carpetbaggers, patriots as well as compatriots, all eager to turn the Irish properties and revenues to their own ends. He was disowned by the Irish bishops whose battle he was fighting. Alone, he fought off each successive attack. Even that defence Murphy would strip him of. 'I hope that he will not say' he wrote to Parker, 'that troubled times have served him ill.'[20] But that remained always Walsh's sole justification. Apart from episcopal approbation, he sought no other. 'I worry little about the judgement of other men' he wrote, 'who could not appreciate my conduct because they had no idea of the difficult circumstances that I encountered.'[21] That he made enemies was inevitable. That he made so many was in the end to prove fatal to his own career.

When Lally Tollendal, in his confidential report to the minister, finally turned his attention to Richard Ferris, he switched from vitriol to honey, a profusion of eulogisms spilling from his pen in his enthusiasm to describe Ferris' accomplishments. 'Enlightenment, education, incisiveness, shrewdness, capacity, precision, such is the amalgam I have found in him.'[22] To this he added, and here his judgment is more than suspect, 'disinterestness and tactfulness.' Later experiences of Ferris were to send him scuttling back to his literary repertoire in search of quite a different set of abstract nouns. Aware that certain objections to Ferris had been expressed to Henry Clarke, Minister of War and newly-created Duc de Feltres, he observed 'that the poison of calumny, distilled by hyprocrisy, can circulate through the purest of channels.'[23] He surmised that Ferris perhaps 'may have occasionally forgotten his priestly character during the revolutionary disorders and the interregnum of ecclesiastical discipline.' 'I have been told' he added, 'that in his horror of the jacobin atrocities, M. Ferris in order to combat them, had bartered his clerical biretta for a grenadier's bonnet.'[24] He warmly recommended Ferris to the minister as the best possible replacement for Walsh as administrator.

Ferris, in fact, was as unprincipled as Walsh was principled. But he was a man of wide culture and enormous charm. Nice people are not always virtuous and more tragically, the virtuous, like Walsh, can sometimes be wanting in humanity. Ferris made friends, usually in high places, while Walsh collected enemies indiscriminately. Maréchal de Beauvais and especially his wife, whom Ferris had spirited out of France to England at the outbreak of the Terror, now brought their considerable influence to bear on the minister in his favour. The Maréchal wrote to the minister reminding him of the written promise he had given him in favour of Ferris and expressed the hope that he would keep that promise.[25]

Lally Tollendal proposed as prefect of studies Charles Kearney who 'sins by excess of goodness as Walsh by excess of callousness'.[26] Kearney 'after having saved the lives of a great number of his compatriots during the reign of terror was exposed to losing his own through the horror of famine when the reign of order was restored.'[27] Kearney had appealed to Walsh to use his influence to secure a pension in the autumn of 1807, a plea which went unheard. Lally now insisted that reparation was due.

The minister continued to hesitate for another nine months. Finally, his department produced in January 1812 a report and two draft decrees,[28] one dealing with the administration of the college and the other exclusively with Walsh. There was a disagreement between the minister and his department, the former proposing the return of the college to the supervision of a bureau while the latter favoured leaving it completely in the hands of the Imperial University. The minister favoured granting a pension to Walsh while also releasing him from his debt to the college. The department preferred allowing him to continue living in the college where all his needs would be met. The minister then proposed Ferris as administrator to replace Walsh as administrator-general while the department argued that such a post was superfluous as there was already a treasurer who fulfilled that function. The report mentioned that at the end of 1811 there were 33 students in the college, of whom only six were studying theology and two medicine. It also added that French families were placing their children in the Irish college in preference to French schools, a practice that should be forbidden. The disagreement between the minister and his department ensured yet another postponement of a definitive settlement. Twelve months later the Maréchal de Beauvais and his wife were still writing to the minister urging Ferris' candidature.[29] The fact that he was also strongly recommended[30] by the grand-master of the Imperial University probably proved decisive with the minister. On 1 April 1813 Richard Ferris was named provisional administrator of the united colleges. The Irish bishops must have greeted the news as some sort of April Fool's gesture on the part of the French government. The pockmarked ex-priest, ex-captain, ex-spy was now in charge of all their colleges, seminaries, properties and revenues in the French empire and in the eyes of the French government their unaccredited 'official' representative. Not only that, he was also in control of all the English and Scots establishments, much to the embarrassment of the church authorities in those countries.

Ferris informed Walsh by letter of the minister's decision and added 'that if he did not evacuate his apartment forthwith he would have a padlock placed on the door.' Walsh commented bitterly: 'In this way, after 34 years of dedicated service, the representative of the insular bishops saw himself thrown out.'[31] Ferris immediately set about preparing luxury quarters for himself commensurate with his new title. He created a large apartment in the English seminary in rue des Postes, where, as Miles Byrne described it, 'he was splendidly lodged'.[32] He kept a carriage and had a Chinese garden specially designed at a cost of at least 20,000 francs,[33] all paid for out of college funds. A library was created to house his collection of 4,000 volumes and considerable number of works of art. Here, he wined and dined his wealthy and influential friends.

Old Father Daniel, the former rector of the great English College of Douai 'was relegated to a tiny dark room over the kitchen.' Here, an English visitor found him 'in that condemned cell' and commented, 'he is often tantalised by the noise of the jack which never turns for him, and the aroma of savoury steams from dainties he is doomed never to taste'.[34] The English historian, Francis Plowden, had a small apartment on the third storey. He was employed as professor of English and, according to Miles Byrne, 'was often in very distressed circumstances'.[35] He handed over the superior's apartment in the Irish college to Dr MacMahon who was ostensibly employed as physician to the college but whom Walsh claimed was put in charge with a handsome salary. Twenty years after the original attempt, the 'Kerry coup-d'etat' was finally successful. Ferris might have lived even more lavishly, had Walsh not wisely taken the precaution, before his appointment, of emptying the coffers of the considerable savings he had made. He used these to buy the building opposite the college, thus ensuring for it 'a good neighbourhood'.[36]

Unfortunately for Ferris political events were rapidly overtaking his stylish living. Ever since the spectacular disaster of his Russian campaign in 1812, Napoleon's star had been declining. He had rushed back from Moscow just in time to snuff out some smouldering conspiracies in Paris, but his over-fatigued armies were too thinly-stretched over too many fronts, making his final defeat inevitable. Besides, most of the conquered states of Europe were now groaning under the burden of his incessant wars which they were compelled to finance. After the disaster of Leipsig in the autumn of 1813 Napoleon was almost surrounded by his enemies but succeeded in hacking his way out and returned to France with them pressing hard on his heels. That November, Madame de la Tour du Pin who was staying in Lally Tollendal's apartment in Paris, called on Talleyrand who informed her that Napoleon 'was a man who is ready to hide under a bed.' After a series of defeats, early in March 1814 and Wellington, by now occupying Bordeaux, the end was in sight. Paris now lay open and the senate, prodded by the allies and Talleyrand, deposed Napoleon and invited Louis XVIII to accept the throne. When Napoleon's marshals refused to serve him any longer he abdicated unconditionally on 11 April.

This was the moment Walsh had been waiting for. The following day he dashed off a petition[37] to the provisional French government. He recalled with gratitude, 'the important favours that a prince had conferred on him' in 1790. The prince in question was none other than Prince de Talleyrand, now head of the provisional government and the most powerful political figure in France. Walsh was not slow to recall 'the protection with which this same prince honoured the Irish seminary and college both when he was a member of the Paris Department and all during his period as Minister of Foreign Affairs.' He drew Talleyrand's attention to the present state of the Irish college under Ferris. 'I must confess that I feel deep pain' he said, 'seeing the collapse of an establishment which was the hope of the insular clergy'. Alluding to the money that Ferris had squandered on his 'spacious apartments' and Chinese garden and his expulsion of five priest-students, he asked : 'How can one abuse so shamelessly the property of others?' In a petition to a government whose president was a renegade priest and a married bishop, it was less than tactful of Walsh to describe Ferris as a man 'who had publicly renounced his priesthood.' He urged the government to place the college under the direction of a commission presided over by the Archbishop of Paris as it was during the *ancien régime*. If the wishes of the Irish bishops did not receive a favourable hearing they would be 'in the sad necessity' of asking their government to seek the return of their funds to be used in their native schools.

Walsh's petition was shelved as the provisional government had more important things to resolve. On 1 May negotiations began on the Treaty of Paris. Two days later Louis XVIII entered the capital and the following day Napoleon began his exile as the absolute ruler of the tiny island of Elba. The restoration of the Bourbons assured Ferris' position in the eyes of the French government: his well-publicised stint as a grenadier captain in the army of the Princes, fighting for the present king's unfortunate brother, guaranteed that. His standing with the Irish bishops was quite another matter and now, with the return of peace, the ball was in their court. Later that month he sent them a statement entitled *The Present State of the British Establishments and Colleges in France and in the Austrian Netherlands.*[38] He began by listing his ecclesiastical titles, which included doctorates in theology and canon and civil law, former almoner of the king of France, former canon of Amiens cathedral and promoter-general of the same diocese.

Despite its title, the document was Ferris' answer to the petition of Walsh to the provisional government, his intention being 'to unmask before the eyes of the Irish bishops a man who for 22 years had been the enemy of his compatriots and had squandered their properties.' He traced Walsh's career from his 'expulsion' from Nantes to his 'usurpation' of the Irish college in Paris. He credited the British ambassador, Lord Gower, with obtaining an exemption for the Irish college from the law of 2 November 1790 confiscating religious houses. Later in 1805 when the English and Scots colleges were united to the Irish, Walsh expelled Kearney and Innis from their respective houses. He solicited and obtained from the French government that none of the foundation funds would be allowed to leave the territory of the French empire, contrary to the wish expressed by Peter Flood who had been sent to Paris for that purpose. Ferris then went on to describe in detail the fraudulent administration of Walsh on account of which the minister had suspended him from his post.

But the bishops had already made their move. With the return of peace they immediately sent Daniel Murray, auxiliary bishop of Dublin, to Paris to carry out an investigation. He set out in May but did not dally in Paris, preferring to press on to Rome to consult the Pope on the British government's request for a say in the appointment of bishops. Ferris wasted no time, haunting the corridors of the Ministry of the Interior, urging them to issue a decree confirming him in his position. His efforts were crowned with success. On 21 June 1814 Louis XVIII signed a decree[39] in the Tuileries dismissing the suspended Walsh and appointing Ferris definitively in his place. A new supervisory bureau was to be created.

Apparently Walsh had still not heard of the new decree when he wrote[40] to Archbishop Troy a week later, sending him a copy of his petition to the provisional government. He was mainly concerned with counteracting the reports which had reached Dublin of his offer to hand over the Irish college to Cardinal Maury. He pointed out that if the Irish bishops renounced their intention, under pressure from the British government, of sending students to Paris, then the college would automatically devolve to the Archbishop of Paris as its spiritual and temporal head from time immemorial. Besides, such a course was preferable to seeing it 'become prey to laymen and others who had dishonoured their cloth'. Unaware of the latest royal decree, Walsh proposed that when the Irish bishops had decided on their course of action, 'I shall then dismiss myself, praying His Majesty to accept my demission, who alone can adopt it.' And he added, 'for my part, I am resolved to spend the rest of my life in personal tranquility.' He was now in his 73rd year.

Ferris, on the contrary, had no plans for early retirement although a new threat had arisen which could evict him from his luxurious apartment and Chinese garden. Following the treaty of Paris the English and Scots churches had sent representatives to Paris to secure the return of their properties, demanding their separation from the Irish college. Late in July Ferris wrote[41] to Talleyrand urging him to reject this demand and in August presented a *Placet*[42] to the king arguing against such a move. He pointed out that in all they comprised seven separate institutions, secular and regular. If each of them were to have a superior, bursar and procurator as they were planning, that would amount to 21 superiors without a single student. Besides, their revenues were extremely modest. The Irish properties alone equalled twice that of all the others combined and they still owed a considerable amount to the Irish section. To expel the students now being educated in the Irish college on their funds would be to violate the decree and would entail lengthy and sordid court cases with the families involved. Furthermore, if the British government submitted subjects of the three nations to one rule at home, they would hardly favour their separation abroad.

The Treaty of Paris decreed that commissioners would be appointed to examine the claims of British subjects against the French government for properties confiscated or losses sustained since 1792. As a result, petitioners flocked back to Paris to press their claims. Dr Bew, the former superior of the English college who had fled France with the advent of Terror, arrived now to reclaim the seminary in which Ferris was luxuriously housed. James Robertson acted on behalf of the Scottish church. The English Benedictine, Henry Parker, supported by two newly-arrived colleagues, produced a *mémoire*[43] in which he answered Ferris' *placet*, point by point. In response to his argument that the other institutions would not be viable if separated from the Irish, the Benedictines sweetly pointed out that 'they were not planning to pay themselves salaries of 24,000 francs a year, with luxurious apartments and fine gardens, at the expense of the foundations.'

The allies were now closing in again, this time on Ferris. 'He is said to have gone off today for London with new machinations' James Robertson told a friend on 12 August.[44] Eight Irish ecclesiastical students had arrived from home and he had refused them admittance to the college. Three were taken into Saint Sulpice, the other five having to book into an hotel. 'Do beseech and conjure Dr Troy' Robertson urged his friend, 'to send immediately with full powers a man of principle and sense to oust such a worthless character from among the sons of Erin.' In September, he denounced Ferris to Troy himself: 'He's disowned by every decent man of the cloth' and he went on to warn the archbishop, more prophetically than either of them were aware, that 'you'll have a battle to fight to get him out of his saddle on the Green Horse.'[45] A similar tale was being recounted by Dr Bew to his master, Dr Poynter of London. 'He is not deficient in cunning' Bew warned, 'and is not sparing in bribes and dinners; he is a total stranger to our concerns and deserves punishment, confiscation and banishment. His reputation among the French clergy is such that no one here in Paris would entrust him with any work concerning religion or education.'[46]

The passing years and incessant disputes were taking their toll of Walsh. 'As my trembling hand will not permit me to write ...' he began his letter[47] to Archbishop Troy at the end of August. He could no longer hold the pen which he had wielded so courageously for over a quarter of a century in defence of the Irish college. In that cause, Walsh's pen had certainly been mightier than many another man's sword. 'Under the auspices of providence during the course of twenty-two years' he reminded the archbishop, 'he had secured the property from final alienation.' Now that peace had finally returned, he intended to 'leave to the solicitude of the prelates themselves the vindication of their rights as he is determined not to take any further concern in the administration.'

In spite of his protestations Walsh was loath to retire from the battlefield at least until he was assured that victory was secure. He had chosen to spend the summer and autumn 'in town as a centre of correspondence which is the only service I can render'. In October, he communicated with Troy, calling on his former colleague, MacNulty, to write the letter[48] this time. His hand may have lost its power but his mind retained all its old vigour:

> When I consider that the efforts of the English and Scots together produce as yet so little effect I am almost tempted to take some merit to myself that I fought the battle all alone for twenty-two years against a faction which has only triumphed because a person vested with proper powers has not been sent at the appointed time.

He proposed that Dr Murray, on his return from Rome, should take up the matter directly with the minister himself 'under the auspices of Lord Wellington if it is necessary to claim the support of His Excellency.' Then he treated the archbishop to a lecture on how such negotiations should be pursued. 'Secondary arguments never appear in my debates when I could have recourse to principle.' The principle in this case was the inherent right of proprietors to choose the administrator of their properties. They should choose such an administrator in Ireland itself and have him presented by the Archbishop of Paris to His Majesty.

The efforts of the English and Scots, however—with the powerful help of the Duke of Wellington—did produce results. On 23 September the king issued a decree[49] separating the three properties. There was, however, a sting in the tail of the royal ordinance. Article 7 decreed that the existing bursary-holders would be permitted to remain until the completion of their studies. These were all native French, and it could entail ten to twelve years' delay before funds became available for Irish students. To avoid disputes mutual debts between the Irish, English and Scots were to be settled, taking 1 January 1809 as the point of departure. Finally, Ferris was rather generously given a year to move out of his apartment in the English seminary. He was reduced to administrator-general of the Irish establishments and colleges alone.

Obviously relishing his previously used metaphor, Robertson reminded Troy in October:[50] 'You have not found it advisable to send a person fit to clean out the Augean stables which the revolution has left to the Green Horse'. Aware of the growing coalition against him and in preparation for the impending arrival of Bishop Murray, Ferris was reduced to desperate measures. He even contemplated renewing his priesthood. With this in mind he approached Charles Kearney. The latter 'was hard put to for permission' as Robertson informed Troy, 'to renew his sacerdotal functions which have twenty-five years rust to rub off.'

Murray arrived in Paris in the autumn of 1814. He spent long sessions[51] closeted with Walsh in his apartment in Collège des Lombards and was thoroughly briefed by him on the approach he should adopt with the French government. His case was based on Walsh's cardinal principle that the right of proprietorship necessarily entailed the right to choose an administrator. In the *mémoire*[52] he presented to the government on 14 November he insisted that the Irish bishops were proprietors, in the strictest sense of the term, of the colleges in Paris. 'Proprietorship would be an empty expression' he insisted, 'if the proprietors had not the right to designate a man of their choice as administrator of their properties.' He requested His Majesty to issue a decree recognising the right of the bishops to choose an administrator and 'his co-operators.' The right of the bishops to present candidates for the bursaries was also requested. The college should be placed under the supervision of a *bureau gratuit* with the Archbishop of Paris as its president. Those presently engaged in the administration should be ordered to submit their accounts to the bureau. In an obvious reference to the big-spending Ferris, accounts should also be rendered of the 'accessory pensions they had received'.

Murray's mission was crowned with success and the king issued, on 16 January 1815, his third decree[53] on the Irish college in less than six months. Ferris was finally unhorsed but the decree was careful to ensure him an honourable discharge. It stated that he was to be replaced as administrator without implying that he had in any way been 'reprehensible either in his conduct, his character or his administration.' It was a notable consolation prize. 'I have noted with pleasure' Abbé de Montesquieu, the minister, wrote to Ferris, 'that the king's ordinance contains an honourable mention of your administration.'[54] And later in a private conversation the minister explained to him 'that because of his cloth he could not refuse the change requested by the bishops and strongly supported by Cardinal Consalvi, but that his ministry would grant him a pension of 2,000 francs as an indemnity.'[55] He was ordered however, to hand over the college in Green Horse street to the full possession of his successor and on request, all documents relative to the establishment. His tenancy in the English seminary had, however, still nine months to run.

Before Murray returned to Dublin he authorised Walsh to publish 'a full refutation of the monstrous composition of falsehoods and calumny published by Mr Ferris.' This he did at the end of 1814.[56] It was, in fact, Walsh's swan-song and amounted to nothing less than an 'apologia pro vita sua'. 'In a word,' he summed up his administration, 'I took over the administration of the Irish section in a state of decay, and I left it flourishing, its buildings repaired and enjoying a revenue of 36,544 francs, not including the rents from the lease of houses in Paris, Louvain, Tournay, Bordeaux, Nantes etc. coming to a total revenue of approximately 60,000 francs.' He had achieved the same for the English and Scots establishments which he had found in an advanced state of dilapidation. Not wishing to engage any further in a *guerre de plume* with Ferris, he took his final bow with the words, 'I pledge here that I will no longer answer any of his charges.'

NOTES

1. A.N. F 19 6237A, 10 Feb. 1811. Walsh to Maury, p6.
2. Ibid. p9.
3. A.N. H 3 2561A, Mar. 1811. Lally Tollendal to Interior, p6.
4. A.N. F 19 6237A, p5.
5. Ibid. p44.
6. A.N. H 3 2561A, Mar. 1811.
7. Ibid. p2.
8. Ibid. p8.
9. Ibid. p10.
10. Ibid. p8.
11. Ibid. p11.
12. A.N. F 19 6237A, p43. This was a play on Napoleon's gibe about Lally as 'the Colossus at Rhodes with one foot on Calais and the other on Dover' (O'Reilly op. cit. p78).
13. A.N. F 19 6237A, p42.
14. *Life of Rev. James Coigly* (1798) p12.
15. I.C.P. 14A, 30 Dec. 1814, *Mémoire pour Walsh*.
16. Douai, Parker Papers, 18 inst. 1812. Murphy to Parker.
17. A.N. BB 70. 320.
18. A.N. H 3 2561A, p10.
19. Byrne, op. cit. 3. p193.
20. Douai, Parker Papers, 18 inst. 1812. Murphy to Parker.
21. I.C.P. 14A, 30 Dec. 1814.
22. A.N. H 3 2561A, p21.
23. Ibid. p22.
24. Ibid. p23.
25. A.H. H 3 2561A, 12 Mar. 1811. de Beauvais to Interior.
26. A.N. H 3 2561A, p28.
27. Ibid. p31.
28. A.N. F 19 6237A, 3 Jan. 1812.
29. A.N. H3 2561A, 17 Dec. 1812.
30. A.N. F 17 2500, 24 April 1813.
31. I.C.P. 14A, 30 Dec. 1814.

32. Byrne, op. cit. 3. p197.
33. I.C.P. 14A, 30 Dec. 1814.
34. D.D.A. and W.D.A. Aug-Sept. 1814, qtd Purcell, op. cit. p55.
35. Byrne, op. cit. 3. p197.
36. I.C.P. 14A, 30 Dec. 1814.
37. I.C.P. 3L12, 12 April 1814.
38. I.C.P. 3L11, 25 May 1814.
39. A.N. F 19 6237A, 21 June 1814.
40. D.D.A. 121/9, 27 June 1814.
41. A.N. F 19 6237C, 25 July 1814.
42. I.C.P. 3L15, 2 Aug. 1814.
43. A.N. F 19 6237A, nd. *Mémoire succinct*.
44. I.C.P. 3Z8, 12 Aug. 1814.
45. D.D.A. 121/9, 18 Sept. 1814. qtd Purcell, p58.
46. W.D.A. & D.D.A., Sept. 1814. qtd Purcell, p57.
47. D.D.A. 121/9, 29 Aug. 1814.
48. Ibid. 18 Oct. 1814.
49. I.C.P. 3L13, 23 Sept. 1814.
50. D.D.A. 121/9, 21 Oct. 1814.
51. I.C.P. 14A, 30 Dec. 1814.
52. A.N. F 17 14761, 14 Nov. 1814.
53. I.C.P. 3L16, 16 Jan. 1814.
54. I.C.P. 3E, 9 July 1815.
55. Ibid.
56. I.C.P. 14A, 30 Dec. 1814.

18
Short Odds on Mr Long

A bas Ferris! Vive M. Long! A bas Napoléon!

–Students, Collège des Irlandais, April 1815.

The person designated as Ferris' successor by the royal decree of 16 January 1815 was Paul Long, parish priest of Coolock, Dublin, who had been sent out to Paris in December to join Bishop Murray. He had been a pupil of Charles Kearney in the Irish college and later served as a curé in the diocese of Laon, from where he tried to make his way back to Ireland during the revolution. On his way he ran short of money and in desperation entered a tavern where he gambled his last few francs on a throw of the dice. Luck was with him and he won enough to get him home safely. He was going to need similar luck to survive his second trip to France. In Ireland he had spent some time as head of the lay school in Maynooth, which appears to have been closely modelled on Collège des Irlandais. Early in February Murray departed for Dublin and the following day Long took possession of the Irish college. Little did he or anybody else realise that the Long administration was destined to be the shortest in the turbulent history of that establishment.

There were 45 bursary-holders in the college. They were almost all French, many of them between the ages of nine and 14 and destined for the army, law and medicine. It was the only victory that Ferris had salvaged from the recent decree which ordered that they continue to enjoy their bursaries until the completion of their studies. For him it meant influential French families in Paris in his debt. For Long it meant, as he pointed out to Troy, that 'several years will elapse before this house can afford essential service to Ireland.'[1] There were, however, 50 vacant rooms which could be occupied immediately by fee-paying boarders and Long impressed on Troy that none should be sent over above the age of 14. There was one final victory that must have pleased Walsh, now content to accept his retirement in Collège des Lombards, his mission finally accomplished. The Minister of the Interior, Abbé de Montesquieu, decreed that the Irish college was to be placed under the department of religion from 1 February.[2] Only one cloud remained on the horizon. A Liverpool newspaper, *The Pilot*, carried a report that the king was planning to set up a new bureau to consist of four honorary members–Duc de Tarente, Duc de Fits-James, Comte Lally Tollendal and Comte O'Mahony–and four ordinary members, headed by Richard Ferris.[3]

By now Vienna had replaced Paris as the glittering capital of Europe, all the crowned heads with their political advisors and courtiers having assembled there to redraw the map of Europe following the collapse of Napoleon's empire. The royal palace hosted at one point two emperors and two empresses, four kings, one queen, two heirs-to-the-throne, two grand duchesses and three princes. Vienna became a carnival for royalty, with an endless series of balls and banquets in the best 18th century tradition. One octogenarian French nobleman who came to Vienna with the intention of quitting this life in style remarked: '*Le Congrès ne marche pas, mais il danse.*'[4] He did succeed in providing the city with the spectacle of a funeral of a Knight of the Golden Fleece. One of the notable English visitors to Vienna was Sir Henry Sidney-Smith, with whose spectacular escape from Paris seven years earlier Charles Kearney had been charged. Serious negotiations however, were held, dominated by Metternich and Castlereagh and of course the inscrutable Talleyrand, intent on ensuring that the sins of Napoleon would not be visited on France. One morning early in March he was handed a note from Metternich which read: 'Bonaparte has left Elba.'

When the news of Napoleon's return reached the Irish college, Long remained unperturbed. 'I did not think' he commented, 'that unexpected events in France and the return of the emperor Napoleon, could have the slightest influence on my position.'[5] He did not have long to wait to learn differently.

> During the greater part of Napoleon's short reign the clergy were in the greatest danger. The fury of the populace was immediately directed against them. The same imprecations that prevailed in '91, '92, and '93 were vociferated in every quarter. The soutane dare not make its appearance nor any dress which indicated a clergyman and if the

> French church had not been stripped of its property already, the scene of jacobinical fury would have been repeated. Several who ventured into the streets were cruelly treated and abused. Hence, a great number quit Paris ... Most of the canons of the cathedral retired into the provinces ... where they were kept under the surveillance of the gendarmerie.[6]

Even before Napoleon's arrival in Paris, Ferris had already stepped up his intrigues to hoist himself once more into the saddle of the Green Horse. 'Strengthened by the support of his numerous friends' Long warned the minister on 27 March, 'he is counting on an easy victory over a man who has no other protection than justice.'[7] With Kerry cunning, Ferris had long since realised that governments change but the civil servants always remain. On these over-worked and underpaid functionaries he lavished his charm and hospitality and the delights of his Chinese garden. 'The minister is led by the nose' John Brewer, superior-general of the English Benedictines informed a colleague in Downside,[8] 'by one of his head clerks who is in the interest of our adversary Mr Ferris.' Long now learned to his cost the power of these 'men who do nothing gratis, whom it would be necessary to bribe with one half of the income to secure the proper application of the other and yet whose report is the only guide of the decisions of ministers.'[9] Ferris' money and charm had been well spent. From Lyon, Napoleon issued a decree restoring all the officials who had been replaced by the king. A mere two days after Napoleon's carriage had clattered up to the hastily-vacated palace of the Tuileries, Ferris had already served a writ on the treasury, freezing the Irish dividends, thus making it impossible for Long to pay his bills. Long sent a petition to the minister asking him to call Ferris to heel and reminding him that Dr Murray had declared that the Irish bishops 'would never risk the education of the catholic youth of Ireland under his direction.'[10] It is doubtful whether his plea ever reached the minister's ear. On 21 April Napoleon issued a decree restoring the united colleges and re-appointed Ferris the administrator-general. The Green Horse had changed riders once more.

A few days later Ferris had a copy of the imperial decree delivered to Long by a process-server. He dismissed the porter and installed the scullion in the lodge, ordering him to allow nothing to be removed without a written order from him, and to take possession of the keys. Thus as Long ruefully remarked, Ferris intended 'subjecting us to the dominion of the lowest servant in the house.'[11] Worse was to follow. This same scullion subjected Long to 'an inconsiderable share of abuse'. One of the students, overhearing the exchange with the scullion, immediately alerted his colleagues. The result was uproar. The students rushed from the study into the courtyard and armed themselves with thick branches torn from the trees, 'and would have wreaked their fury on the unfortunate scullion had he not luckily made a timely escape into the town.' They then turned their attention to the other servants who had fortunately barricaded themselves in the kitchen. 'The whole college was in a state of tumult and confusion not to be described. *À bas Ferris! vive M. Long! à bas Napoléon!* was heard in every quarter.'[12] Long eventually succeeded in appeasing them.

Ferris took advantage of the incident to denounce Long to the minister as the author of the student insurrection and 'the enemy of the government, instilling into the minds of the students rebellious principles.'[13] He also tried to evict him from the college.

> His first attempt was to reduce me by famine. He ordered that nothing should be furnished to me from the kitchen. This method not succeeding to his wish, he next endeavoured to take me by storm. He sent a thundering letter to begone and next day ordered the sheets to be taken off my bed. As I however did not relish sleeping without them, he at length made application to the minister ... and obtained an order from him for my departure in the course of eight days.

The parish priest of Coolock accepted this harsh treatment with christian resignation and begged Dr Murray 'not to conclude from these observations a want of charity on my part or the least animosity towards Ferris. Be assured that I entertain for him every christian sentiment and wish most sincerely his true happiness.'[14]

Notwithstanding, Long appealed against the decree to the emperor.[15] He claimed Ferris had secured it by taking advantage of the minister by 'intrigue and trickery' and by putting it out in ministerial offices that Long was an enemy of the present government and a former *émigré*. To prove that Ferris' own credentials in this regard were not above suspicion he quoted from the latter's pamphlet to the Irish bishops in which he referred to Napoleon as a tyrant and praised Lally Tollendal for publicly declaring the same. Ferris had used this argument then to discredit Walsh who boasted of being described in the British parliament as 'a man devoted to Napoleon.' Long should have profited from Ferris' mistake. Published statements have a nasty habit of rebounding on their authors in a volatile political situation. Long's statement was hardly calculated to please any French government, least of all that of the returned emperor.

> As an Irishman I am bound to the constitution of England and to the King of Great Britain. As administrator of a seminary-college, I am bound to keep good order in my house. Such is my profession of faith. After that, what type of constitution France chooses to give itself, whether it be democratic or monarchical, absolute or constitutional monarchy, aristocratic or oligarchic, is a matter of complete indifference to me.

Unfortunately for Paul Long his fate was just then a matter of complete indifference to the emperor. The great powers assembled at Vienna quickly patched up their quarrels. Before the Congress dispersed it issued a proclamation, prompted by Talleyrand, denouncing Napoleon as a 'usurper' and the enemy and disturber of the peace of the world, whom they handed over to public vengeance. The great powers agreed to field 150,000 men each until 'Bonaparte should have been rendered absolutely incapable of stirring up further trouble'. While they mobilised their forces, Napoleon prepared to strike a swift blow. With an army of 120,000 he arrived at the Belgian frontier on 14 June before the allied commanders, Wellington and Blücher, had time to unite their larger forces. He defeated Blücher on the road to Brussels but inexplicably allowed him to retreat in good order. Two days later he took on Wellington at Waterloo and after a bitter engagement he was defeated because Blücher and his Prussians arrived at a crucial stage of the battle.

With incredible optimism Napoleon returned to Paris, still believing that he might arouse the people to conjure up another army to take the field. But the French would have no more of the 'little Corsican.' For a second time in a little over a year he was forced to abdicate. In any event, the allies had encircled Paris. Paul Long, whose prospects brightened as those of Napoleon declined, was a more than interested spectator of these events. Like other Parisians he experienced

> the greatest alarms while Paris was in a state of siege. We were then between two fires, the rabble to whom arms had been distributed and the allied forces. St Denis, Belleville, Chaumont and Montmartre were strongly fortified. Wellington left in these quarters only troops sufficient to keep them in check. He approached with the strength of the

army to about 150,000 on the defenceless side of Paris by Saint Germain, Versailles, Saint Cloud, until he at length advanced to Vaugirard, Meudon, Villejuif, Montrouge most of which are but a quarter of a league from the boulevard. The remains of the French army was about 50,000 men and the attack was on the point of beginning. The British and Prussian troops were drawn up for battle when, fortunately, the French sent commissioners and the capitulation was signed. Had the city been taken by storm it would probably have become a second Moscow.[16]

This time the allies were determined that the world would never again resound to the roar of Napoleon's cannon. He was packed off to the island of St Helena, 5,000 miles away in mid-Atlantic.

While the armies had been drawn up for battle on the outskirts of Paris, an incident[17] took place in the Irish college which could have proved embarrassing for the superior in a world of sudden changes of loyalty and political intrigue. Before the issue had been finally decided somebody had placed the white Bourbon flag on the roof. Eighteen-year-old Arthur Barker climbed onto the roof, took the flag down and burnt it in the courtyard in front of all the students. Long reacted swiftly and promptly expelled Barker. It was a bad break for young Barker. His father, the one-armed veteran of the '98 rising in Wexford, had died a few years earlier and his widowed mother was trying to raise two children on a very small pension. His hopes of a military career were blighted by this incident and he was obliged to follow less profitable literary pursuits.

Ignoring the pleas of Talleyrand, who begged him to cross the border into France unescorted by the allies, Louis chose to enter Paris on the coat-tails of the Prussians. The reception he received showed little trace of the hurt he inflicted on French national pride by such a gesture. The Bourbons had never been renowned for their tact. However, the Irish Paul Long had every reason to celebrate his return:

You have no idea of the enthusiasm manifested at the king's entrance. I saw the procession at three different places, at the barrière Saint Denis, the boulevards and the Tuileries. The cries of *Vive le roi!* were incessant and not a window without a white flag. It was easy to see that he was beloved by all, except the Jacobins and the army. Not a private soldier of the time nor a French uniform is to be seen in Paris. The streets are crowded with English, Russian, Austrian and Prussian troops. The city is full of the last who have behaved very badly. At

> the beginning they plundered their posts and paid for nothing. The Ponts d'Iena, d'Austerlitz and the pillar in Place Vendôme gave them particular umbrage. They considered them as monuments disgraceful to their country, were resolved on their destruction and had already begun to demolish the bridge of Iéna. The arrival of the king of Prussia put a stop to these excesses but to appease them the king was obliged to change the names of these bridges.[18]

The eve of his return to Paris, '*Louis le Desiré*', as Long now preferred to call him, issued a decree at Saint Denis authorising all functionaries accredited up to 1 March last to resume their responsibilities. Long promptly notified Ferris who chose to ignore it. He then approached the Minister of the Interior for a decree expelling Ferris. The secretary of the department promised him that such a decree would be issued within 24 hours. Several days passed and a worried Long approached the department once more to be informed that the matter was not as simple as it first appeared. He even managed with great difficulty to get an audience with the minister himself but had to be content with 'vague and general' answers. 'How is it' Long exclaimed in exasperation, 'that I have to wait several days for an audience with the minister, while Ferris can enter the minister's office at any hour of the day under the pretext of making a social call'.[19]

Ferris, wearing his lawyer's cap, presented his own case to the minister.[20] Trumps had once more changed suit and he took delight in drawing the minister's attention to the passage of an earlier *mémoire* where he had referred to Napoleon as a 'tyrant'. This was the same passage that Long had sent to Napoleon and to Carnot, his minister. Long 'knew well' he added, 'that it was enough to tell Bonaparte that an individual had called him a tyrant to make him liable to capital punishment.' Having thus established his royalist credentials, he went on to dispute the legal basis of the bishops' claim to be proprietors of the Irish college and revenues. 'The Irish bishops have no right' he declared, 'either as proprietors or as so-called nominators of bursaries.' In the event of suppression the original right of the founders devolves upon the crown.

At the end of July Ferris was still in possession of the Irish college. Long wrote to the Archbishop of Rheims[21] asking him to intervene with the king to resolve the matter. 'The King's sense of religion and justice' he informed the archbishop, 'will never permit him to sanction a man so fatal to the interests of Irish catholics.' He urged the archbishop to remind His Majesty of the reasons for his earlier decree, which 'the extraordinary events since January' had obliterated from his memory. He informed Dr Murray at the same time that it would take another month or six weeks before the ministry took action. He impressed on him the urgency of sending over an episcopal delegation from Ireland. 'The present moment is the most favourable that can occur' he told Murray, 'and no time is to be lost. Lord Castlereagh, the Duke of Wellington and the English ambassador are here. Some strong recommendations can be had from their friends in England and Ireland and if yourself and the reverend Dr Everard were to come over immediately, I have not the smallest doubt of the certainty of success.'[22]

He raised another question with Dr Murray which was going to occupy the college for many years to come. 'Other matters of the highest importance urge the journey,' he pleaded. 'The indemnities are soon to be taken into consideration, which are to be made in compensation for the British property dilapidated during the French revolution. The Irish losses at the most moderate computation amount to two million French *livres*.'[23] Negotiations were just then taking place in Paris between France and the allied powers which led to the signing of a convention on 20 November 1815. It was agreed that claimants would be indemnified for properties or rents sequestrated, confiscated or sold since 1 January 1791 at their value of that year. Commissioners were to be appointed, two French and two British, to adjudicate the claims which were to be submitted within three months. Ferris was quick to become involved, issuing a pamphlet entitled *Observations on the claims of British subjects for property lost during the Revolution.*[24] He ended it with a scathing attack on the bishops who 'have lost almost 300,000 francs, a sum which would have ... maintained in France 300 extra students, furnishing Ireland with some brilliant ecclesiastics of which she seems to be greatly in need.'

At the end of July the department of the interior had submitted a long report[25] to the minister on the respective claims of Ferris and Long. It was heavily prejudiced in favour of Ferris 'who had proved by his year in office that he was very capable of fulfilling with dignity the functions which had been entrusted to him.' He had all the qualities required by the constitutive decree 'while Long, completely ignorant of these establishments, is far from fulfilling the necessary conditions.' He was not even a master in arts. He had pursued his classical studies in Ireland while the decree required that the superior should have done so in France. Here the report, on information supplied by Ferris, was factually incorrect. Long had been awarded his MA in Paris on 25 September 1790.[26]

The minister went so far as to ask the French ambassador in London to report on Ferris' activities in England. He sent in a glowing account of Ferris 'who had never served any but the royal cause and whose conduct is very far from meriting the least reproach.' After serving in the army of the Princes, Ferris had crossed to England where he was engaged as a captain on the staff of the army of Lord Moira, destined for La Vendée. As such, he was sent to General Charette, to facilitate the disembarking of the English and he contributed a loan of 24,000 francs for the support of the war in La Vendée. 'There is no proof that Ferris had married' the ambassador added, 'like so many of the curés and ecclesiastics of La Vendée.'[27]

On 30 October, 'His Majesty, wishing to put an end to all the claims addressed to him on the administration of the British colleges',[28] established a new *bureau gratuit*. It consisted of four honorary members: Maréchal MacDonald, Duc de Tarente, Duc de Fitz-James, Comte Lally Tollendal and Comte O'Mahony, Lieutenant-General of the king's armies. Among the eight ordinary members were Richard Ferris and his friend, Dr MacMahon. The Minister of the Interior charged the bureau with drawing up a report as soon as possible on the rights of the bishops to nominate the superior; whether these rights had devolved to the crown following the suppression during the revolution; and on the candidates, conditions, persons and mode of presentation of the superior. The bureau duly made their report and on 25 January 1816 the king signed a decree in the Tuileries confirming the separation of the colleges and nominating Paul Long as administrator-general of the Irish establishments. For the fourth time in one year the Green Horse had changed riders.

NOTES

1. K.D.A., 6 Feb. 1815. Long to Troy.
2. A.N. F 19 6237A, 26 Jan. 1815.
3. Douai, Parker Papers, 4 Dec. 1815.

4. Cooper, *Talleyrand*, p201.
5. A.N. F 19 6237C. Long to Napoleon.
6. D.D.A. 121/9, 20 July 1815. Long to Murray.
7. A.N. F 19 6237A, 27 Mar. 1815. Long to Interior.
8. Douai, Parker Papers, 26 Sept. 1816. Brewer to Lawson.
9. D.D.A. 121/9, 20 July 1815. Long to Murray.
10. A.N. F 19 6237A.
11. D.D.A. 121/9, 20 July 1815.
12. D.D.A. 121/9, 20 July 1815. Long to Murray.
13. Ibid.
14. Ibid.
15. A.N. F 19 6237C. nd. Long to Napoleon.
16. D.D.A. 121/9, 20 July 1815. Long to Murray.
17. Byrne, op. cit. 3. p26.
18. D.D.A. 121/9, 20 July 1815. Long to Murray.
19. I.C.P. 3L17, 24 Aug. 1815.
20. I.C.P. 3E, 9 July 1815. Ferris to Interior.
21. A.N. F 19 6237A, 30 July 1815. Long to Abp. of Rheims.
22. D.D.A. 121/9, 20 July 1815. Long to Murray.
23. D.D.A. 121/9, 20 July 1815. Long to Murray.
24. D.D.A. 121/9, 1815, Ferris, qtd Purcell, op. cit. p63.
25. A.N. F 19 6237C, 31 July 1815.
26. R.I.A. Brockliss & Ferté, *Prosopography*.
27. A.N. F 19 6237C, 4 Nov. 1815. Ambassador to Interior.
28. A.N. F 19 6237A, 16 Nov. 1815. Interior to President of Bureau.

19
Sic Transit...

For myself, I would scorn to ask indulgence of the mongrel minister, who is only Irish on his father's side.

–Richard Ferris

The first task of the government of the second restoration was to summon a parliament. It was decided to have two chambers on the English model. The upper chamber, the Chamber of Peers, was to be hereditary and hand picked from among the royalists and former *émigrés*. Talleyrand lightheartedly drew up the list and included his former companion in exile in London, Comte Lally Tollendal. Popular elections, with a limited franchise, returned the Chamber of Deputies. The royalists succeeded in sweeping the country and the lower house had a large majority of deputies who were even more royalist and reactionary than the king himself. It was the end of the French revolution: France was content to slip back into the old ways. The memory, however, lingered on and spasmodically agitated French political life for the next century and a half. Like French wine it travelled well and often found more congenial society abroad in the 19th century.

In this new political climate in France Charles Kearney was at last prepared to break his long silence and recount his story of what had happened during the revolution. He could now safely reveal the part he had played in the secret mission sent by the French court to London in the autumn of 1792. 'That voyage' he now declared, 'exposed me to all the persecutions I suffered during six or seven years after.'[1] In reply to the criticisms of his maladministration of Collège des Irlandais he claimed that the modest income of the house was in no way commensurate with the needs of the college and its young students. When fees were not forthcoming Kearney had not the heart to turn the young offenders away. 'I listened too easily' he said, 'to the prayers of the boys and their families.' And he declared–and nobody could dispute it–'that I have quitted the house much poorer than I was when I was placed at the head of it, that what I spent was spent on the boys of the house, that I made no reserve for myself or family, that I had neither the will nor the intent of speculating on the house.'[2] Now in the autumn of his life, Kearney could at last come in from the cold and end his days in whatever modest comfort the new regime would provide him.

It was his friend, Abbé Edgeworth, who had recommended Kearney for the dangerous mission to London. Edgeworth himself went into hiding shortly after the execution of the king. He stayed on in France awaiting the call of the king's sister which never came and after her execution crossed to England. Here, the retiring Edgeworth was feted much to his surprise and more to his discomfort. Offers were made to him, including a pension from Pitt and the presidency of Maynooth, all of which he politely declined. Early in 1797, he was summoned by the king's brother, then in exile in the duchy of Brunswick. The future Louis XVIII pressed him to remain on as chaplain to the royal family. They settled finally in Mittau, which the delicate Edgeworth described as the 'land of ice'.[3] From here, he continued to write regularly to his old friend, Bishop Moylan of Cork. 'Here I am, my dear friend,' he wrote: 'pinned down to the most unfortunate family upon earth; and resolved, if providence don't open a door, to share its fate to the last.'[4] His release came sooner than he expected. In the winter of 1806 Napoleon had advanced to Warsaw in an effort to crush what remained of Prussian resistance. In the rigours of that winter campaign, considerable numbers of French soldiers contracted fever. Some of them were left at Mittau. Abbé Edgeworth went immediately to minister to them despite the warnings of his friends and as a result caught the infection. He died on 22 May 1807, nursed to the end by the daughter of the king whose last night on earth he had shared. He was buried 'in the land of ice' at Mittau and the Latin inscription on his tomb was composed by the future Louis XVIII.

It was in that year too that Miles Byrne met the gallant MacKenna for the last time when the Irish legion was based at Boulogne-sur-Mer prior to their departure for the Spanish campaign. MacKenna had acted as spokesman for the six Irish students arrested following the incident on Champ de Mars nearly 20 years earlier. Having seen service on two of the French expeditions to Ireland he abandoned the army and reverted to civilian life. In 1807 he was a wealthy ship-owning merchant, had married a widow and was living in style. He was always eager to render a service to any of his former comrades-in-arms. One of the Irish officers who had previously fought with Humbert in Killala was court-martialled for insulting a superior officer, a Prussian. MacKenna, 'a worthy Irish patriot',[5] as Byrne called him, informed of the incident, prepared a written brief for the defending officer. The French major in question later declared that 'none but a first rate French scholar could have drawn up such a document'[6] and Miles Byrne added the comment: 'It was very true that at that time those who studied at the Irish college became very good French scholars.'[7] The court-martial found in favour of the Irish officer and to celebrate the victory MacKenna put on a splendid breakfast for his French and Irish friends. It was quite an affair. '"Erin go bragh" was toasted in bumpers of sparkling champagne.'[8] MacKenna was a great peacemaker, according to Byrne, though he was himself occasionally challenged to a duel. 'He was a first rate swordsman and had nothing to dread, though not very young and getting quite corpulent.'[9] It was a long breakfast as the Irish officers did not take leave of MacKenna until evening when they returned to their camp 'in high spirits'.

Jeremy Delany from the Kerry mountains was two years junior to MacKenna and had spent four years in the Irish college when he became involved in the Champ de Mars incident. The bloody nose he got on that occasion may well have deterred him from pursuing a military career in later life. He was considered a young man of talent and an accomplished scholar,[10] and he became private secretary to a French councillor of state. In despatches of the English agent in Paris he is referred to simply as 'Delany of the Irish college.'[11] He became an intimate friend of Thomas Russell and Thomas Addis Emmet in whose home in Saint Germain-en-Laye Miles Byrne met him. Byrne recalls him recounting to the Emmets 'the cruel privations suffered by the catholic population of Munster, particularly as regarded education'.[12] When Byrne returned from his Spanish campaign in 1812 he tried to look up Delany in Paris, only to discover he had died three months previously. 'He left no fortune and no debts. He spent his money in the most generous manner and he was surrounded by his Irish friends at his last moments.'[13]

As for the other four, the Champ de Mars was their only moment in the limelight. They later slipped quietly into oblivion. Not all are destined to encounter those generous dispensers of immortality, chroniclers of their time, like a Miles Byrne or a Wolfe Tone. The rebel students of 1792 achieved a higher average. Of the ten involved in that incident at least six led reasonably well-documented lives. Nicholas Madgett, elected superior on that occasion, left to posterity the secret reports he sent to Dublin Castle as an English agent. Later he figured on the prison registers in Paris and as the subject of a debate in the National Convention. He returned to respectability of sorts when he joined Richard Ferris as a member of the *bureau gratuit* of the united British colleges. Subsequently he completed the circle, resuming his ministry as a curé in the diocese of Bordeaux,[14] which he had left almost a quarter of a century earlier.

Bernard MacSheehy was the first of the group to die, killed by a cannon ball at the snow-driven battle of Eylau on 7 February 1807 while serving as a colonel on Napoleon's staff. It was that same army which had carried the fatal disease to Abbé Edgeworth. MacSheehy was described as 'a brave officer with military talents of the first order, a vast erudition, and capable of speaking and writing several languages.'[15] His fellow officer in the Irish legion, Major James Bartholomew Blackwell[16] from Ennis like him also quit the legion in its early days. He rejoined the main French army and served in the cavalry corps in the Prussian and Austrian campaigns of Napoleon. Ill-health forced him to retire as a colonel on half-pay to Paris where he died in 1812. He was buried in the cemetery of Père Lachaise.

Those who became doctors, as might be expected, weathered better the ravages of time. Dr John O'Neill made his career as the physician attached to the hospital in Saint Denis and figured little in later Irish circles. Dr MacMahon, on the contrary, followed his profession for the most part in the Irish milieu, first as medical attendant in Abbé MacDermott's Academy and later as physician to the Irish college. He served for many years as an Irish member of the *bureau gratuit*. He was a valuable acquisition to the supervisory board of the college, because 'having studied there when young, and having a perfect knowledge of the many changes which took place in the establishment subsequent to the revolution, Marshal MacDonald and the other members of the commission were generally guided by the information they got from him respecting those who had a right to "bursaries" in this rich seminary'.[17] Later, at Byrne's prompting, he applied for the post of head librarian of the medical school. Through the influence of a former student of the college, Laurence Lewins, now head of personnel in the Ministry of Education, he obtained an interview with the minister, Abbé de Frayssinous, and was given the job. He continued, however, to practise and 'had no lack of Irish clients among the poor exiles of Erin'.[18] He died in December 1835. 'He was born in Ireland, and ever did honour to the land of his birth: his friendship was sincere and lasting, and no difficulty could prevent him rendering a service to a friend in distress.'[19]

William Duckett, so maligned by Wolfe Tone in his Diaries, continued to furnish the French government with valuable reports on Ireland until interest in that cause finally petered out. While in Hamburg as private secretary to Léonard Bourdon he married Frederica Georgina Volmeister from a prominent Danish family. On returning to Paris, he was appointed professor in Collège de Sainte Barbe. He applied unsuccessfully for a bursary for his son in the Irish college. He died in Paris in 1841 at the age of 74, 'quoting his favourite Horace on his death-bed and receiving extreme unction.'[20] An appreciation of him was written by Charles Durozoir, a former pupil and a notable literary figure; and published in *Le Moniteur Universel*. His one-time employer and mentor, Léonard Bourdon, also returned to the teaching profession after the revolution. His bloodthirsty record as a revolutionary had few equals. Always in favour of extreme measures, he had voted for the execution of Louis XVI, played an active role in the arrest of Robespierre and had the remains of Marat taken from the Panthéon and dragged through the gutters of Paris.

Richard Ferris, who once had risked his neck by calling Napoleon a tyrant, continued to meddle with the Irish college, much to the displeasure of the Irish bishops. By now he had become a Chevalier of France, one of only 22 persons, outside the royal family, upon whom this distinction was conferred. Two other Irishmen were also recipients, Colonel Count Daniel O'Connell and Count O'Mahony. So disillusioned had the bishops become with Ferris and the lay board he manoeuvred so expertly that they sent Archbishops Murray and Curtis to Paris to negotiate with the French government to have their funds transferred to Ireland and Maynooth. Ferris promptly organised a petition signed by all the leading Irish in Paris protesting vociferously against such a move. Miles Byrne's only explanation of this 'strange' attempt on the part of the bishops was that 'it was one way of shewing their devotion to their taskmasters, to deprive the Irish rebel and exile of the means of having his son well-educated in France'.[21]

In any event, he had nothing to fear as the French government would never condone such a transfer of funds and the bishops 'were obliged to renounce their scheme'.

When the battle-weary Paul Long elected to return to the less demanding pastoral life in Dublin, Ferris had himself once more placed at the head of the Irish college. He had been enthusiastically recommended for the position by Hely d'Oisel, of Irish extraction, who was appointed president of the bureau in August 1819. In a lengthy confidential report[22] to the minister he warmly defended Ferris against the criticism of the Irish bishops. 'I know of no class of people in the world,' he wrote, 'more prone to calumny and more self-opinionated, than Irish priests.' What he conveniently forgot then was that Ferris himself belonged, more or less, to that class. Now, subject himself to the inspection and criticism of the bureau, his charm was less in evidence. Lally Tollendal was the first to become disillusioned and regret his earlier extravagant praise of Ferris. Lally quarrelled with the other members of the bureau 'calling them robbers, dogs, intriguers, dilapidators who ruined the best establishment in Paris.'[23]

Differences soon arose between Ferris and d'Oisel which led to heated exchanges at a meeting. Ferris, considering himself insulted, approached Miles Byrne to act as his second: he was determined to challenge d'Oisel to a duel. It was a foolhardy act as d'Oisel was a minister and councillor of state. Byrne, then on half-pay and liable to expulsion from France as a foreigner if he became involved, tried to dissuade Ferris. 'I thought it quite impossible for him to hold a pistol in his hand on account of the palsy with which he was afflicted.' But Ferris was determined: "Never mind" he replied, "I'll rest my pistol on my left arm and let my antagonist do the same".'[24] In spite of Byrne's pleas Ferris persisted and issued the challenge: 'This letter was written in the most gentlemanlike style, as indeed every letter dictated by Mr Ferris was.' The answer was swift and sharp, couched 'in terms more insulting than the verbal insult which caused it.' D'Oisel also declared that 'if he could discover the addresses of the *spadassins* (hired assassin) seconds, he would have them forthwith sent sixty leagues from Paris.' Stung to the quick, Ferris retorted that 'a coward who is afraid to fight is always the most vindictive and dangerous as an enemy.' He took the liberty of naming Count MacNamara, deputy governor of the king's pages and Lieutenant General Count O'Mahony as his seconds without consulting them.

The 'fire-eating abbé' Ferris realised he had overstepped the limit when he received d'Oisel's reply; 'If they prove, as I suspect they will, other than native-born Frenchmen,' d'Oisel threatened, 'they shall be forthwith expelled from French territory.'[25] Ferris' chief concern now was the fate of his unsuspecting seconds. He informed them of the liberty he had taken with their names and called on General Count Daniel O'Connell for advice. 'For myself' he told O'Connell, 'I would scorn to ask indulgence of the mongrel minister, who is only Irish on his father's side.'[26] O'Connell advised Ferris to apologise and agreed to settle the matter of the seconds. Together with General O'Mahony he intimated to Hely d'Oisel that 'if he desired to know further respecting the persons who had presented the hostile message he had received they were ready to answer him in any way he might require.'[27] And there the incident ended—and also the career of Richard Ferris as administrator of the Irish college.

Incredibly, he was succeeded in 1822 by none other than Charles Kearney who had first occupied the post 40 years earlier and who was now the last surviving signatory of the original deed of the college of 1772. Now in his late seventies, it was a fitting end to a long and persecution-ridden career. Unlike his predecessors he was universally loved. Miles Byrne knew him well and left a kindly drawn pen-picture[28] of him:

> Abbé Carney(sic) was temperate, and cared little about what he had to eat or drink himself, tho' generous and hospitable to his guests, whom he used to entertain whilst at table with many amusing anecdotes, as well as good cheer; he was always gay and good humoured, never speaking harshly of any one. He was low in stature, well-made, with a very agreeable, benevolent countenance, tho' not handsome. He had very little to live on before he became superior of the Irish college and still with that little, he was ever endeavouring to be useful to his friends and countrymen. I met him one day, with a rather large parcel under his arm; he told me it was one of his pantaloons he was taking to a poor exile of Erin. He hoped it would fit him, for he was to present him at ten o'clock to a French family where he expected to have him placed as tutor or preceptor.

Kearney died on 22 April 1824 and Miles Byrne attended the obsequies:

> His funeral service was celebrated in the chapel of the college, where were assembled a great concourse of his countrymen, with numbers of the French nobility; the Castelbacjacs family attended and were anxious to have the religious ceremony executed with all the pomp

> of the Roman Catholic Church. Ladies were allowed to be present in the gallery of the chapel, and a special permission was obtained to have him buried in the vault of the chapel, and after making three rounds of the college courtyard, in the most solemn manner, the procession returned to the chapel, when the coffin was descended into the vault; and there the remains of the worthy Abbé Carney lie, enclosed in a double coffin, a lead one inside.[29]

The simple inscription on the coffin reads: 'Kearney 1824.'

A little over a year later, his former colleague and one-time adversary John Baptist Walsh followed him to the grave. He ended his life in splendid isolation, the sole Irish occupant of Collège des Lombards. In retirement, the old lion probably stirred and growled in his Lombardian lair at each new Ferris triumph, but he kept the pledge he made in 1814, to engage no further in controversy. Here, on 18 October 1825, he drew up his will.[30] After thanking God for his long life—he was then in his 84th year—he bequeathed his most prized possession, a ciborium given him by Madame Elisabeth, to the Archbishop of Paris. He provided for his housekeeper and shared his silverware among a few convents and devoted the rest of his wealth to the education of native Irish students. Instead of founding bursaries 'which experience had taught him, proved of little value to the Irish mission', he devised what he called 'annual pensions of encouragement.' Candidates had to be at least sub-deacons, which shrewdly reduced the risk of drop-outs. Ironically, with all his shrewdness, he made one mistake. He named the Archbishop of Paris as his sole legatee and consigned to him and his successors the administration of his foundation. The history of that office during his lifetime should have left him wiser. The See of Paris continued to be a high-risk investment for the rest of the 19th and early 20th century. Following the separation of church and state in 1905 the Walsh foundation was disposed of. It was the only loss suffered then by the Irish college. In his will, Walsh expressed a desire to be buried 'among the ecclesiastics at Mont-Calvaire.' He was the last Irishman ever to occupy the once famous Collège des Lombards. Strangely, he never took down the sign 'Property for Sale' placed on the chapel door in 1793. Perhaps he kept it as a reminder of his long battle to save the Irish college.

Ferris, his arch-rival, spent the remainder of his life doing what he was best at, making money for himself. His last intervention in the affairs of the Irish college was towards the end of 1822, when he addressed a *placet*[31] to the king, arguing against the attempt by the Irish bishops to have their funds transferred to Ireland. It was a finely-argued legal case alleging that the bishops had little or no legal rights to the foundations. 'His ambition was to shew to ... the Irish bishops that he had more influence with the French government than they had'.[32] He concluded his address to the king by paying a tribute to 'so many generous benefactors who wished to devote their wealth to providing education in France for their relatives who could adopt the principles and liberty of the Gallic church, which is invoked today by all who are attached to our holy religion.'[33]

From then on he concentrated on his legal practice in which he was very much in demand, particularly among British subjects claiming compensation for losses sustained during the revolution. It was apparently highly remunerative for he purchased a handsome country house and land near Soissons. Here, in the house he named *La Maison Blanche*, Richard Ferris from Tuoght, Co. Kerry, died at nine o'clock in the morning on 16 June 1827 in his 75th year. Two months previously, being 'of very sound mind, memory and judgement',[34] he drew up his will in Paris. It was a substantial document running to ten large pages detailing the disposal of his considerable fortune. To each of his two executors he gave a diamond worth 1,200 francs. His estate was divided mainly between a French family called Paulmier and his nephew, Captain Richard Maurice Ferris, who also inherited his library.

In a strange way, the three men, Kearney, Ferris and Walsh—the saint, the sinner and the accountant—who dominated the history of the Irish college during the revolution—by their wills wrote their own epitaphs on their relationship to that institution. Of his vast wealth, Ferris left nothing to the college. Kearney left it all he had at the end of his life, his remains. Walsh devoted his modest savings to providing an endowment for the college. It was neither the saint nor the sinner but the accountant alone who preserved the college from final extinction during that turbulent period.

Lally Tollendal died in 1830 from a fit of apoplexy but not before he had seen the Irish college become the type of institution he had always strongly advocated.

> Establishments founded by catholics for their catholic posterity should contain uniquely catholics, for tolerance would be odd indeed which would hand over the schools of its religion to a foreign religion, and fraternity would be indeed strange which would rob its catholic brothers to give to its protestant brothers. Religious studies must and should always have first place in these establishments, the other liberal

> studies, which have already been admitted there, can, depending on new circumstances, compete with them to a larger degree.[35]

Lally himself was showered with honours in the autumn of his life. He became a marquis and was admitted as a member of the French academy where he read his five act tragedy entitled *Tuathal-Teamar, ou la restauration de la monarchie en Irlande*. Thirty years earlier he had read another of his tragedies at Juniper Hall to a brilliant coterie of French *émigrés*, including Talleyrand. He was described then as 'large, fat, with a great head, small nose, immense cheeks'[36] and Talleyrand labelled him rather unkindly, *un très honnête garçon et rien de plus.*[37] He may well have, like good wine, improved with age.

All that the revolution had left now to be resolved was the matter of the indemnities.[38] In 1818 the French government paid a lump sum to Britain, leaving it the task of adjudicating the claims of its own subjects. In 1824 the claim of the English college in Douai was examined and rejected. This was taken to apply also to the Irish colleges and Paul Long was accordingly notified in 1825. Two grounds were given for the rejection. Firstly, their purpose was directly opposed to British law, and secondly, they were deemed to be French establishments. An attempt was made to have this decision reversed in 1832. Daniel O'Connell succeeded in having the case appealed to the Privy Council where he managed to demolish the first ground, pointing out that Irish law was totally dissimilar to the law of England on the subject of these foundations. However, the Privy Council upheld the second ground that they were deemed French establishments and thus not subject to indemnification. O'Connell described the decision as a 'most atrocious violation of justice'.[39] In 1790, the National Assembly had exempted the Irish college from confiscation on the ground that it was the property of British subjects; in 1793 the Convention had confiscated it as the property of British subjects. Now, Britain twice refused to acknowledge what France had twice admitted.

Over 40 years were to pass before the Irish made another attempt to redress the balance of justice. This time the case was handled by Isaac Butt. He introduced a motion in the House of Commons on 30 April 1875 for a select committee to inquire into the claims of the Irish college. It was defeated by 116 votes to 54. Treating of a similar case, some years earlier, Lord Lyndhurst had stated that 'neither lapse of time nor technicalities nor any inconvenience of being called upon to pay a sum however large ought to prevent the discharge of such a claim on the part of this country.'[40] Informing the rector of the Commons vote, Isaac Butt wrote: 'I am quite sure this ought not to be our final effort.'[41] With decisions like these the British government were bound to have had surplus funds to dispose of. The money in fact was spent on three projects, paying off the debt on Brighton Pavilion, refurbishing Windsor Castle and building the Marble Arch. The latter, among other things, serves to mark the site of the martyrdom of St Oliver Plunkett, who played a major part in the acquisition of Collège des Lombards in Paris.

In spite of its losses Collège des Irlandais continued to thrive for another century and a half, turning out priests, and sometimes turbulent ones, for the Irish mission. It was producing so many of the latter at one period that Cardinal Cullen, after a visit in 1850, remarked ruefully: 'Poor Ireland has much to fear from its future ministers.'[42] The college was to witness other revolutions which Paris seems destined to produce with almost predictable regularity. Sometimes, it became involved as in 1848, when 'the whole community, priests and students, with banner unfurled, paraded with the "Reds" from end to end of the city–*deux rouges* supporting each soutane ...,'[43] much to the scandal of clerical Paris. It survived that and the siege of Paris some two decades later and two world wars in the 20th century.

With the disbandment of the Irish legion in September 1815, the Irish college was all that remained of the once strong Franco-Irish tradition. It survived thanks to the courage and tenacity of John Baptist Walsh who saved it from revolutionary confiscation and to the bureaucratic genius of Napoleon who ensured that not even the Irish could dispose of it. Lurking in terror inside the great door of the college, while the communards were assembling menacingly outside in 1871, the French administrator began to muse on the strange and turbulent history of the building he was left to protect. It consoled him then to believe 'that this noble college, already three hundred years old would yet survive many more centuries.'[44] It occurred to him then that it would be often buffeted but never wrecked and that it had earned the right to adopt the motto of the city of Paris itself: *Fluctuat nec mergitur.*

NOTES

1. D.D.A. 121/9 169, 29 Jan. 1816.
2. Ibid.
3. England, *Edgeworth*, p148, 13 Mar. 1804.
4. Ibid. p150.
5. Byrne, op. cit. 2. p50.
6. Ibid. 3. p165.
7. Ibid. pp165-6.
8. Ibid. p165.
9. Ibid. p168.
10. Ibid. p169.
11. Hayes, *Biog. Dict.* p56.
12. Ibid. p169.
13. Ibid. p172.
14. Hayes, *Biog. Dict.* p196.
15. De La Ponce Mss. qtd Hayes, op. cit. p192.
16. Hayes, op. cit. pp13-14.
17. Byrne, op. cit. 3. p150.
18. Ibid. p158.
19. Ibid.
20. N.L.I. pos.210 *Life of Duckett*.
21. Byrne, op. cit. 3. p195.
22. A.N. F 19 6237B, 4 April 1820. Hely d'Oisel to Interior.
23. D.D.A. 121/9, 11 April 1816. qtd Purcell, *Richard Ferris*, p64.
24. Byrne, 3. p198.
25. O'Reilly, op. cit. p243.
26. Ibid.
27. Ibid. p244.
28. Byrne, op. cit. 3. pp200-1.
29. Byrne, op. cit. 3. p203.
30. Boyle, 'Abbé John Baptist Walsh', I.E.R. XVII (1905) pp450-3.
31. A.N. F 19 6237B, 26 Dec. 1822. Ferris to Louis XVIII.
32. Byrne, op. cit. 3. p196.
33. A.N. F 19 6237B, 26 Dec. 1822.
34. Purcell, *Richard Ferris*, p74.
35. A.N. H 3 2561A, Mar. 1811. Tollendal to Interior, p7.
36. Qtd. Cooper, *Tallyrand*, p52.
37. Ibid.
38. Boyle, op. cit. pp73-5, 80-4, 100-3.
39. Qtd. ibid. p84.
40. Boyle, op. cit. p102.
41. Qtd. ibid. p103.
42. Swords, *Irish-French Connection*, p110.
43. Qtd. ibid. p108.
44. I.C.P. 64J. qtd. Swords, op. cit. p126.

STUDENTS OF COLLEGE DES IRLANDAIS 1790–1795

Ahearne,		Aug. 1792				
Barrett,						
Bowe, Sr.		Aug. 1792				
Bowe, Jr.		Aug. 1792				
Callan,		Aug. 1792				
Costello, William,	6 Dec. 1790	Aug. 1792				
Cruise,		Aug. 1792			8 Sept. 1793	4 April 1795
Curtayne, Jeremy,		Aug. 1792	13 Oct. 1792	24 Nov. 1792		
Delany, Jeremy	6 Dec. 1790					4 April 1795
Ferris, Edward		Aug. 1792	13 Oct. 1792	24 Nov. 1792		
Fitzpatrick,					8 Sept. 1793	4 April 1795
Foley,					8 Sept. 1793	4 April 1795
Graham,		Aug. 1792				
Hickey, John,	6 Dec. 1790	Aug. 1792				
Hurley,	6 Dec. 1790					
Ingolsby, Peter,	6 Dec. 1790					
MacCurtain,		Aug. 1792			8 Sept. 1793	4 April 1795
MacDonough,		Aug. 1792				
MacKenna, Thomas,	6 Dec. 1790	Aug. 1792			8 Sept. 1793	4 April 1795
MacMahon, Jeremy,				6 Feb. 1793	8 Sept. 1793	4 April 1795
MacMahon, John						4 April 1795
MacSheehy, Bernard		Aug. 1792	13 Oct. 1792	24 Nov. 1792		4 April 1795
MacSheehy, John		Aug. 1792				4 April 1795
Magennis,		Aug. 1792				
Maginn,	6 Dec. 1790	Aug. 1792				
Molony, James				6 Feb. 1793	8 Sept. 1793	4 April 1795
Moriarty,		Aug. 1792			8 Sept. 1793	4 April 1795
Murphy,		Aug. 1792			8 Sept. 1793	
Murry, Bartholomew		Aug. 1792	13 Oct. 1792	24 Nov. 1792		4 April 1795

Appendix 1 (cont'd)

O'Berne, Francis	6 Dec. 1790	Aug. 1792			6 Feb. 1793	8 Sept. 1793	4 April 1795
O'Carroll,		Aug. 1792			6 Feb. 1793	8 Sept. 1793	
O'Connor,		Aug. 1792					
O'Diggan,						8 Sept. 1793	
O'Neill, John							4 April 1795
O'Reilly,	6 Dec. 1790						
O'Ronan,						8 Sept. 1793	
O'Shaughnessy, Terence					6 Feb. 1793		

*6 Dec. 1790. Incident on the Champ Mars.
*Aug. 1792. List of students submitted by J. Maher to Ministry of Foreign Affairs.
*13 Oct. 1792. Students who took part in the election.
*24 Nov. 1792. Students who signed the congratulatory address to the National Convention.
*6 Feb. 1793. Students who petitioned the National Convention re burses.
*8 Sept. 1793. Students who signed petition to National Convention.
*4 April 1795. Those listed as in need of help.

PRISONERS IN COLLEGE DES IRLANDAIS Oct 1793-Sept 1794.

Surname	*Name*	*Profession*	*Age*	*Entered*	*Left*	*Freed*
Audibert	Auguste Desiré	Cons. d'Aix	48		3 Mar. 1794	
Audibert	Thomas Albin Joseph				3 Mar. 1794	
Barbaré	Madeleine	Ex-noble	70	27 April 1794	17 May 1794	
Beaufils	Nicholas Louis				3 Mar. 1794	
Beaufils, Angelique Jeanne			44		3 Mar. 1794	
Betz	J.F.			25 Oct. 1793		
Carte					17 May 1794	
Cepoy					17 May 1794	

Chalendar	Louis Charles	Ex-captain	44	26 April 1794		
Clutterbuck	Charles	Language teacher	38	25 Oct. 1793		
Cousin	Guillaume Jacques					
Dargaud	Charles				2 Mar. 1794	
David	Pierre Louis Honoré				17 May 1794	
Dejean					17 May 1794	
Delaunay	Gilbert Fougeray				17 May 1794	
Ferry	Louis H. Joseph	Judge	30	31 Jan. 1794	17 May 1794	
Fitzsimmons	Dominick	Language teacher		25 Oct. 1793		24 Sept. 1794
Garnet	George	Mechanic		25 Oct. 1793	4 Nov. 1793	
Gauthey	Paul Françoise	Lt.-Gen.	60		2 Mar. 1794	
Guermante	Adelaide Marie	Ex-noble	72		2 Mar. 1794	
Hunt	Edward	Domestic	33	25 Oct. 1793		24 Sept. 1794
Jourdan	Adrien Felix	Royal Guards		27 Mar. 1794	17 May 1794	
Joussineaux la Tourdonnet	Jean	Col.		25 April 1794	17 May 1794	
Juge	Alexandre	Musician, noble		26 April 1794	17 May 1794	
Larbouste	Comte				17 May 1794	
Laval	Comtesse de				17 May 1794	
Leberton	André Jacques Hiacinthe		82	6 Jan. 1794	4 Mar. 1794	
Leconteur	François Joseph	English	22	25 Oct. 1793		
Lepinet	Jacques	English interpreter	27	4 Nov. 1793		
Lewal	Charles Cerf	Banker	46		31 Jan. 1794	
Lewal	Leon	Banker	49		31 Jan. 1794	
Lort	Guillaume Auguste de	*Vicaire* de Valence			3 Mar. 1794	
Lynch	John Baptist	Pres. Parl. Bordeaux	45	6 Jan. 1794	21 April 1794	
Lyster	Robert			25 Oct. 1793		22 Dec. 1793
Malard					27 May 1794	
Merigot	Jean Baptiste	Lawyer			17 May 1794	
Michel				25 Mar. 1794	27 May 1794	

Montferrant	Leroux				27 May 1794	
Montignie					27 May 1794	
Moore	John James	English		5 Nov. 1793		
Morsan	Mrs.	English	52		17 May 1794	
Nazon	Jean Charles	Planter, St. Domingue		26 Mar. 1794	17 May 1794	
O'Connor	James	Medical student	27		17 May 1794	
Parker	George	English		25 Oct. 1793		
Pauck	James	English, delph seller	45	25 Oct. 1793	2 Oct. 1794	
Perrin				26 Dec. 1793		
Pierrecourt	Abel Alexandre			26 Mar. 1794	17 May 1794	
Pigott	Jean			25 Oct. 1793		24 Sept. 1794
Promoteur	(William Proctor)	English teacher		25 Oct. 1793		
Reeves	John	English		25 Oct. 1793		
Roland	Nicolas Legaré	Writer			3 Mar. 1794	
Roland	Marie Anne					
St Amand	Prudent Galbois				2 Mar. 1794	
Therant					17 May 1794	
Therou	Jean Nicolas				17 May 1794	
Thibaut					17 May 1794	
Tournier	Urbain Grégoire				17 May 1794	
Tournon	Antoine	Journalist	40		17 May 1794	
Vanhoff	Charles	Dutch clockmaker	19	8 April 1794	17 May 1794	
Vendeuil	Marie-Charlotte				17 May 1794	
Vendeuil	Adelaide				17 May 1794	
Weld				4 Nov. 1793		
Wild	William	English, groom	37	25 Oct. 1793	4 Nov. 1794	
Williams	Thomas	English teacher		25 Oct. 1793		
Woulf	Francis	Servant (La Tour du Pin)		25 Oct. 1793		

*Foregoing list compiled from the register in Archives de la police judiciare, Paris.

Bibliography

PRIMARY SOURCES

England

BODLEIAN LIBRARY OXFORD
Bland Burges Papers.

BRITISH MUSEUM
Huskisson Ms. 38769; Dropmore Papers, 58857 vol. III June 1792-1793.

DOUAI ABBEY, READING
Parker Papers.

PUBLIC RECORD OFFICE, LONDON F.O.
Foreign Office 27/40, 27/42, 27/43.

WESTMINSTER DIOCESAN ARCHIVES

France

ARCHIVES DES AFFAIRES ETRANGÈRES
Correspondance Politique Angleterre.
vol. 559, f62, 176.
vol. 582, f41, 80, 119, 125, 135, 330-1, 341-2, 350, 353rv, 358, 359-60.
vol. 583, f103, 106-7, 110-11, 131, 147, 237, 266-7, 273-4.
vol. 587, f20, 45, 137, 159, 169, 292, 296-300, 306-7, 312, 314, 319r & v, 325, 326, 334.
vol. 588, f3, 14, 19, 43, 186, 262, 270, 484.
vol. 589, f78, 135, 155, 157, 260.
vol. 592, f43r, 61, 80, 84-5, 128r, 129-30, 151, 152r & v, 288r, 375, 377-83, 395r & v, 396r, 400r & v-401r, 402rv, 403r, 404r.
vol. 593, f3rv, 4rv, 5rv, 6rv, 8rv, 11rv, 12r, 20rv, 37rv, 143r, 144rv, 145rv, 383rv, 384rv, 410r, 451rv, 452rv, 465r.
Correspondance Politique Hambourg.
vol. 111, f311-312.
Mémoires et documents, Angleterre, 55, f189, 196.

ARCHIVES OF THE IRISH COLLEGE PARIS
3E, 3J, 3L 2, 3, 4, 5, 11, 12, 13, 15, 16, 17, 3U 1, 4, 3V 1, 3W 1, 2, 3Z 8, 14A; 64J.

ARCHIVES NATIONALES PARIS
AF. 11. 288.
AF. 11 290 f63, 65r.
AF. 111. 186b. doss. 860
BB 3. 54.
BB 3 81 A. f345-9, 355-7
BB 4 123, f193-8.
C 134. doss. 3, 5.
C 241.
DXL 3 no. 60.
DXIX. 44 no. 702.
AF. 111 149 doss. 701 f67, 71
AF. 111 58 doss. 228.
AF IV, carton 1671 f129v.
BB 3. 56.
BB 3. 70 320.
C 58 no. 590.
C 163 f6624v.
C 271. 666.
DXIX. 30 doss. 472.
E 2654 no. 184.

F 7 2514 p84.
F 7 4774 51.
F 7 4474 28 doss. 1.
F 7 4624.
F 7 4753 doss. 1.
F 7 4774 55 doss. 3.
F 7 4774 60 doss. 1.
F 7 4774˙63 doss. 4.
F 17 1162.
F 17 14760.
F 17 14764.
F 19 6237A.
F 19 6237C.
M 147.
T 1259.
W 308. 401.
W 345. 676.
W 411. 945.
W 429. 965.
Z 3 81, 84.
F 7 4706 doss. 1
F 7 4474 27.
F 7 4474 59, doss. 1.
F 7.4720 doss. 5.
F 7 4774 39 doss. 3.
F 7 4774 59.
F 7 4775 50 doss. 3.
F 7 4775 52 doss. 2.
F 17 2500.
F 17 14761
F 19 471.
F 19 6237B.
H 3 2561A.
T 452.
T 1636.
W 335. 585.
W 389 no. 904 pièce 13.
W 414. 949.
W 430. 966.

ARCHIVES DE LA PREFECTURE DE LA POLICE

A A/198 Observatoire, 19 Mar. 11, 15 April, 9, 10, 11, 16 Oct. 1791, 6 May 1794.

A A/200 Panthéon, 25 Sept., 8 Dec. 1791, 2 Feb. 1792, 28 Mar. 7 & 8 Sept. 1793.

A B/330 f79, 16 Oct. 1797; f83 & 87, 21 Oct. 1797; f88, 92, 27, 31 Oct. 1797.

A B/334, f25, 15 April 1800.

A A/86 Butte-des-Moulins, 15 Oct. 1791.

Labat. Léon, Documents à consulter pour l'histoire de la Révolution Française-Ordres d'arrestation, de transférments, de mise en liberté, 1789-An 5 (1797) Catalogue Alphabétique. (unpublished manuscript) 1879.

ARCHIVES DE LA SEINE

6AZ 404 pièce no. 8
D 13 U 1.
DC 6 17 f33r.
DC 6 19 f95r.
DC 6 27 f64v.
DC 6 28 f45v.
DC 6 29 f131v.
DC 6 31 f135r.
DC 6 32 f82r.
DC 6 32 f155r & v.
DQ 10 5 doss. 3222.
DQ 10 35 doss. 10892.
DQ 10 108 doss. 2086.
DQ 10 131 doss. 3577.
DQ 10 699 doss. 2562.
VN 4 carton 144 19.
D 12U 1 23.
DC 6 14 f92v.
DC 6 18 f66r.
DC 6 25 f32v.
DC 6 28 f9r.
DC 6 31 f117r.
DC 6 31 f143v.
DC 6 32 f167v.
DC 6 252 f205.
DQ 10 6 3592.
DQ 10 5 doss. 3592.
DQ 10 94 doss. 1291.
DQ 10 117 doss. 2627.
DQ 10 603 doss. 751.
DQ 10 791 & 1312.

BIBLIOTHÈQUE HISTORIQUE DE LA VILLE DE PARIS

7502, 12272, 953548, 959775, 959784.

BIBLIOTHÈQUE NATIONALE
B.N. 395; Lb 39 9585, 9586, 4407, 4408; Lc2 2453.
Fonds Français 11697 fos. 109v. & 110r.

Ireland

DUBLIN DIOCESAN ARCHIVES
D.D.A. 121/8 Irish college Paris Papers 1718-1812.
Ibid. 121/9, 1812-1853.
Troy Papers, 4 Nov. 1788; 17 April 1802.

CASHEL DIOCESAN ARCHIVES
Papers of Butler 11, 9 Aug. 1785.

KERRY DIOCESAN ARCHIVES
6 Feb. 1815, Long to Troy.

MAYNOOTH COLLEGE
Papers of the Irish College Paris.
Ms 60, 18 Nov. 1801.
Mémoire à consulter, nd.

NATIONAL LIBRARY DUBLIN
Manuscript Life of William Duckett, microfilm pos. 210.

ROYAL IRISH ACADEMY
Brockliss & Ferté, 'Irish clerics in France in the seventeenth and eighteenth centuries: a statistical survey.' Typescript.

Italy

ARCHIVES OF PROPAGANDA FIDE
SC Irlanda 1788-1801, f85-6, 191-2, 238, 580rv.

VATICAN ARCHIVES
Francia, 583.

PUBLISHED WORKS AND SECONDARY SOURCES

NEWSPAPERS
La Feuille du Jour, 7 & 8 Dec. 1790.
London Evening Post, 5 Mar. 1807.
Mercure de France, 15 Oct. 1791.
Moniteur, 4, 24 July 1789, 29 Oct. 1790, 23 Oct. 1791, 29 Nov. 1792, 24 Jan., 8 Sept., 10 Oct. 1793, 21 Oct. 1794, 4 April 1795, 8 July 1795, 18 April 1796, 21 April, 9 June, 28 Oct., 8 Nov. 1798, 3 Jan., 19 Oct. 1799.
Morning Chronicle, 17 Nov. & 3 Dec. 1794.
Northern Star, II, no. 304.
The Pilot (Liverpool).

Anonymous, 'The Irish College Paris' I.E.R. 1. III. (1866) 180-5, 252-62.
Amadou, Robert, 'Saint-Ephrem-des-Syriens du Collège des Lombards à nos jours' in Paris et Ile-de-France Mémoires, Tome 37, 7-152, 1986.
Archives parlementaires. Recueil complet des débats législatives des Chambres françaises, 91 vols. 1879-1976.
Aulard, A. Recueil des actes du comité de salut public, 33 vols. Paris 1889-1951.

Paris sous le Consulat. Recueil des documents.

Bolster, E. 'Moylan Correspondence in Bishop's House, Killarney, Collect. Hib.XIV (1971) 82-143, & XV (1972) 56-109.

Bournon, F. La Bastille.

Boyle OP, Leonard F. San Clemente Miscellany 1, Rome, 1977.

Boyle CM, Patrick. The Irish College in Paris from 1578-1901, London, Dublin, New York, 1901.

'The Irish College in Paris 1578-1901' I.E.R. 4. XI. (1902) 193-210.

'Glimpses of Irish collegiate life in Paris in the seventeenth and eighteenth centuries' I.E.R. 4. XI. (1902) 432-50.

'Irishmen in the university of Paris' I.E.R. 4. XIV. (1903) 24-45.

'The Irish College Paris during the French Revolution' I.E.R. 4. XV. (1904) 48-73.

'Abbé John Baptist Walsh' I.E.R. 4. XVII, XVIII. (1905) 431-54.

'Abbé Kearney' I.E.R. 4. XXIII. (1908) 454-66.

'Irish ecclesiastics at the seminary of St Nicholas Paris' I.E.R. 4. XXVIII. (1910) 480-91.

'Documents relative to the appointment of an archbishop to the See of Cashel in 1791 and a coadjutor to the Bishop of Waterford in1801'. Arch. Hib. VII. (1918-22) 1-19.

'Dr Hussey and the Concordat of 1801' I.E.R. April 1915.

Brock, F.W. van. 'Captain MacSheehy's Mission' Irish Sword, X (1972) 215-28.

Brockliss, L.W.B. & P. Ferté. 'Irish clerics in France in the seventeenth and eighteenth centuries: a statistical study' Proceedings of the Royal Irish Academy, vol. 87. C. no. 9. (1987).

Burke, Edmund, Works of the Rt Hon. Burke 15 vols. London, 1826.

Byrne, Miles. Memoirs of Miles Byrne, 3 vols. Paris, New York, 1863.

Carles, Lt. Col. Pierre, 'Le corps irlandais au service de la France sous le Consulat et l'Empire' Revue historique des Armées, 2 (1976), 25-54.

Cogan, A. The ecclesiastical history of the diocese of Meath. 3 vols. Dublin, 1867-74.

Coigly, James. The Life of the Rev James Coigly, London, 1798.

Conlan OFM, Patrick. Saint Anthony's College of the Irish Franciscans at Louvain, Dublin, 1977.

Cooper, Duff. Talleyrand, London, 1958.

Daumet, G. Notices sur les établissements religieux anglais, écossais et irlandais, fondés à Paris avant la Révolution' Mémoires de la Société de l'histoire de Paris et de l'Ile-de-France, t. XXXVII (1910) 1-184, XXXIX (1912) 1-224.

Debidour, A. Recueil des actes du Directoire exécutif, 4 vols, Paris, 1910-17.

Delarc, Abbé, L'église de Paris pendant la révolution française, Paris s.d.

Documents inédits sur l'histoire de France. Procés-verbeaux de la commission temperaire des arts.

Elliot, Marianne. Partners in Revolution. The United Irishmen and France, Newhaven and London, 1982.

England, T.R. Letters from Abbé Edgeworth, London, 1818.

Fitzpatrick, W.J. Secret service under Pitt, London, 1892.

Flood, J.M. 'Dr Plunkett, bishop of Meath, 1779-1827' I.E.R. LXXII (1949) 234-42.

Gorce, M. de la. Histoire religieuse de la révolution française, Paris, 1909.

Guillaume, M.G. Collection de documents inédits.

Hayes, Richard. Ireland and Irishmen during the French Revolution, London, 1932.
Irish Swordsmen of France, Dublin, 1934.
The last invasion of Ireland, Dublin, 1937.
Old Irish Links with France, Dublin, 1940.
Biographical dictionary of Irishmen in France, Dublin, 1945.
'Irish links with Napoleon' Studies, XXXV (1946) 71f.
'Priests in the independence movement of 1798' I.E.R. 5. LXVI (1945) 258-70.
Henchy, Monica. 'The Irish college at Salamanca' Studies, Summer/Autumn, 1981.
Hussey, T. A Pastoral Letter to the clergy of the united dioceses of Waterford and Lismore, Waterford, 1797.
Jennings, B. Louvain Papers 1606-1827.
La Montagne Sainte-Geneviève et ses abords, no. 196, octobre 1976.
Lecky, W.E.H. History of Ireland in the eighteenth century, 5 vols., London, 1892.
Lefebvre, G., M. Bouloiseau, M. Reinhard. Procés verbaux des séances de la Convention Nationale (table analytique), Paris, 1961.
Le Grand, L. Les sources de l'histoire religieuse de la révolution aux Archives Nationales, Paris, 1914.
Lestra, A. Le P. Coudrin, fondateur de Picpus, Lyon, 1952.
Martin, André, & Gérard Walter. Catalogue de l'histoire de la Révolution française, Paris, 1940.
McDonald, Wm. 'Irish colleges since the Reformation' I.E.R. XI (1874).
McEvoy, Brendan, Father James Quigley, Seanchas Ard Mhacha, 247-68.
Nolan, P.L. 'Irishmen in the French Revolution' Dublin Review, XXIII (1890) 368-85.
O'Boyle, J. The Irish colleges on the continent, Dublin, 1935.
O Fiaich, Cardinal Tomas. 'The Irish Colleges in France' The Humbert Summer School, 1988.
Ó Néill, Eoghan. Gleann an Óir, Dublin, 1988.
O'Reilly, A. The Irish abroad and at home, New York, 1956.
O'Riordan, M. The Irish colleges in Paris and the French Revolution, unpublished Ph.D. thesis, UCG, 1973.
Pisani, P. L'église de Paris pendant la Révolution, 3 vols., Paris, 1908.
Power, T.P. 'Dr Thomas Hussey' I.E.R. 5. XLV (1935) 561-75.
Procés-verbaux de la Convention Nationale.
Purcell, Mary. 'Richard Ferris, 1754-1828' Journal of the Kerry Archaeological and Historical Society, 18 (1985) 5-77.
Salamon, Abbé de. Correspondence secrète Paris 1898.
Scott, Samuel F. & Barry Rothaus, ed. Dictionary of the French Revolution, 1789-99, Westport, Connecticut, 2 vols., 1985.
Sneyd-Edgeworth, C. Memoirs of the Abbé Edgeworth, London, 1815.
Swords, Liam, ed. The Irish-French Connection 1578-1978, The Irish College Paris, 1978.
'History of the Irish College Paris, 1578-1800' Arch. Hib. XXXV (1980) 3-233.
Soldiers, Scholars, Priests, The Irish College Paris, 1985.
Theiner, A. Documents inédits relats aux affairs religieuses de la France, 1790-1800, Paris, 1857-8.

Tierney OSB, Mark, 'Calendar of the papers of Dr James Butler II' (typescript).
'Calendar of Dr Bray's papers' (typescript).

Tuetey, A. Répertoire général des sources manuscrites de l'histoire de Paris pendant la Révolution, 11 vols., 1890-1902.
L'Assistance publique à Paris pendant la Révolution.

Wallon, H. Histoire du Tribunal Révolutionaire de Paris.

Walsh, Micheline. 'Irish soldiers and the Irish college in Paris' The Irish-French Connection, 63-87, & Seanchas Ard Mhacha vol. 9 no. 1 (1978) 95-122.

Walsh, T.J. The Irish continental college movement, Dublin & Cork, 1973.

Chronology

1789

February	Elections to the Estates-General.
5 May	Opening of Estates-General.
17 June	Third Estate declares itself the National Assembly.
20 June	Oath of the tennis court.
11 July	Dismissal of Necker.
12 July	Crowd urged by Camilles Desmoulins invaded Tuilerie Gardens.
13 July	Irish priest nearly murdered at Hôtel de Ville.
	Joseph Cavanagh on deputation to Hôtel de Ville.
14 July	Taking of the Bastille.
	Whyte released.
16 July	Necker recalled.
4-11 August	Abolition of feudal rights and privileges.
26 August	Declaration of the rights of man and the citizen.
24 & 28 Sept.	Irish colleges donate silver to national mint.
29 September	Decree requiring church to donate its silver.
8 October	Lally Tollendal presents receipts of Collège des Irlandais to National Assembly.
2 November	Nationalisation of ecclesiastical property.
19 December	Issue of *assignats*.

1790

20 February	John Baptist Walsh makes declaration of Collège des Lombards property.
19 June	Abolition of hereditary titles.
12 July	Civil constitution of the clergy.
14 July	*Fête de la Fédération.*
14 September	Ecclesiastical committee decrees that Collège des Lombards is to retain management.
	Walsh mémoire requesting confirmation by National Assembly.

29 October	Chasset reports to National Assembly in favour of Irish colleges.
7 November	National Assembly decree preserving Irish colleges.
27 November	Clerical oath to the nation declared.
6 December	Irish student incident on Champ de Mars. Collège des Irlandais attacked. Charles Kearney saved by National Guard.
7 December	Bailly instructs Lafayette to protect Irish colleges.
8 December	Pamphlets published on incident.

1791

10 March	Pius VI condemns Civil Constitution.
31 March	National Assembly grants Walsh sole administratorship of Collège des Lombards.
15 April	Police place seals on Collège des Irlandais.
16 April	Police place seals on Collège des Lombards.
17 April	Seals lifted on Irish colleges.
18 April	Irish priests prepare to leave Collège des Lombards.
20-25 June	Flight to Varennes and return of the royal family to Paris.
17 July	Champ de Mars 'massacre'.
27 August	Declaration of Pillnitz.
14 September	Louis XVI takes oath to the new constitution.
25 September	Riot outside Collège des Lombards.
30 September	Final session of the National Assembly.
9 October	Riot outside Collège des Irlandais. Pamphlet 'Exact account of the great revolution'.
10-11 October	Rioting continues. Arrests.
12 October	Department of Paris condemns the outrages.
15 October	Walsh's letter published in Mercure de France.
16 October	Rioting outside Collège des Irlandais. Arrests.
19 October	Decree permitting re-opening of churches under police supervision.
November-December	French retreats in Collège des Lombards.
8 December	People attacked after mass in Collège des Lombards. Police warnings.

1792

2 February	Women attacked outside Collège des Lombards. Police mount patrols.
4 March	Pierre de Coudrin ordained in library of Collège des Irlandais.
20 April	War of the first coalition.
13 June	Louis XVI vetoes decree against refractory priests.
20 June	Parisian crowd invades the Tuileries.
28 July	Brunswick's manifesto reaches Paris.
30 July	*Fédérés* from Marseilles arrive singing *La Marseillaise*.
9 August	Formation of insurrectional commune.

10 August	'Second' French revolution. Tuileries invaded, Louis suspended and imprisoned.
	Collège des Irlandais invaded. Students flee.
	Thomas MacKenna appeals to the mob.
12 August	Irish college again invaded by armed mob led by Truchon.
	Kearney's mission to England.
19 August	Defection of Lafayette.
1 September	Lally Tollendal flees to England.
2-6 September	September massacres.
	Peter Flood rescued and presented to the National Assembly.
20 September	French win the battle of Valmy.
	Monarchy abolished. First session of Convention.
	Kearney arrested. Walsh in hiding.
1 October	Safe conduct for Walsh to pay creditors.
29 October	Student election, 'Kerry coup d'état'.
3 November	Keys handed over to Duckett.
5 November	Seals placed on Kearney's property.
6 November	French win the battle of Jemappes.
16 November	Kearney restored.
18 November	Banquet in White's Hotel.
19 November	First propaganda decree offering fraternal aid to subject peoples.
28 November	Congratulatory address by English-speaking residents of Paris to Convention.
2 December	Irish 'rebel' students present petition to Convention denouncing superiors.
6 December	Convention orders Citizen Rovère to compile report.
20 December	Charles Kearney presents defence.
26 December	Trial of Louis XVI.

1793

14-17 January	Louis found guilty.
20 January	Abbé Edgeworth attends the king.
21 January	Louis XVI executed.
1 February	France declares war on England.
4 March	Irish student mission sent to England. Arrested.
10 March	Rising in La Vendée.
	Revolutionary Tribunal established.
18 March	French lose the battle of Neerwinden.
March-April	Walsh detained at Mairie.
6 April	First Committee of Public Safety established by Convention.
9 May	Committee of General Security orders arrest of Walsh and Kearney.
12 May	Walsh arrested.
17 May	Kearney arrested on orders from Marat. Detained for a week.

24 June	Constitution of 1793 accepted but never put into effect.
13 July	Charlotte Corday murders Marat in his bath.
2 August	Decision to send Richard Ferris on secret mission to England.
23 August	General mobilisation ordered.
5 September	Terror becomes officially the order of the day.
6 September	Léonard Bourdon denounces Kearney to National Convention.
	Decree ordering arrest of foreigners.
	Kearney detained at Irish college.
8 September	Irish students petition Convention to be allowed continue studies.
	Seals placed on Collège des Lombards.
22 September	Republican calendar begins.
28 September	Student denunciation of superiors sent to Committee of General Security.
10 October	Convention decrees arrest of all British subjects.
15 October	Walsh imprisoned in Chateau of St Germain-en-Laye.
16 October	Marie Antoinette executed.
25 October	First batch of prisoners arrive in Collège des Irlandais.
13 November	Charles Kearney and Arthur Dillon interned in Luxembourg palace.
22 November	Closing of all catholic churches in Paris.

1794

1 February	Convention decrees sale of foreign-owned property.
2-4 February	Papers seized in Collège des Irlandais.
15 February	Papers seized in Collège des Lombards.
26 Feb-3 Mar.	Ventôse decrees authorise seizure of property of suspects.
5 April	Dantonists executed.
13 April	Arthur Dillon and Lucille Desmoulins executed.
25 April	Convention decrees departure of Irish students for Ireland.
27 April	Committee of Public Safety order Irish students to be placed on neutral ship to Hamburg.
6 May	Seals placed on Kearney's effects.
10 May	Madame Elizabeth executed.
18 May	Committee of Public Safety orders arrest of Irish students at Dunkirk.
10 June	Law of 22 Prairial increases power of revolutionary tribunal.
26 June	French win battle of Fleurus.
27-28 July	Thermidorian reaction. Robespierre executed.
17 August	Irish students petition Convention to be released.
24 September	First prisoners released from Collège des Irlandais.
17 October	Convention orders release of Irish students in Toulouse.

1795

17 February	Armistice in the Vendée.
21 February	Separation of church and state decreed by the Convention.

1-2 April	Food insurrections in Paris.
4 April	Irish assimilated to refugees from invaded colonies.
30 May	Furniture of Collège des Lombards auctioned.
8 July	National Convention denounces Nicholas Madgett as spy.
22 August	Five-man Directory established.
18 September	Kearney and Walsh restored in possession of Irish properties.
5 October	Royalist insurrection repressed by Napoleon.
26 October	Last session of the National Convention.
25 November	Nicholas Madgett released.

1796

1 February	Wolfe Tone arrives in Paris.
19 February	*Assignats* abolished.
14 March	Tone meets Carnot and General Clarke.
27 March	Napoleon takes command of army of Italy.
10 May	French win the battle of Lodi.
20 September	Tone arrives at Rennes. Bernard MacSheehy appointed his adjoint.
8 November	MacSheehy mission to Ireland.
15 December	Hoche expedition leaves for Ireland.
18 December	MacSheehy arrives back from Ireland.
21 December	Bantry Bay.
26 December	Expedition sets out to return to France.

1797

April	Rev. James Coigly leaves Ireland.
	Royalist landslide in French elections.
June	Napper Tandy arrives in France.
4 September	Coup of Fructidor against royalists.
5 September	Charles Kearney arrested.

1798

28 February	Coigly arrested at Margate.
25 April	Escape of Sidney-Smith from Temple.
	Kearney interrogated.
19 May	Egyptian expedition leaves Toulon
21 May	Trial of Coigly.
7 June	Coigly executed.
1 July	Napoleon lands in Egypt.
22 August	Humbert lands in Killala.
17 September	Tandy's expedition reaches Rutland Bay.
	Arrest of Tone and Blackwell in Hamburg.
12 October	Tone's expedition reaches Lough Swilly.
19 November	Death of Tone.

1799

16 October	Napoleon in Paris.
4 November	Prytanée annexes Irish college.
9-10 November	Coup d'état of 18 Brumaire. End of Directory.

12 December	The consulate.
22 December	Council of state.
27 December	Senate.

1800

15 April	Richard Ferris imprisoned in Temple.
15-23 May	Second Italian campaign.
24 May	Consular decree provisionally annexes Irish college to Prytanée.
5 November	Concordat negotiations open.
24 December	'Infernal machine'. Kearney interrogated.

1801

15 July	Concordat signed.
16 September	Consular decree restores Irish college under bureau.

1802

25 March	Treaty of Amiens with Britain.
	Peter Flood arrives in Paris.
2 August	Napoleon named consul for life.
14 October	Irish and Scots colleges amalgamated.

1803

18 May	War resumes between France and Britain.
22 June	English colleges united to Irish and Scots.
13 August	Napoleon establishes Irish Legion.

1804

2 December	Coronation of Napoleon as emperor.

1805

18 May	Imperial decree regulating the united colleges.
September	Opening of united colleges.
21 October	Battle of Trafalgar.
2 December	Battle of Austerlitz.
31 December	End of Republican calendar.

1806

10 May	Imperial University established.
5 June	Louis Bonaparte king of Holland.
21 November	Continental blockade.
11 December	Bonaparte enters Warsaw.

1807

22 January	Irish bishops condemn Walsh.
7 February	Battle of Eylau. MacSheehy killed.
22 May	Death of Abbé Edgeworth.
30 November	General Junot enters Lisbon. Beginning of Peninsular War.

1808

7 July	Joseph Bonaparte crowned king of Spain.
16 September	Irish college annexed to Imperial University.

5 November	Napoleon assumes personal command of the army of Spain.
	1809
20 April	Wellesley lands at Lisbon with British army.
17 May	France annexes Papal states.
11 June	Pius VII excommunicates Bonaparte.
6 July	Pius VII arrested.
28 July	Walsh suspended as administrator-general.
	1810
17 February	Rome annexed to French empire.
21 May	Foreign ecclesiastics in Rome ordered to Paris.
15 July	Roman priests arrive in Irish college.
	1811
January	Preparations for Russian campaign.
11 February	Walsh petitions Cardinal Maury.
March	Lally Tollendal sends confidential report to Minister of the Interior.
	1812
24-25 June	French invade Russia.
22 July	Wellington wins battle of Salamanca.
14 September	Napoleon enters Moscow.
19 October	Retreat from Moscow begins.
	1813
1 April	Richard Ferris appointed administrator-general of united colleges.
26 June	Allied peace offer to Napoleon.
12 August	Final grand alliance against Napoleon.
	1814
1 January	Allies cross the Rhine.
12 March	Wellington enters Bordeaux.
2 April	Senate deposes Napoleon.
11 April	Napoleon abdicates unconditionally.
1 May	Treaty of Paris. Louis XVIII restored.
4 May	Napoleon in exile at Elba.
21 June	Decree of Louis XVIII sacking Walsh and appointing Ferris.
23 September	Decree of Louis XVII separating the three colleges.
	Bishop Daniel Murray in Paris.
	1815
16 January	Royal decree removing Ferris and appointing Long.
25 February	Napoleon leaves Elba.
13 March	Congress of Vienna outlaws Napoleon.
20 March	Napoleon in Paris. Hundred days begin.
21 April	Decree of Napoleon re-uniting the colleges with Ferris as administrator-general.
18 June	Battle of Waterloo.
22 June	Napoleon's second abdication.
7 July	Allies enter Paris.

1816

25 January Decree of Louis XVIII separating the colleges and appointing Long administrator-general of the Irish college.

Index